Recognition Politics

This pioneering work explores a new wave of widely overlooked conflicts that have emerged across the Andean region, coinciding with the implementation of internationally acclaimed indigenous rights. Why are groups that have peacefully cohabited for decades suddenly engaging in hostile and, at times, violent behaviours? What is the link between these conflicts and changes in collective self-identification, claim-making and rent-seeking dynamics? And how, in turn, are these changes driven by broader institutional, legal and policy reforms? By shifting the focus to the 'post-recognition', this unique study sets the agenda for a new generation of research on the practical consequences of the employment of ethnic-based rights. To develop the core argument on the links between recognition reforms and 'recognition conflicts', Lorenza Fontana draws on extensive empirical material and case studies from three Andean countries – Bolivia, Colombia and Peru – which have been global forerunners in the implementation of recognition politics.

LORENZA B. FONTANA is Associate Professor of International Politics in the School of Social and Political Sciences at the University of Glasgow. Her research has addressed questions around the ethnic politics of socio-environmental conflicts, the domestic politics of human rights of vulnerable groups and, more recently, the contentious politics of wildfires.

T0370694

Cambridge Studies in Comparative Politics

General Editor
Kathleen Thelen *Massachusetts Institute of Technology*

Associate Editors
Catherine Boone *London School of Economics*
Thad Dunning *University of California, Berkeley*
Anna Grzymala-Busse *Stanford University*
Torben Iversen *Harvard University*
Stathis Kalyvas *University of Oxford*
Margaret Levi *Stanford University*
Melanie Manion *Duke University*
Helen Milner *Princeton University*
Frances Rosenbluth *Yale University*
Susan Stokes *Yale University*
Tariq Thachil *University of Pennsylvania*
Erik Wibbels *Duke University*

Series Founder
Peter Lange *Duke University*

Other Books in the Series

Christopher Adolph, *Bankers, Bureaucrats, and Central Bank Politics: The Myth of Neutrality*

Michael Albertus, *Autocracy and Redistribution: The Politics of Land Reform*

Michael Albertus, *Property without Rights: Origins and Consequences of the Property Rights Gap*

Santiago Anria, *When Movements Become Parties: The Bolivian MAS in Comparative Perspective*

Ben W. Ansell, *From the Ballot to the Blackboard: The Redistributive Political Economy of Education*

Ben W. Ansell and Johannes Lindvall, *Inward Conquest: The Political Origins of Modern Public Services*

Ben W. Ansell and David J. Samuels, *Inequality and Democratization: An Elite-Competition Approach*

Ana Arjona, *Rebelocracy: Social Order in the Colombian Civil War*

Leonardo R. Arriola, *Multi-Ethnic Coalitions in Africa: Business Financing of Opposition Election Campaigns*

Continued after index

Recognition Politics

Indigenous Rights and Ethnic Conflict in the Andes

LORENZA B. FONTANA

University of Glasgow

CAMBRIDGE
UNIVERSITY PRESS

Shaftesbury Road, Cambridge CB2 8EA, United Kingdom

One Liberty Plaza, 20th Floor, New York, NY 10006, USA

477 Williamstown Road, Port Melbourne, VIC 3207, Australia

314–321, 3rd Floor, Plot 3, Splendor Forum, Jasola District Centre, New Delhi – 110025, India

103 Penang Road, #05–06/07, Visioncrest Commercial, Singapore 238467

Cambridge University Press is part of Cambridge University Press & Assessment, a department of the University of Cambridge.

We share the University's mission to contribute to society through the pursuit of education, learning and research at the highest international levels of excellence.

www.cambridge.org
Information on this title: www.cambridge.org/9781009265508

DOI: 10.1017/9781009265515

First published 2023
First paperback edition 2024

A catalogue record for this publication is available from the British Library

Library of Congress Cataloging-in-Publication data
NAMES: Fontana, Lorenza B., 1980– author.
TITLE: Recognition politics : indigenous rights and ethnic conflict in the Andes / Lorenza B. Fontana.
DESCRIPTION: Cambridge, United Kingdom ; New York, NY : Cambridge University Press, 2023. | SERIES: Cambridge studies in comparative politics | Includes bibliographical references and index.
IDENTIFIERS: LCCN 2022044006 (print) | LCCN 2022044007 (ebook) | ISBN 9781009265539 (hardback) | ISBN 9781009265508 (paperback) | ISBN 9781009265515 (epub)
SUBJECTS: LCSH: Indians of South America–Andes Region–Ethnic identity. | Indians of South America–Civil rights–Andes Region. | Identity politics–Andes Region. | Ethnic conflict–Andes Region. | Andes Region–Ethnic relations.
CLASSIFICATION: LCC F2230.1.E84 F66 2023 (print) | LCC F2230.1.E84 (ebook) | DDC 980/.00498–dc23/eng/20221019
LC record available at https://lccn.loc.gov/2022044006
LC ebook record available at https://lccn.loc.gov/2022044007

ISBN   978-1-009-26553-9   Hardback
ISBN   978-1-009-26550-8   Paperback

In memory of my mother.

Contents

Figures

Tables

Acknowledgements

This book was inspired by a passion and an intuition. When I first landed in Bolivia, it was not to conduct research or to stay any longer than an eleven-month fellowship to work at the United Nations. A week after I arrived in La Paz, on 25 January 2009, an historical referendum approved a new Constitution. Alongside a multitude of Bolivians, *huipalas* (Andean flags) and occasional tourists, I was in the Plaza Murillo that evening to listen to the speech of President Evo Morales. Bolivia was discarding its old republican clothes to become a plurinational state. The new Constitution opened an exciting (and conflictive) time of institutional changes and political reforms. Given my passion for politics, these recent developments offered a good excuse to postpone my return to Europe as well as an excellent topic for my developing PhD project. I spent the following three years trying to adapt to the altitude and enjoying the chaotic charm of La Paz, with field trips to remote regions where my case studies were located. The conflict in Apolo, in North-East Bolivia, which is described in detail in the book, was my first encounter with the complex and changing relationship between land and identity. In a way, I owe the people I met in Apolo, and this conflict, for the inspiration underlying what became a decade-long project. My intuition was that Apolo was not an isolated case. Indeed, I found other similar inter-communal conflicts in Bolivia, which became the core of my PhD dissertation. The next step was to see how far my intuition would travel across countries. It took me five years, a number of trips to Latin America and the generous support of the British Royal Geographical Society and the Sheffield Institute for International Development to gather the rest of the empirical material for this book.

Throughout my fieldwork, my interactions with people have been incredibly rich and rewarding. Without the generosity of the over 200 people I interviewed and their willingness to share their stories, knowledge, thoughts and opinions, this book would not exist. I am particularly grateful to those who had been directly affected or involved in conflicts, for whom talking about it was a potentially painful and challenging experience. These conversations were for me a stark reminder of how these conflicts have real-life consequences for many people, particularly among already poor and marginalised communities, and of the neglect that often surrounds them. This was ultimately what convinced me of the importance of writing this book. I hope my attempt to report, interpret and explain the stories I gathered does them justice and provides some clues on how to improve the chances of fair settlements and peaceful futures for these communities.

Conducting field research in three countries, with limited budget and means, was an exciting and challenging endeavour. Being able to spend over three years in total in these countries was fundamental not only to gather data but also to embed myself in the cultures and politics of the places I visited and called home for some time. All this would not have been possible without the support of friends, colleagues and a network of local contacts that helped my project in many different and fundamental ways: from being crucial informants and network builders, to providing hospitality, to helping me navigate complex logistics in remote locations, to sharing their insights and views on Latin American politics, society and culture. In Bolivia, I am grateful to my colleagues at the United Nations, particularly Isabel Arauco, Santiago Daroca, Cielo Morales, Jonna Lundwall, Andrea Nelli Feroci, Armando Ortuño, Iñigo Retolaza, Eliana Quíroz, Antonella Spada and Yoriko Yasukawa; to Nelly Arista for being so generous to bring me along to many meetings and to introduce me to key informants; to Simona Sansone, Lilia Grosso, Agustín Vásquez, Fernando Molina, Caroline Cotta de Mello Freitas, Gabriel Zeballos, Mariana Bueno, Daniela Sánchez-López for their friendship; to Attilio Aleotti and Silvio Mignano for their institutional and 'uninstitutional' support; to Annibale Ferrini and Daniela Leyton for the research assistance; to Alejandro Nató for hosting me as an intern at the Carter Center office in Bolivia. In Peru, I would like to thank Lidia and Ramón Gallardo for making me feel at home in Barranco and Vladimir Gil and Loïc Cecilio for the friendship and intellectual exchange. In Colombia, my gratitude goes to Sara Tufano for the friendship, research assistance and endless and inspiring conversations about Colombian history and politics;

to Juan Quiroga for being such a great host in Bogotá; to the researchers at the Pontificia Universidad Javeriana de Cali – particularly Tania Rodríguez and Maria José Rota Aguilar – for sharing their knowledge on inter-ethnic conflicts in the Cauca; to Myriam Mendez-Montalvo, Maca Gómez and Karina Banda for making crucial contacts with local institutions and community leaders; and to Carlos Quesada for sharing his insights and early findings on peasant recognition.

While developing my career as a social scientist, I soon realised that the research process, at least for the kind of research I do, goes in waves. There are the big exceptional waves, which come with the time in the field: it is hectic and exciting and exhausting. Time to think is limited, and it is mostly action and a lot of logistics on how to get from one place to another chasing the next interviewee (the hours I spent in various means of transport – from taxis to buses to the backs of unstable and crowded trucks to even a poor skinny horse one time – is probably more than the time it took me to write the first draft of this book). Once back in the office, there are long, solitary and quiet periods to work through the material, let it sediment, read some more and eventually face the blank page. This is like the toing-and-froing of the backwash upon the shore-line. It takes time, and a natural inclination towards self-discipline, to learn to enjoy it. Unlike fieldwork, it is predictable. You trust the next wave will brush up the shore at the same rhythm, but the repetition can become boring, obsessive and even frightening at times.

I was lucky enough to find some perfect retreats to face the post-fieldwork backwash, gather my thoughts and write: first at the École des Hautes Études en Sciences Sociales in Paris, where Yvon Le Bot kindly hosted me at the Centre d'Analyse et d'Intervention Sociologiques for the final year of my PhD; and then, right when I was ready to turn this project into a book, a European Commission–funded Marie Skłodowska-Curie Fellowship (655710) that brought me to Harvard University for two years. The Weatherhead Centre for International Affairs (WCFIA) and the WCFIA Scholar Program represented an ideal environment for my project. My thanks go to Beth Simmons, Kathryn Sikkink and Michèle Lamont for their mentorship and support. The seminar series at the WCFIA and the David Rockefeller Center for Latin American Studies constituted inspiring breaks during my writing retreat in combination with the entertaining and caffeinated company of my colleagues, particularly Darja Djordjevic, Sophie Lemiere, Eva Østergaard-Nielsen and Mireille Paquet. The Research Cluster on Comparative Inequalities and Inclusion was not only an intellectually stimulating venue but also a nurturing environment for friendly and supportive exchange throughout my fellowship.

As my research and writing unfolded, I had the opportunity to present some of the book's key arguments and empirical cases at conferences, seminars and workshops at the European Commission's Joint Research Centre at Ispra; Edinburgh University; Fundação Escola de Sociologia e Política de São Paulo; Harvard University; Newcastle University; New York University in Paris; Northumbria University; Open University; University of Cape Town; Universidad de Córdoba; University of Oxford; University of Sheffield; University of Sussex; University of York and Universidad Mayor de San Simón. Papers related to this research were presented at the Latin American Studies Association conference, Royal Geographical Society congress, ISS-CEDLA conference, International Political Science Association conference, conference of the Italian Association of Political Science, IPSA-ECPR joint conference, Northern Latin American Network conference, II Jornadas Internacionales de Problemas Latinoamericanos, II Jornadas de Jóvenes Americanistas and III Jornadas Andino-Mesoamericanas. My thanks to all the conveners, discussants and participants as these were all opportunities to refine my arguments and crystallise some of the ideas presented in these pages.

The book in its current form owes a great deal to the incredibly insightful and critical comments in the framework of a book workshop hosted by the WCFIA at Harvard University. I am indebted to Candelaria Garay, Alisha Holland, Jean Jackson, Ronald Niezen, Mireille Paquet and Prerna Singh. Their thorough engagement with the book's arguments and empirics and their generosity in sharing suggestions and ideas were crucial for transforming an early version of the manuscript into a publishable piece of research. I am deeply grateful to former WCFIA director Michèle Lamont for hosting the workshop and, more importantly, for believing in this project and for her tireless support and encouragement over the years.

After my time at Harvard, I moved back to the UK to take up a permanent position at Newcastle University. Here I met colleagues and friends who provided an amazing intellectual and support network, which pushed me through a challenging time coinciding with the processes of review and revision of the book's manuscript. My thanks go in particular to Laura Routley, Derek Bell, Valentina Feklyunina, Maarja Luhiste, Tony Zito, Una McGahern, Jemima Repo, Sorana Jude, Diana Burlacu, Andrew Walton, Rosario Aguilar, Alistair Clark and Sebastian Popa.

My editors at Cambridge University Press, first Sara Doskow and then Rachel Blaifeder, have been a professional and supportive presence since the initial book submission. Two anonymous reviewers provided detailed comments and suggestions that helped me improve the book's clarity and structure. I would like to thank Simon Davies for copyediting and Rohan Bolton for indexing the manuscript. I am grateful to the Fundación Tierra in Bolivia and the Instituto de Estudios Interculturales at the Pontificia Universidad Javeriana de Cali for granting permission to use maps and shape files for the book's figures, and to Iain McNicol and Kyle Dexter for producing some of the maps.

During the process of writing this book, I have incurred many intellectual debts with friends and colleagues who have nurtured inspiring conversations over the years and offered insightful and critical comments to an early version of book chapters and related articles. I thank, in particular, Arun Agrawal, Tony Bebbington, Francesco Bogliacino, Stefan Collignon, Johan Crabtree, Cecilie Dyngeland, Hervé do Alto, Sofia Donoso, Veronica Herrera, Denise Humphreys Bebbington, Margo Huxley, Sue Iamamoto, Pablo Lapegna, Roberto Laserna, Steve Levitsky, Matias López, Fernando Mayorga, Danilo Martuccelli, John-Andrew McNeish, Angelo Miramonti, Fernando Molina, Jojo Nem Singh, Johan Oldekop, Huáscar Pacheco, Tom Perreault, Christopher Raiche, Thiago Rodrigues, Federico Rossi, Luana Russo, Davide Sparti, Pablo Stefanoni and Agustín Vásquez.

Deep gratitude goes to Jean Grugel for being an outstanding mentor since I first met her when I arrived at the University of Sheffield, soon after my PhD. By considering me a fellow academic, she gave me the courage and confidence to try and become one. Many of the ideas developed in this book are grounded on the fruitful conversations and joint research we entertained over the years.

Acknowledgements are mostly a way to say thank you. However, they are also an insight on the journey behind these pages. As such, they might also hide less rosy stories. There are what some might consider egregious omissions in these pages. These are not oversights. I have omitted the names of people and institutions that have, particularly at the very start of this journey, hindered my chances to become a researcher and of producing this work, by corroding my self-esteem, through power abuse, harassment, negligence and a lack of accountability and professional ethics. This book and my career were possible in spite of them. I am grateful to the #MeToo movement for helping me find words to start elaborating my traumas and for giving me some hope that academia will be a better, safer and fairer place for the next generation of fellow female students and researchers.

On a more personal – and positive – note, I would like to acknowledge the support of some of my dearest and long-lasting friends. Thanks for welcoming me back every time all my moving around made me feel dizzy and when I am in need of a solid ground to stand still and rest: Betta Astori, Ilaria Franco, Lele Bosticco, Manu Dinunno, Patrizio Anisio, Silvia Ottone, Claudia Mazzá, 'il Comitato', le 'famiglie' di Cascinetta e Lignod.

This research journey spanned over a decade. It started with grief and loss and is ending with a new family and two new lives. I dedicate this book to my mother, Giuse Verri, who died too young when I was preparing for my first trip to Bolivia. As a primary school teacher, her passion for education and her commitment to my early learning laid the grounds for my own academic interest and trajectory. My father, Gabriele Fontana, and grandmother, Giovanna Gamaggio, cheered me in the most difficult times. Even if they eventually gave up on asking what it is that I 'do for a living exactly', they were a source of tireless and unconditional support throughout the years.

In the middle of the book's journey, I met my partner, Kyle Dexter. His intellectual curiosity, open mindedness, stimulating comments and irreverent defiance contributed to making this book, and our dinner conversations, more compelling and entertaining. Our common passion for Latin America brought us a long way, although we are still figuring out how we can work in the same place if I study social communities made of people, and he studies plants where there are no people. While we worked on this dilemma, we welcomed Liam and Gabo. Without Kyle's unconditional support and firm commitment to an equal partnership and distribution of care and domestic responsibilities, this book would not likely have materialised. The book would have certainly seen the light earlier without the new family additions, yet I would have missed out on the most exciting, intense, if exhausting, years of our lives.

Acronyms and Abbreviations

AA	affirmative action
ACIT	Asociación Campesina del Municipio de Inzá (Peasant Association of the Inzá Municipality)
AIDESEP	Asociación Interétnica de Desarrollo de la Selva Peruana (Association for the Development of the Peruvian Rainforest)
AIOC	Autonomía Indígena Originaria Campesina (Indigenous Native Peasant Autonomy)
ANUC	Asociación Nacional de Usuarios Campesinos (National Association of Peasant Users)
ANZORC	Asociación Nacional de Zonas de Reserva Campesina (National Association of the Peasant Reserve Zones)
APCOB	Apoyo Para el Campesino Indígena del Oriente Boliviano (Support for the Indigenous Peasant of the Bolivian East)
APG	Asamblea del Pueblo Guaraní (Guaraní People's Assembly)
ASCAMCAT	Asociación Campesina del Catatumbo (Peasant Association of the Catatumbo)
CART	Central Ashaninka De Rio Tambo (Ashaninka Council of the Rio Tambo)
CCP	Confederación Campesina del Perú (Peasant Confederation of Peru)
CIDOB	Confederación de Pueblos Indígenas de Bolivia (Confederation of Indigenous Peoples of Bolivia)

CIPLA	Central Indígena del Pueblo Leco (Indigenous Council of the Leco People)
CNA	Confederación Nacional Agraria (National Agrarian Confederation)
CONACAMI	Confederación Nacional de Comunidades del Perú Afectadas por la Minería (National Confederation of Communities Adversely Affected by Mining)
CONAIE	Confederación de Nacionalidades Indígenas del Ecuador (Confederation of Indigenous Nationalities of Ecuador)
CONAMAQ	Consejo Nacional of Ayllus y Markas del Qullasuyu (National Council of Ayllus and Markas of the Qullasuyu)
CONAP	Confederación de Nacionalidades Amazónicas del Perú (Confederation of Amazonian Nationalities of Peru)
CRIC	Consejo Regional Indígena del Cauca (Regional Indigenous Council of the Cauca)
CSCIB	Confederación Sindical de Comunidades Interculturales de Bolivia (Syndicalist Confederation of Intercultural Communities of Bolivia)
CSUTCB	Confederación Única de Trabajadores Campesinos de Bolivia (Unified Confederation of Peasant Workers of Bolivia)
FARC	Fuerzas Armadas Revolucionarias de Colombia (Revolutionary Armed Forces of Colombia)
FPIC	Free Prior and Informed Consent/Consultation
FSUTC-FT	Federación de Campesinos de la Provincia Franz Tamayo (Peasant Federation of the Franz Tamayo Province)
IBE	intercultural bilingual education
ILO	International Labour Organization
INCODER	Instituto Colombiano para el Desarrollo Rural (Colombian Institute for Rural Development)
INE	Instituto Nacional de Estadística (National Institute of Statistics)
INRA	Instituto Nacional de Reforma Agraria (National Institute of Agrarian Reform)
IWGIA	International Work Group for Indigenous Affairs
MNR	Movimiento Nacional Revolucionario (National Revolutionary Movement)

ONAMIAP	Organización Nacional de Mujeres Indígenas Andinas y Amazónicas del Perú (National Organisation of Andean and Amazonic Indigenous Women of Peru)
ONIC	Organización Nacional Indígena de Colombia (National Indigenous Organisation of Colombia)
TAN	Tribunal Nacional Agrario (National Agrarian Tribunal)
TCO	Tierra Comunitaria de Origen (Native Communal Land)
TIOC	Territorio Indígena Originario Campesino (Indigenous Native Peasant Territory)
TIPNIS	Territorio Indígena and Parque Nacional Isiboro Sécure (Isiboro Sécure Indigenous Territory and National Park)
UN	United Nations
UNCA	Unión de Comunidades Aymaras (Union of Aymara Communities)
UN-REDD	United Nations Programme on Reducing Emissions from Deforestation and Forest Degradation
VAIPO	Vice-Ministerio de Asuntos Indígenas y Pueblos Originarios (Vice-Ministry of Indigenous Issues and Native Peoples)
VRAEM	Valles de los Rios Apurímac, Ene y Mantaro (Valleys of the Apurímac, Ene and Mantaro Rivers)
ZRC	Zona de Researva Campesina (Peasant Reserve Zone)

Introduction

Shortly after midnight, early on Christmas Day 2010, the Cultural Centre of San Andrés Pisimbalá, a small town nestled in Colombia's western mountain range, was transformed into a battlefield. Celebrations were interrupted by gunshots that left four people seriously injured, and machete attacks that left another dozen with minor wounds. This would be the first of many violent episodes in a conflict between indigenous and peasant residents over territorial control and the implementation of ethnocultural education in schools. For almost a decade now, life in San Andrés has been disrupted by a series of land invasions, house and crop burnings, forced displacement, and threats. Ten years after that fateful episode, the local school is still closed to peasant children and the conflict remains unresolved.

In a similarly remote region, this one bordering the northern Bolivian Amazon, in the early morning of 16 May 2007 around 600 peasants marched from the town of Apolo towards Madidi National Park. Armed with chainsaws and rifles stolen from the local police, they threatened to start logging this internationally famous biodiversity hotspot, in protest against the issuing of a land title that granted a large portion of the community territory to a newly constituted indigenous organisation. The park's occupation marked the culmination of a long-lasting dispute between the local peasant union and the Leco indigenous people that completely altered the coexistence of families and communities, who were suddenly split along new ethnic boundaries.

A few years earlier, some 3,000 km north of Apolo along the western edge of the Peruvian Amazon, a conflict between an Awajún indigenous community and peasant settlers ended in one of the deadliest episodes of civil violence in recent Peruvian history. On 17 January 2002, a few dozen peasant families living in a settlement called Flor de la Frontera awoke to find themselves under siege from a group of armed Awajún. The siege, intended to evict the settlers from illegally occupied indigenous land, left sixteen people dead and seventeen wounded – most of them women and children.

These three episodes are paradigmatic examples of inter-communal conflicts that have emerged over the last thirty years across the Andean region. These disputes are between peasants and indigenous peoples – groups identified along class and ethnic lines – who occupy remote rural areas characterised by widespread poverty, social marginalisation, environmental fragility and a deep colonial history. Most of these conflicts tend to become endemic and protracted over time, generally remaining at relatively low-intensity levels with occasional escalations and peaks of violence. That they take place in remote settings and have relatively moderate levels of violence may help explain why they fall outside the radar of the national media, public debate and scholarly attention.

Yet these conflicts deserve attention not only because of the negative impact they have on local communities, but also because they open up new and important questions in contemporary debates on equality and diversity. Why are groups that have peacefully cohabited for decades suddenly engaging in hostile and violent behaviours? What is the link between these conflicts and changes in collective self-identification, claim-making and rent-seeking dynamics? And how, in turn, are these changes driven by broader institutional, legal and policy reforms? To address these questions, this book employs extensive empirical material that delves into stories of recent inter-communal conflicts in three Andean countries: Colombia, Peru and Bolivia. It maps the actors, motives and time frames of these conflicts and situates them in the broader context of the socio-political transformation that the region has undergone in recent decades. In particular, the book shows how the rise in inter-group competition is linked to the implementation of a new generation of legal, institutional and policy reforms that, since the early 1990s, have introduced special rights and protection for ethnic (indigenous) groups.

A new consensus on the need to grant legal guarantees to ethnic minorities was forged at the international level in the 1980s and, since then, has trickled down to domestic policy across the world. The approach has become particularly influential in Latin America, where vibrant indigenous movements have successfully pressured governments to respond to their demands for recognition, rights and, in certain cases, self-government. Contentious indigenous politics has led to a new model of citizenship and statehood, in stark contrast with the assimilationist paradigm that had prevailed since the mid-twentieth century. Inspired by globally famous theories of recognition (Taylor 1992; Kymlicka 2001), this new model postulates that the formalisation of differentiated rights for ethnic groups is a precondition for social coexistence on peaceful and equal grounds. Over the last thirty years, Latin America, and the Andean countries in particular, have pioneered the implementation of the recognition agenda mainly through constitutional reforms that formally recognised the multicultural or plurinational nature of their societies. These reforms introduced new ethnic-based rights, granting indigenous peoples certain degrees of territorial and administrative autonomy, political representation, direct participation in decision-making processes and access to special social provisions. In this context, I include within the 'recognition reform' category a broad set of institutional, legal and policy changes, ranging from more moderate versions inspired by neoliberal multiculturalism to more radical plurinational regimes, while I understand recognition as the process of institutionalisation of special rights to social collectivities determined along ethnic lines.[1]

As has been extensively documented, recognition reforms have had an empowering effect on traditionally marginalised indigenous groups and, in turn, have strengthened democratisation and improved the quality of political communities in countries traditionally beset by persistent discrimination and inequality. Yet these positive effects have come with unforeseen social costs. In contrast to the mainstream progressive interpretation of the politics of recognition as offering more peaceful and inclusive arrangements for ethnically diverse societies, this book argues

---

[1] This is a rather narrow definition of recognition as it focuses specifically on ethnicity and institutionalised politics. In the literature, recognition has been understood in very different ways. As many as twenty-three different usages of the notion 'to recognise' have been identified, grouped into three main categories, namely recognition as identification, recognising oneself and mutual recognition (Ricoeur 2005). While left-Hegelian political philosophers have tended to emphasise the positive normative dimension of recognition as a precondition for the fulfilment of a 'vital human need' (Taylor 1992, 26; see also Honneth 1995; Kymlicka 1995), Marxist and post-structuralist philosophers have conceptualised recognition as a potential source of estrangement and as an inhibitor of social transformation (Sartre 1943; Althusser 1971). Sociological literature has tended to focus on recognition claims as the expression of struggles of marginalised social groups for social incorporation (Bauman 2001; Hobson 2003), and more recently on recognition gaps, defined as disparities in worth and cultural membership between groups in a society (Lamont 2018).

that these politics contain seeds of conflict. While they aim to improve
social inclusion, under certain conditions they increase social differentiation in cultural and socio-economic terms, expand the gaps between
communities of rural poor, reduce incentives to cooperate, and generate
new types of social conflict, which I call recognition conflicts.

I define *recognition conflict* as a pattern of behaviour in which social
groups consistently engage in contests with each other over goods, services, power, social boundaries and/or leadership as part or as a consequence of the recognition of specific ethnic rights. Parties in competition
self-identify as members of distinct and bounded communities, divided
along ethnic and/or class lines. Although public authorities are often
called into question in the framework of these conflicts, state involvement
is not a condition for recognition conflict to happen. To be sure, the high
volume of disputes in which groups (particularly ethnic groups) claim
different forms of legal and social recognition by the state are excluded
from this definition. These 'vertical conflicts' have been crucial triggers of
wider recognition reform in Latin America and beyond, and have been the
subject of extensive investigation (Davalos 2005; Yashar 2005; Lucero
2008; Merino Acuña 2015). The definition of 'recognition conflict' proposed here aims to uncover instead the horizontal dimension of recognition claims, that is, those situations in which the main dispute occurs
between two (or more) social groups or communities in conflict with each
other. This horizontal dynamic has seldom been the object of research in
its own right. Although conflicts are often complex phenomena and both
horizontal and vertical dimensions are sometimes coexisting features of a
single dispute, I argue that there is an added value in untangling those
axes and identifying inter-communal conflicts as a distinct phenomenon
within broader struggles for recognition.

The rather broad definition proposed here seems pertinent to studying
a phenomenon with common roots but outcomes and material implications that vary greatly. The recognition conflicts studied in this book
range from increased inter-group competition to open violence and
involve a broad spectrum of actions: from hatred discourses and political
competition to discriminatory acts, threats and blackmail, and to outbreaks of violence and physical aggression. This book constitutes the first
attempt to provide an empirically grounded analysis and a theoretical
framework for understanding these widely overlooked types of conflict,
which have emerged over the last twenty years alongside the
strengthening of ethnic-based rights. It challenges the primary logic of
recognition, according to which the granting of minority rights should

reduce conflict, revealing that, under certain conditions, recognition can become the main source of conflict itself.

ETHNIC CONFLICT IN THE AGE OF RECOGNITION

Throughout history, multi-ethnic communities have been the norm rather than the exception. This is true also for the contemporary world. It is estimated that more than 90 per cent of modern territorial states contain two or more ethnic communities of significant size (Connor 1973). Esman (1994) identifies three main sources of ethnic pluralism: conquest and annexation, European colonisation and decolonisation, and cross-border population movements. In modern times, ethnic heterogeneity has often been the source of conflict and political instability. Throughout the twentieth century, the doctrine of national self-determination inspired anticolonial struggles and legitimised autonomy claims by ethnic minorities within national borders. Over the past few decades, economic globalisation has also favoured the movement of people, at times increasing social tensions in receiving societies. These instabilities have made it urgent for states to explore new strategies for ethnic diversity governance. Recognition has been one of these. Despite the fact that moral principles, a sense of justice and just struggles vary widely within and across human societies (Eckstein & Wickham-Crowley 2003), the paradigm of recognition has had a reach across different and diverse countries. This is probably because it addresses some of the most urgent anxieties of modern democracies concerning how to guarantee the peaceful and fair coexistence of ethno-cultural groups within liberal state architectures.

Recognition of ethnic groups through institutional and legal reform has been the object of important national debates from Canada to Argentina, from Kenya to Norway and from Nepal to the Philippines. But the most audacious steps to institutionalise recognition of ethnic groups have been taken in Latin America. The region, which hosts approximately 50 million indigenous peoples (UNDP 2013), has the highest rate of ratification of Convention 169 on the Rights of Indigenous and Tribal Peoples (fifteen out of twenty-two countries),[2] the only binding international norm on ethnic-based rights. This enthusiasm can at least partially be explained by the need to overcome the dark past of dictatorial regimes in the 1970s and 1980s, which provided an

---

[2] Argentina, Bolivia, Brazil, Chile, Colombia, Costa Rica, Dominica, Ecuador, Guatemala, Honduras, Mexico, Nicaragua, Paraguay, Peru, Venezuela.

incentive for the ratification of conventions in general, as part of Latin American countries' international rehabilitation (Panizza 1995; Lutz & Sikkink 2000). The impact of international law on domestic legislation, however, has been more than symbolic. Since the early 1990s, constitutional reform took place across the region to formally recognise the multicultural or plurinational nature of Latin American societies, while introducing ethnic-based rights which granted a degree of territorial and administrative autonomy, political representation, and access to special social provisions (e.g. in education and health) to indigenous peoples (including, in certain cases, Afro-descendants; see Hooker 2005; Paschel 2016). Where constitutions were not amended, indigenous rights were often included in legal frameworks and nationwide policies through, for example, systems of quotas for political representation and affirmative action in the education sector (Van Cott 2005b; Rousseau and Dargent 2019).

These reforms were not only the result of 'norm cascade' mechanisms, in which the chance of ratification increases once a norm has proven internationally successful (Finnemore & Sikkink 1998); they also stemmed from bottom-up pressure from a growing number of indigenous movements active at national and international levels. Since the 1980s, organisations representing indigenous peoples have been founded in a number of Latin American countries, including Bolivia, Peru, Ecuador, Colombia, Mexico and Nicaragua. The so-called indigenous 'awakening' or 'resurgence' (Albó 1991; Bengoa 2000; Le Bot 2009) occurred in tandem with the rise of global indigenous movements and thanks to the financial and advisory support of a myriad of non-governmental organisations and activists, mostly foreigners, that formed alliances with local communities to win battles of recognition (Jackson 1995, 2019; Andolina et al. 2009; Canessa 2018). Throughout the 1990s, indigenous organisations consolidated and, in certain cases, made their first steps into national political arenas, while ethnic identities regained traction as sources of self-identification and markers of social differentiation and group belonging (Rivera Cusicanqui 1984; de la Cadena 2005). The rise of indigenous movements and their politicisation has been linked to the new opportunities enabled by the democratisation processes that followed the collapse of dictatorial regimes across the region, and particularly the efforts to generate more open electoral and party systems (Yashar 1998; Van Cott 2005a) and to strengthen local governance and participation (Andolina et al. 2009; Rousseau & Dargent 2019).

The positive assessment of recognition in the framework of democratisation processes in Latin America has meant that, in practice, the effects of these reforms on social and political ethnicisation (and therefore more rigid social boundaries) have been read almost exclusively through the lens of the empowerment of traditionally marginalised and impoverished communities and their enhanced participation and social inclusion. Indeed, as research on indigenous politics has amply shown, these reforms were a key step towards the rebalancing of a system of exclusion and discrimination rooted in the colonial past (Brysk 2000; Hale 2002; Sieder 2002; Postero 2007; Lucero 2008). They were key factors in strengthening the social and political organisation of indigenous peoples and converting them into political actors in many Latin American countries, from Mexico to Colombia, Ecuador to Bolivia (Van Cott 2005a; Yashar 2005). Latin America is therefore considered the region in which the recognition agenda has been implemented most successfully and in a relatively unproblematic and peaceful way. In this context, and in the absence of major ethnic conflict of the kind frequently seen in other parts of the world (Yashar 2005), scholars have generally been reluctant to focus on the effects of the ethnicisation of social conflict and collective identities on the overall cohesion of societies and communities.

This attitude has contributed to widening the gap between continentally siloed debates on ethnic politics. Indeed, mirroring the position of the vast majority of governments in Asia and Africa, scholars studying ethnic politics in these continents have remained somewhat sceptical about recognition. If in Latin America the focus has been on the emancipatory potential of indigenous rights for social inclusion and on fighting old discrimination rooted in the colonial past, in Africa and Asia discussions have revolved around the destabilising potential of ethnic politics and its malleability vis-à-vis political and economic change (Posner 2005; Comaroff & Comaroff 2009). Scholars have been especially sensitive to the potential for indigenous politics to exacerbate local inter-ethnic conflicts and reinforce class hierarchies that further marginalise the poorest people (Li 2002; Pelican 2009; Shah 2010; Sylvain 2014). What are the roots of this continental divide on recognition? I argue that politics rather than ethnic demography is the key factor at play here. This is rooted in a very pragmatic assessment of the potential for geopolitical destabilisation linked to ethnic appraisals, which is related to the relative power of ethnic groups with respect to central government, as well as to their loyalties, interests and sense of belonging to the nation-state. Even a very rapid assessment of these features leads to the conclusion that both the fragilities in the process of consolidation of national identities and the disruptive potential of irredentist claims are much more serious in most African and Asian countries than in Latin America (Gutiérrez Chong 2010). Also, in most Latin American countries, no single ethnic group makes up more than 20 to 30 per cent of the population. Without a clear discriminated-minority-vs-ruling-majority divide, the very claim for autonomy based on discrimination loses traction (for an in-depth analysis of factors that might explain these divides see Kymlicka 2007).

It is hardly a coincidence, then, that in Africa and Asia minimalist approaches have prevailed, which means that few groups are treated as 'indigenous' and the term is chiefly reserved for scattered and nomadic minorities. In Latin America, however, maximalist interpretations dominate (with some exceptions, such as Peru), which suggests that all the populations that existed before colonisation should be considered 'indigenous'. Countries' different attitudes have also been influenced by the role of international organisations, which have certainly been more pro-active in the implementation of indigenous rights in Latin America compared to any other region. In particular, in the African context, international organisations have been framing indigenous rights as a humanitarian matter, focusing on very specific minorities (those living in remote regions, hunter-gatherers and those particularly marginalised even among multiple ethnic minorities) and trying to avoid issues around self-determination for national minorities (such as the Kurds, the Tamil, the Tuareg, etc.). A minimalist attitude is also mainstream among anthropologists and subaltern studies scholars focusing on Asia and Africa, who have often denounced the essentialist idea of culture and identity embedded in the concept of indigeneity, although they disagree on whether essentialism could, in certain cases, benefit social struggles (e.g. through strategic essentialism, Spivak 1990) or foster new inequalities (Kuper et al. 2003).

In the effort to bridge this continental divide, this book finds inspiration in the work of scholars focusing on other world regions that have, in recent years, started to document the unforeseen and troubling effects of recognition reforms. In certain cases, what Shah (2007: 1806) calls the 'dark side of indigeneity' means that local use of global discourse by well-intentioned urban activists can in fact reinforce a class system that further marginalises the poorest. In others, the effort to 'become tribal', motivated by access to affirmative action and autonomy, has generated new tensions among local communities over the determination of what constitutes tribal culture and competing claims for authenticity

(Middleton 2015). My aim is to contribute to this body of literature by advancing a broader theoretical and conceptual framework that will identify and understand the under-researched phenomenon of recognition conflict in Latin America, while supporting my claims through cross-national empirical evidence.

This book puts forward a new perspective on the study of recognition and ethnic politics by introducing three major shifts: (1) from recognition to post-recognition; (2) from indigenous groups claiming recognition to broader social communities; and (3) from the Global North to the Global South.

From the 'Epic' to the 'Tragedy' of Recognition

Scholarship on recognition and ethnic mobilisation in Latin America can be divided into three main generations. The first generation of research, which I analyse in detail in Chapter 2, considered ethnicity a relatively marginal category for social action and subsumed the study of ethnic groups within a broader approach to the rural question through class lenses. This reflected in part the prominence of peasant movements across Latin America between the 1950s and early 1970s. Following the crisis of these movements and the initial rise of new social actors with strong ethnic associations throughout the 1980s, the attention of scholars (especially anthropologists) became more explicitly focused on the ethnic question, in many cases with sympathetic if not militant attitudes in support of cultural and identity-based claims and forms of organisation. Identities suddenly became central concerns for activists, scholars and practitioners alike, while ethnic differences could no longer be ignored nor reduced to class differences. Although they may greatly overlap in practice, they began to be perceived as 'qualitatively different' (Orlove & Custred 1980: 167). This differentiation had two interpretative implications for the understanding of the rural poor as political actors: on one hand, the rural poor went from being perceived as reactionary to being the progressive vanguards of social change; on the other, the material differences that were used as traditional markers of social boundaries were assimilated into cultural and identity cleavages, blurring the distinctions between poverty, class and ethnicity. With the age of recognition reforms that started in the early 1990s, political scientists in particular became very interested in questions around when and under what conditions indigenous movements were created, and how their claims relate to broader democratic arrangements, potentially constituting a 'post-liberal turn'. The debate, opened by influential works such as Yashar's *Contesting Citizenship in Latin America* (2005), was followed by a vast amount of scholarly production trying to understand the new political role of ethnic movements in Latin America and their impressive successes in moving from recognition claims to recognition reforms (see, e.g., Van Cott 2002 on multicultural constitutionalism).

The focus on recognition as either a normative principle to guide institutional reforms or a framework for claim-making means that most academic work has so far concentrated on the period preceding recognition, while scholarly interest has generally waned once recognition is granted. It is understandable that the *epics* of recognition struggles have been of great inspiration to scholars. Historic indigenous mobilisations and social uprisings, such as the Zapatista rebellion in Mexico in 1994 and the first march for dignity and territory in Bolivia in 1990, were paradigmatic turning points in the entire Latin American political scenario. Yet recognition is not the end of the story, but rather the beginning of a different, perhaps less epic, tale.

By shifting the focus to the post-recognition phase in order to capture the practical consequences of the implementation of indigenous rights, this book is setting the agenda for a fourth generation of research on recognition, one that focuses on post-recognition. In this endeavour, I draw inspiration from recent work across the social sciences that has embarked on the task of dismantling well-established assumptions around the relationship between ethnicity and political and economic processes. In particular, constructivist approaches have highlighted how ethnic identities and boundaries are often the product of political and economic change, rather than key variables that explain that change (Chandra 2012; Wimmer 2013; Singh & Vom Hau 2016). More specifically, scholars have explored the impact of state institutionalisation of ethnic categories (i.e. formal recognition through, e.g., census forms or systems of national ethnic certification) on inter-group relationships and violence. The argument, in brief, is that institutionalisation boosts ethnic differentiation, creating a competitive dynamic that increases the likelihood of spiralling aggression (Lieberman & Singh 2012; 2017). In line with the constructivist turn in ethnic studies (Wimmer 2013), the empirical cases presented in this book illustrate how recognition reforms have major performative effects on identity and social boundaries, which in turn can increase inter-group competition and, in certain cases, lead to outbreaks of violence.

Performative effects that emerge if we shift focus to the post-recognition phase can be of different kinds. I identify three here, all represented by the case studies in this book:

(1) A *genesis effect*, whereby new identities are created or become salient in response to contextual change. This effect describes, for example, the ethnogenesis of new indigenous identities, as in the case of Apolo (Chapter 5), or the process of revitalisation of ethnic markers, as for the Quechua settlers in Peru (Chapter 7).

(2) A *crystallisation effect*, which creates an interruption in the flow of cultural and identity innovation. An equilibrium among multiple identities is reached and remains stable for a given period of time, as long as enabling conditions are maintained, while the tension between identity fluidity and resilience is at least temporarily resolved. As I illustrate in Chapter 3, in Latin America, crystallisation effects have shaped the alternation of peasant and indigenous identities as the main referents for social mobilisation and self-identification over the past fifty years.

(3) A *hierarchical effect*, which triggers situations where not only do identities crystallise in a new equilibrium, but this equilibrium is sustained by the primacy of one identity over another. In the history of indigenous and peasant identities, there have been different moments characterised by hierarchal relationships (class over ethnicity and vice versa), as described in Chapters 2 and 3. These effects are not exclusive of recognition reforms (assimilationist models had the same effects but on different identities), yet they have not been fully acknowledged in the case of recognition.

Although the chain of actions and reactions triggered by recognition is not linear, changes in the way groups self-identify most likely lead to the redefinition of social boundaries and inter-group relationships. As I demonstrate throughout this book, recognition reforms tend to create stronger and more exclusive inter-group boundaries, particularly in contexts characterised by high social heterogeneity and economic fragility. Markers of difference become more relevant than markers of similarity in a process of mutual construction of exclusions. 'Indigenous' is therefore defined in opposition to 'peasant', and vice versa; 'autochthonous' is defined in opposition to 'migrant', and vice versa; 'highlander' is defined in opposition to 'lowlander', and vice versa. As I illustrate in the two historical chapters (2 and 3), these dichotomies have not always existed and have not always had the same relevance as they do today. Historical trajectories of articulation and disarticulation between these collective identities highlight how recognition conflicts are likely the product of the contemporary reshaping of norms of inclusion and exclusion, recognition and redistribution.

From Actors to Social Communities

The second shift introduced by the book is from a focus on those groups either 'recognised' or 'claiming recognition' to a focus on a broader social aggregate, which I call a social community. This is an ensemble of different ethnic and class groups that share the same physical space but that may or may not have access to recognition. Expanding the theatre to social communities allows the researcher to better capture the boundary-making processes in the operationalisation of recognition, or how in practice recognition involves redefining social relationships and collective identities. Once again, the focus here is on horizontal inter-group relationships rather than vertical relationships with, for instance, the state, private companies or international actors. The horizontal dimension, however, does not imply that there are no power imbalances between these groups, but that the imbalances are contingent to specific social configurations rather than institutionalised or intrinsic to a given relationship.

As I mentioned earlier, I define recognition as the act of granting special rights to culturally distinct social groups. In the logic of recognition, group differentiation is indeed instrumental to achieving social justice. Hence, one of the key steps in the operationalisation of recognition involves defining what characteristics a group should have in order to deserve differential treatment. The challenge here is that recognition is a discrete mechanism, while most ethnic markers are continuous variables (i.e. skin colour, adherence to distinct cultural features, language proficiency). In practice, although abstract criteria can be more or less strict and rely on more or less undisputed markers, a cut-off point needs to be set. Depending on where the threshold falls, different social groups will be considered more or less suitable for being granted recognition. Both the relative arbitrariness of the criteria for recognition and the 'in or out' type of outcome mean that the very implementation of recognition is likely to be a contentious and highly politicised endeavour, with the state, social actors and other stakeholders trying to shift the cut-off point towards what they consider a more favourable outcome. This also means that groups of rural poor are not entering the 'recognition battleground' on an equal footing and, therefore, there are likely to be winners and losers in the post-recognition phase (both aspects have generally been neglected by scholars of recognition). Indeed, even when the criteria of inclusion are rather lax, social differentiation will make it easier for certain groups to gain recognition compared with others. For example, those groups that have more credible and visible ethnic markers or that have managed to preserve an identity perceived as distinct within the national context and that is acceptable for local communities will be better equipped to adapt (i.e. or have *fitness*, to borrow the fortunate Darwinian concept) to the new political environment than others. In this context, fitness not only implies entitlement to new rights but also easier access to the globalised world of recognition, made up of networks, international organisations and activists that can provide different types of material and non-material support.

The second problem with the operationalisation of recognition, at least in the Latin American context, is that while target groups are defined in terms of collective identity and ethnic markers, policies that stem from recognition reforms entail in general a heavy redistributive component that ranges from land titling to monetary transfers to control over strategic resources (e.g. hydrocarbon, forest, water). Quantitative evidence generally supports the assumption that indigenous communities are the poorest and most marginalised within Latin American societies (Freire et al. 2015), which would in turn justify the overlapping of recognition and redistribution measures. Yet, in practice, micro-sociological realities are much more complex than what appears in World Bank figures. Not only is there an increasing number of indigenous urban dwellers that are making a decent living, if not heading towards the top of the economic pyramid, by controlling crucial import/export sectors of Andean economies (Tassi 2010), but the number of rural poor in these countries definitively exceeds the number of 'recognised' indigenous peoples. These discrepancies make it harder to justify the redistributive component of recognition if we take equality as a moral horizon, as I will elaborate on in my conclusion. These dilemmas become clearer in those contexts in which different groups of rural poor (whether indigenous, peasant or Afro-descendant) do not live in isolation from each other. Often as a result of more or less recent processes of migration and displacement, these groups share the same geographical space and relatively similar conditions of marginalisation and economic precarity. In such socially heterogeneous contexts, recognition introduces demarcation lines across communities, and sometimes families, which not only crystallise symbolic boundaries but also set up differentiated mechanisms in regard to accessing key resources. It is not surprising, therefore, that many of these communities have been experiencing increased inter-group competition in the post-recognition phase.

Finally, given the complexity of social communities, we might wonder whether identity fitness constitutes a good metric for social justice at all. Indeed, all the conflicts described in this book entail moral dilemmas around the subject and the scope of recognition. If identities are fluid and endogenous to the institutional process of recognition, then identity does not seem a good enough criterion in itself to justify access to special protection and resources. Additional elements may need to be added to the equation, particularly an intersectional analysis that considers other variables such as class and gender. The argument here is not against recognition *tout court* but for an empirically grounded assessment of recognition that can highlight its successes as well as its limitations within a particular social community in a given historical and geographical context. This brings us to the third shift of perspective, which invites us to rethink recognition beyond Western boundaries.

From the Global North to the Global South

It is now clear that indigenous movements across Latin America have fully embraced the struggle for recognition and the human rights discourse associated with it. Without bottom-up pressure, those constitutional changes that have reshaped the very nature of Latin American states and societies would simply not have been possible. Yet it is equally undeniable that the roots of recognition of ethnic diversity, as implemented through these reforms, are mainly grounded in the international codification of indigenous rights as human rights, and in the globalised network of actors that have been instrumental in 'translating' recognition discourse into the language of social struggle. As Kymlicka (2007: 4) notices in a rare attempt to look at the 'internationalisation' of recognition, its global diffusion through both political discourses and legal norms has been 'fundamentally reshaping the traditional conceptions of state sovereignty, nationhood, and citizenship that have underpinned the international system of nation-states'. But surprisingly, despite this global dimension, academic discussion of recognition has rarely been influenced by experiences beyond Western borders. Yet how recognition is claimed, granted and contested outside of the West constitutes an important part of the journey of recognition as a philosophical, legal and political category. Indeed, while the liberal perspective of most of the advocates of recognition and their biographical origins has meant that the geographical focus and the empirical observations that inspired their theories were driven mainly from Western post-industrial democracies (particularly Canada, the United States, Australia and Europe), the most audacious steps to institutionalise recognition of ethnic minorities have in fact taken place in the Global South and particularly in Latin America.

By shifting the empirical focus to economically fragile and relatively young democracies, this book consciously tries to overcome a divide in the literature and academic thinking on recognition between the Global North and the Global South. While the underlying principles of recognition may have universal value (for instance, in their ambition for inclusion and non-discrimination), when applied to specific socio-historical contexts, their rather homogeneous and a priori evaluation of the causes and remedies for oppression and misrecognition fails to account for important variations. Institutional and state capacity, the availability of public resources, levels of economic development, and ethnic demographic and categorisation variables (density and volatility of ethnic population and politicisation of ethnic identities) are all relevant conditions that affect the outcome of recognition reforms (Storper 2005; Guibernau I Berdún & Rex 2010; Telles & PERLA 2014). In this sense, introducing recognition measures in Western democracies with relatively stable and efficient institutions, high levels of economic development, and low poverty rates is a very different endeavour from implementing similar policies in developing countries and young democracies. Yet, as Wimmer (2013) observes, advocates of recognition tend to support the propagation of this model across the globe, regardless of whether the conditions under which it originally emerged (in Western developed democracies) have been met.

I argue that indigenous rights (as implemented in the Latin American context) should be more fully integrated in the theoretical and normative discussion on recognition politics for at least three reasons: they are one of the fields in which recognition politics have achieved a greater degree of formalisation and practical implementation; they have gathered significant support and consensus in their potential to advance the social justice agenda, without seriously scrutinising their practical outcomes; and they can be studied in a variety of national contexts across the developed/developing divide. Critically, an empirical focus is instrumental for raising issues of contextual and historical variation. In other words, recognition principles and politics might not lead to the same outcomes in terms of social justice everywhere. While recognition theories and policy recipes have often raced along the path towards universalisation, local, domestic and regional variations have rarely been considered. By focusing on countries in the South, this book argues for the need for a more nuanced assessment of recognition politics, which accounts for historical and contextual variations, and a more cautious generalisation of their normative prescriptions.

EXPLAINING RECOGNITION CONFLICTS

This book examines how progressive and globally acclaimed recognition reforms can trigger protracted social conflict affecting poor and marginalised communities. One key reason to study cases where recognition is contested 'stems from the general rule that researchers who want to learn about a given institution should focus on its margins and instances where things don't work' (Jackson 2019: 225). Indeed, the defining feature that distinguishes recognition conflicts from other types of ethnic conflict is their close link with the implementation of specific legal or policy measures related to broader recognition reforms. The object of these measures varies significantly, ranging from land titling to education policies and affirmative action, administrative autonomy, and participatory governance. Whether at the national, regional or local level, these measures are all part of the project of incorporating ethnic groups into the framework of multicultural or plurinational models of citizenship and statehood. In order to do so, they adopt different measures and systems that I broadly divide between what I call 'means of recognition' and 'means of redistribution'. The former includes those provisions that clearly allow for the differentiation of one group from the rest of society based on ethnic criteria, and, from there, allocate this collective subject differentiated rights. The latter are the mechanisms through which recognition norms institutionalise the allocation of material resources on an ethnic basis. The institutionalisation of ethnic categories through recognition reforms has the downstream effect of hardening potentially fluid categories. At the same time, the redistributive effects of recognition through, for example, land tenure increase the stakes for the rural poor. Indeed, many recognition reforms offer access to very concrete resources, including land, and (in certain cases) direct monetary transfers from central government, which can make a big difference in conditions of widespread poverty or indigence. In these scenarios, horizontal inter-group relationships are often completely altered, mechanisms and incentives for cooperation are greatly debilitated, and access to new rights (and resources) becomes a zero-sum game, whereby it is important not only to be granted recognition, but equally to exclude other groups from enjoying the same rights. In certain cases, even relatively homogeneous communities have become battlegrounds, as a result of the new salience suddenly attributed to ethnicity and the emergence of brand-new identities.

The link between rising competition and conflict and the introduction of legal recognition and policy reforms is not always easy to assess. In the cases of the conflicts I discuss in this book, I treat this as an empirical question and I identify two facts that substantiate this relationship: firstly, none of the conflicts I analyse existed prior to the implementation of recognition reforms; secondly, the link is clearly and openly acknowledged by the vast majority of informants. Indeed, this is one of the few points of agreement between the parties in conflict. Another important finding that corroborates the link is the strikingly similar features of the conflicts analysed across three countries – Bolivia, Colombia and Peru – which, despite being part of the same geographical sub-region (the Andes), are in fact quite different from one another in terms of economic development, political orientation and stability, history of civil violence, and ethnic demographics. These countries have, however, followed relatively similar paths towards the implementation of recognition reforms. The comparison represents a compelling framework in which to link the new wave of inter-communal conflict with the implementation of recognition reforms. I discuss the comparative dimension of the book in detail in Chapter 1.

Although the link between conflict and recognition reform appears strong in the cases analysed, I am far from suggesting that such reforms always lead to conflict outcomes. In fact, I identify other concurrent conditions that can increase the likelihood of recognition conflict. In other words, normative changes are necessary but not sufficient conditions for recognition conflict to happen. The first condition is the presence of heterogeneous social communities (i.e. different social groups sharing the same local spaces) or, in some cases, the existence of different ethnocultural roots that can be mobilised to strengthen social differentiation. Demographic change, such as migration inflow, is one of the factors that can contribute to an increase in social heterogeneity and hence trigger recognition conflicts. The second important condition that can fuel recognition conflict is the endemic lack of resources linked to widespread poverty, precarious livelihoods and/or environmental fragilities that characterise many rural communities. This in turn exacerbates the competition for resources, particularly land, and the sensitivity around the distributive outcomes of recognition reforms.

In Chapter 1, I elaborate on the mechanisms that underpin recognition conflicts and I offer a typology of such conflicts that results from the interaction between the two key mechanisms embedded in recognition norms (means of recognition and means of redistribution) and the two key characteristics of social communities: social heterogeneity and resource scarcity. The four types of recognition conflicts that emerge are discussed in detail and with examples in the four empirical chapters (4–7).

ALTERNATIVE EXPLANATIONS

Situations of conflict among rural communities are not new and were frequent across the Andean region well before the rise of recognition politics. It is therefore legitimate to wonder if the conflicts described in this book in fact represent new and different kinds of dispute, or whether they are yet another manifestation of long-standing trends and socio-political processes. Institutionalist perspectives have been particularly valuable in identifying how the endemic weaknesses of Latin American states and the challenges to effectively controlling and governing vast and remote territories have been linked to social instability (Burt & Mauceri 2004; Yashar 2005; Brinks et al. 2019). Relying on evidence mainly from socio-environmental conflict involving rural communities, the state and private companies, scholars have explained the existence of protracted social tensions as the result of inadequacies and dysfunctionalities in the political and institutional system, a lack of transparency, and inappropriate management of conflict; in sum, problems of 'governance' (Panfichi 2011; Vergara 2011; Tanaka 2012). Weak state presence is also considered responsible for the rise of illegal activities and disruptive operations by external actors in the attempt to access and exploit strategic resources through, for example, logging, mining, illicit crop planting and hydrocarbon extraction. All these activities can be very disruptive for local communities and can also contribute to rising social tensions (Bebbington & Bury 2013; Rettberg & Ortiz-Riomalo 2016).

Recognition conflicts, and particularly conflicts involving land claims (which goes here mainly under the category of 'social reproduction conflicts'), are indeed at least in part the result of state failures, weaknesses and slowness in granting land and other rights to rural communities. However, as Merino Acuña (2015: 87) argues: 'fixation on these explanations ... explicitly or implicitly den[ies] structural analysis and deeper understandings of phenomena'. It fails to explain, for example, why, even when efforts are made to strengthen accountability and institutionality, conflicts do not automatically vanish. As Li (2015) illustrates in the case of mining conflicts in Peru, efforts to resolve conflict through institutional mechanisms often fail to account for factors that remain 'outside the frame of visibility', that is, cultural and social structural factors that underpin the value assigned to things. The incompatibility between institutional or mainstream factors and local indigenous ones (or political ontologies, as Merino Acuña (2015) calls them) is at the root of conflict perpetuation. Furthermore, while institutional explanations work well for vertical conflicts, in which social groups mobilise in protest against state actions (or inaction), state inefficiencies do not fully explain why communities are in conflict with each other.

By focusing on the specific impact of recognition reform, I offer an additional explanation for inter-communal conflicts that complements, and adds to, other analyses focused on state and institutional weaknesses. In other words, I argue that state inefficiencies are an important factor, but not one that in itself can explain the rise of these particular kinds of horizontal conflict. Indeed, if the main issue in these conflicts was inefficiencies in implementation, rather than the norm itself, I would expect to find more widespread alliance, rather than conflict, between communities of rural poor that would be similarly impacted by those very inefficiencies and implementation weaknesses. Why then, instead of building alliances to lobby the state, do these communities end up on different conflict fronts? Why are these conflicts often accompanied by the strengthening of identity boundaries and social closure? And why do they not always match the map of old colonial and corporatist disputes? I argue that, to answer these questions, closer attention ought to be paid to the very epistemology of recognition norms, or the way ethnicity is conceived of within the recognition framework, as well as to its operationalisation and the implications it has for the redistribution of key resources.

A second recent line of investigation focusing on social conflict in Latin America has been driven by critical development studies of multicultural reforms. Some of the most common formulations of these critiques have explained the rise in social conflict as a symptom of the dysfunctional implementation of recognition norms. A particularly prolific field in this regard has been around resource governance and participation. Some of these scholars have been highly critical of participation processes in mining and hydrocarbon activities rooted in the International Labour

Organisation (ILO)'s convention and national legal framework, arguing
that these mechanisms result in 'mundane performances of bureaucratic
action' (Perreault 2015: 447) or 'invited spaces dominated by the state'
(Flemmer & Schilling-Vacaflor 2016: 182), rather than fostering participation and genuine dialogue between the state, private companies and
marginalised communities. Power asymmetries, lack of trust and reliable
mediators, and the manipulative role given to technical brokers have
progressively led to a disempowering effect of recognition reforms on
marginalised ethnic groups, as well as to local actors abandoning the
participatory process because of the inability and unwillingness of the
state to address the underlying issues of consultation (Merino Acuña
2018; Torres Wong 2018). At the same time, an opposite trend is
emerging that points towards the exacerbation of socio-environmental
and socio-legal conflicts over prior consultations and extractive endeav-
ours more generally (Merino Acuña 2015; Torres Wong 2018).
Although, at least in certain cases, consultation procedures seem to be
able to deter the use of state repression against indigenous groups
(Zaremberg & Torres Wong 2018), the persistence of social conflict
undermines the promise that Free Prior and Informed Consent/
Consultation (FPIC) could work as a mitigation and resolution tool.
Some of these conflicts associated with extractive industries include
demands for structural change at the state level and are used to promote
broader public discussion on the necessity of recognition policies such as
indigenous territorial and participation rights (an example is the
2009 Baguazo conflict in Peru) (Merino Acuña 2015; 2018).

Taken together, this body of literature has offered an array of explanations for the rise in social conflict across the Andes in recent decades.
This book builds and expands on these authors' findings by showing how,
under certain conditions, recognition reform has the potential to fuel
conflict rather than contributing to conflict prevention and mitigation
across different countries and in a broader range of issue areas (not only
in the extractive industry but also in service provision and territorial
demarcations). The book also shifts the focus from vertical conflicts
characterised by structural power asymmetries (i.e. conflict between social
groups and the state or private companies), which have been the object of
the literature on socio-environmental conflict, to horizontal conflicts
characterised by a relative power equilibrium between parties (i.e. conflict
among social groups themselves). I argue, indeed, that horizontal
conflicts should not be considered as proxies for vertical conflicts but as
conflicts that deserve attention in their own right. This is, I argue, an

important limitation of critical and institutional approaches that have tended to more or less consciously link inter-communal conflicts to broader struggles where social (particularly indigenous) organisations mobilise in protest against the state or petition state authorities for reform. As I mentioned earlier, these kinds of conflict have attracted much scholarly attention in recent years. They have commonly been considered movements of resistance against neoliberalism and what Harvey calls 'accumulation by dispossession' (Kohl & Farthing 2006; Harvey 2007: 34; Remy 2010; Rice 2012), attempts to forge alternative public spheres emancipated by liberal institutions (Stephenson 2002; Albro 2006; Postero & Zamosc 2006), or rebellions against entrenched racism, discrimination and neo-colonial practices (Richards 2003; Paschel & Sawyer 2008; Rivera Cusicanqui 2015).

Such interpretations are not in question here. All these analytical angles can indeed contribute to explaining some aspects of the types of social conflict that have become widespread in the Andean region over past decades. Yet, as de la Cadena (2010: 241) notes, citing Chakrabarty (2000), 'what is accurate is not necessarily sufficient, and questions remain [open]'. Why do social groups that suffer from similar conditions of marginalisation and the negative effects of neoliberal and neo-colonial politics not manage to build sustainable social and political coalitions? Why, at the local level, does conflict erupt in situations where neoliberalisation is similarly affecting communities belonging to different social groups? Why do communities that previously entertained long-standing peaceful relationships end up in conflict in a period characterised by a decline in neoliberalism and the emergence of new national-popular paradigms such as plurinationalism? And why are inter-communal conflicts of the kind that I call recognition conflicts happening across countries with very different political trajectories? A necessary condition to answer these questions, I argue, is to focus on the horizontal dimension of conflict as an object of study in its own right, rather than as reflections of other vertical struggles and claims.

Another popular angle from which to explain ethnic-based social tension in the Global South is embedded in postcolonial theory. In particular, the concept of strategic essentialism, first coined by the Indian scholar Gayatri Chakravorty Spivak (1990), represents a rare example of cross-continental spread in ethnic studies, as it became very influential in Latin America as well. There it has been used as an alternative to institutionalist approaches in accounting for a trend towards the ethnicisation of social struggle. In particular, it is used to describe how subaltern groups decide to subscribe to a shared identity in order to increase their chances of success in public battles for rights (Buchanan 2010). It has the merit of introducing a strategic dimension to recognition struggles – one that accounts, at the same time, for the rarely considered performative effects of institutional change. Yet it falls short in explaining why certain subaltern groups are not able, or do not choose, to act strategically. This comes once again through neglecting the horizontal dimension of recognition struggles. In the context of indigenous rights, for example, why do some groups with clear indigenous markers choose not to self-identify as indigenous? As we shall see, this behaviour is not uncommon across the Andean region and can be understood only by looking at the 'deep history' of collective identities. In the Apolo conflict that I analyse in Chapter 5, for example, more than half of the local peasant union's leaders and members did not join the indigenous organisation, although they could be considered to be just as indigenous as those that self-identified as such. Resistance to embracing ethnic identities is also common across the Peruvian highlands, albeit this has been slowly changing in recent years. These cases do not have one single and generalisable explanation. Opposition to indigenous identity is not uncommon where indigeneity evokes negative associations linked to a colonial past and a derogatory conception of contemporary indigenous peoples. As an Apoleño Quechua peasant told me:

They want to get us back as we were just getting civilised, as in the Eastern lowlands. There, there are true indigenous that do not even have their legal dressing as we have. We already know how to pray the 'Lord's Prayer', we are Catholics, Christians. … How could they convert us if we believe we are syndicalised, organised peasants!? We feel they are trying to convert us! (Interview, Apolo, July 2010)

But resistance to indigenous self-identification is not always driven by emotion. As I will show, it can also be a deliberate strategy to gain a portion of local power in opposition to the rise of competing actors (e.g. new indigenous movements). In sum, norm-driven performative effects on identity change are not always predictable and depend on the contingent responses of different social groups to evolving circumstances. The agency of subaltern groups has been strongly revindicated by Latin American 'decolonial' scholars. The Bolivian sociologist Rivera Cusicanqui has formulated one of the most elaborate critiques of multiculturalism in Latin America, identifying multiculturalism as an 'ongoing practice of coloniality' that recognises ethnic groups only as idealised static subjects. This aspect of Rivera Cusicanqui's argument does in part resonate with this book's claim that recognition reform has contributed to social closure and hard ethnic boundaries, although I tend to consider this a 'side effect' of recognition rather than a deliberate attempt to control subaltern masses, as Rivera Cusicanqui argues (2012; 2015).

After this brief summary of the main argument of the book and discussion of alternative explanations, two clarificatory notes are in order. Firstly, social conflict and competition are not considered here as negative in and of themselves; conflict can be understood as symptomatic and inevitable in any process of social and political change. This book argues that it is equally important to acknowledge the unintended effects of ethnic recognition regimes, with the aim of moderating their potentially disruptive impact on communities that are among the most marginalised and poorest in Latin America.

Secondly, this book does not argue against the politics of recognition *tout court*, nor is its intention to provide 'ammunition to enemies' (Jackson & Warren 2005: 566) of recognition, particularly those states still reluctant to engage in the fight against the exclusion and discrimination of ethnic minorities. It does, however, challenge the dominant narrative about the effects of recognition in terms of inclusion and conflict mitigation. By exploring the links between global, national and, particularly, local politics, a more nuanced picture of recognition outcomes emerges. These nuances, and in particular the trade-offs between strengthening cultural and ethnic rights and increasing inter-group competition and socio-economic differentiation, should be fully acknowledged and incorporated both in a theory of recognition and within international and domestic policymaking. It is indeed 'in the shadow' of recognition that a more balanced understanding of the complex relationship between diversity and equality emerges.

ORGANISATION OF THE BOOK

The book contains one theoretical chapter, two historical chapters, four empirical chapters and a conclusion.

The first three chapters provide the theoretical framework and historical background. They offer a brief introduction to Latin American and Andean rural politics for those not familiar with the subject, while developing an original analytical framework in which to situate key historical processes.

In the first chapter, I propose a framework for analysis of recognition conflicts, through establishing a typology of such conflicts that results from the interactions between key mechanisms that underpin them, related to both recognition norms and the characteristics of social communities. The chapter also provides details on the country case studies, offering an overview of recognition reforms and other relevant national features such as ethnic demography, economic performance, and institutional and political context across the three countries. Finally, it presents the methodology and some necessary conceptual and terminological clarifications.

The second chapter provides an overview of the different strategies adopted by Latin American states in dealing with the incorporation of the rural poor into nation-building processes. It proposes a chronology of implementation of four different models of citizenship and development from the early twentieth century to the present: (1) indigenism and *mestizaje* (1920–1950); (2) national corporatism (1950–1970); (3) neo-indigenism and multiculturalism (1980–1990); and (4) plurinationalism (2000–2010). The historical accounts that illustrate these models focus particularly on Bolivia, Peru and Colombia, with the aim of providing important background information for the case studies that are the focus of this book. Yet, with some variations, these models have been implemented across Latin America more widely over the past century.

Changes in state-building regimes have been key determinants in reshaping the modes of interaction and even the identities of rural communities. Chapter 3 analyses how collective identities and inter-group relationships have changed since the 1950s, commensurate with shifts in citizenship regimes. It focuses in particular on the alternation between class and ethnicity as the two main referents for social organisation in rural Latin America. Four main phases in the evolution of the class-ethnic relationship are identified: (1) hierarchical articulation (class over ethnicity); (2) hierarchical articulation (ethnicity over class); (3) organisational disarticulation; and (4) pragmatic articulation. These phases are illustrated through concrete examples, mainly from the Andean region. The chapter provides a historical narrative and an analytical lens through which to understand the complex and thus far only partially told story of the relationship between peasant and indigenous movements in Latin America.

Chapters 4 to 7 focus on recognition conflict. The empirical material and case studies are organised according to the types of recognition conflict identified in Chapter 1: participation conflicts, social reproduction conflicts, demographic conflicts and access conflicts. All the chapters have an introductory section offering more specific background information about contextual and normative changes. Each chapter discusses at least two empirical cases of conflicts from different countries and provides a brief conclusion.

Chapter 4 deals with recognition conflicts around participatory governance. As an example of participation conflict, I provide a close analysis of the debates that led to the introduction of Free Prior and Informed Consent/Consultation (FPIC) in national legislation and policy in Bolivia, Colombia and Peru. Rooted in international human rights law, the FPIC mechanism is designed to regulate and operationalise the participation of indigenous peoples in environmental decision making and political processes on questions in which their interests are directly affected. The implementation of FPIC illustrates the tensions around key aspects of the recognition agenda, particularly on how to define the 'legitimate' subjects of recognition.

Land is perhaps the most obvious and widespread of the motives behind recognition conflicts, as territorial control and land access have been central claims for both indigenous and peasant movements. Chapter 5 discusses the links between land reform and identity change as examples of social reproduction conflicts. It describes paradigmatic cases from Colombia and Bolivia in which identities have increasingly become salient tools in social conflicts, eventually having an impact on the way people self-identify and the very nature of land struggles.

Chapter 6 illustrates how both exogenous and endogenous changes in rural demographics, namely sustained internal migration and growing indigenous population rates, fuel social tensions around new settlements, as well as in contexts where communities have peacefully coexisted for decades. Relying on empirical cases from Peru and Colombia, I explore changes in local demographics as roots of new recognition conflicts.

Chapter 7 focuses on access conflicts linked to recognition reforms in the education sector. Policy initiatives that seek to account for ethnocultural diversity in education and schooling, including affirmative action measures and bilingual education models, have become increasingly popular over the past few decades. I draw on empirical case studies from Colombia and Peru to show how identity education policies can increase social tensions and lead to outbreaks of violence.

In the conclusion, I first highlight the contributions of the book to a broader cross-continental perspective on recognition that could help to bridge long-standing gaps in the literature on ethnic politics. I argue that findings about the Latin American case have particular value to this discussion, showing how the subcontinent shares more similarities with other contexts than scholars have generally assumed. I then discuss how empirical evidence should encourage new thinking around the way in which recognition is theorised as a justice principle. Finally, I offer some recommendations on how to incorporate the book's findings into a policy agenda, or more precisely how to tackle these empirical and moral puzzles through concrete action and policy measures.

Recognition Conflicts

In this chapter, I offer an original analytical framework for what I call recognition conflicts. I propose a definition and a typology that can help identify these conflicts beyond the specific geographical and temporal boundaries of my empirical cases. The second part of the chapter is intended as a methodological and conceptual framework to orient the reader throughout the remainder of the book. I provide a rationale for the country case selection, a description of methods used and my methodological approaches, and a brief discussion of key concepts and terminology.

A FRAMEWORK FOR ANALYSIS

The conflictive outcomes of recognition are relatively recent phenomena, at least in Latin America, and have generally received minimal scholarly attention. I therefore begin by offering a definition of recognition conflict. A *recognition conflict* is a pattern of behaviour in which social groups consistently engage in contests over goods, services, power, social boundaries and/or leadership as a part or consequence of the recognition of specific ethnic and cultural rights. Parties in conflict self-identify as members of distinct and bounded groups divided along ethnic/race and class lines. As mentioned above, the focus here is on the horizontal dimension of conflict, whereby parties' relationships are characterised by a relative balance of power and understood as 'peer to peer', rather than vertical, as in the case of social groups' claims on the state and other more powerful actors. This is a relatively broad definition that allows for the inclusion of a wide range of conflicts at different stages of intensity –

Competition					Violence
Competing identities/narratives	Discrimination	Threats	Land Invasions	Physical injuries	Killings
Competing organisations	Hate speech	Blackmail	House/crop burnings		Massacre
	Physical segregation				

FIGURE 1.1. Recognition conflicts spectrum

from competition to open violence – and a broad set of actions – from the presence of competing organisations to hate speech, land invasion and killings. Figure 1.1 offers an overview of the broad spectrum of actions and levels of violence across which recognition conflicts discussed in this book fall. The main feature that distinguishes recognition conflicts from other kinds of ethnic conflicts is the fact that they happen in response to or as a consequence of recognition reforms. As I mentioned in the Introduction, the main goal of this book is to illustrate how and under what conditions recognition conflicts emerge.

I identify two sets of mechanisms that underpin different types of recognition conflicts that have to do with (1) the features of the norm; and (2) the features of social communities. I discuss the two sets of mechanisms below and subsequently the resulting typology (Figure 1.2). Each ideal type of recognition conflict will then be discussed in the empirical chapters (Chapters 4–7).

Recognition Reforms

The first set of mechanisms focuses on the link between recognition reform and conflict. Following well-known concepts in contentious politics studies, I argue that recognition reforms open new 'windows of political opportunities' that people may use to trigger social action (McAdam et al. 2001). Although this concept is often applied to explain social movements' engagement with the state apparatus, it is also useful in illuminating the importance of external conditions in regard to whether or not conflict will occur. The implementation of recognition reforms can be seen as a window of opportunity in both a situational and structural sense (Tarrow 1998). The rise of recognition politics generally coincides with a period of democratic consolidation and political opening, which implies less repressive and more favourable conditions for protest and social conflict. Likewise, it introduces a structural change in the way certain social groups can access rights and resources. Both these situational and structural conditions make an increase in intra-group conflict, as well as its visibility, more likely.

However, I am far from considering the step from recognition to conflict an automatic one. As I have already mentioned, not all recognition reforms lead to conflict, and, when they do, the process is not instantaneous. It is often some time after the ratification of new multicultural constitutions, agrarian reforms and other recognition policies that conflicts emerge. This is because, in order for people to be willing to respond or capable of responding to external changes (legal reforms, policy implementation, political shifts), these changes ought to be relevant and identifiable, that is, they ought to be having an impact on people's lives. As Frances Fox Piven and Richard Cloward (1979: 20–21 cited in Lapegna 2016: 8) pointed out, 'it is the daily experience of people that shapes their grievances, establishes the measure of their demands, and points out the targets of their anger'. As a result, the most contentious phase of recognition, at least in terms of horizontal contention, often coincides with the implementation of new laws and policies (post-recognition), rather than with national debates and the approval of recognition reforms.

I now introduce a distinction between two different elements that coexist in most recognition reforms in order to untangle the different ways in which mechanisms embedded in these reforms can increase social tensions. I argue that recognition norms work as triggers of recognition conflicts in two different ways through what I call (1) means of recognition; and (2) means of redistribution.[1] These are provisions of recognition norms that set up different actions or systems through which recognition can be achieved.

The 'means of recognition' concept describes all those tools that, by mobilising symbolic resources (e.g. conceptual distinctions, classification and interpretation strategies, cultural traditions), create and institutionalise social differences on ethnic/cultural grounds.[2] This in turn favours the crystallisation of historically situated identity hierarchies, as I discuss in Chapter 3. Taylor's (1992: 25–26) famous argument rests on the

---

[1] In formulating this distinction, I draw inspiration from Nancy Fraser's (1995: 73) differentiation between 'redistributive remedies' and 'recognition remedies'.
[2] I rely here on the influential definition of 'symbolic resources' and 'symbolic boundaries' offered by Lamont and Molnár (2002: 168).

assumption that 'our identity is partly shaped by recognition or its
absence', and recognition becomes therefore a 'vital human need'.
Citizens' equal treatment within a given society cannot thus be achieved
other than through differentiated sets of rights, which account for
people's identity specificities. Means of recognition are therefore all those
provisions that clearly allow for differentiation between one group and
the rest of society based on ethnic/cultural criteria and, from there,
allocate different rights to this new collective subject. Indeed, one of the
most important ways in which means of recognition function is through
the definition of the 'subject' of recognition, or the collective that may be
entitled to a differentiated set of rights. Examples are the inclusion of
questions on ethnic belonging in a national census or the definition of
criteria and institutional mechanisms to identify and classify ethnic
groups within laws and constitutions. I also include under the 'means of
recognition' category those provisions which are critical moulders of
social relationships with a relatively weak redistributive component.
Examples of these provisions are cultural and linguistic rights, such as
intercultural (bilingual) education, and affirmative action measures. As
constructivists have extensively shown, in practice, norm-making influences the process of boundary-making with which social actors are constantly occupied (Barth 1969; Lamont & Molnár 2002; Wimmer 2013),
with possible effects on political competition and social conflict
(Lieberman & Singh 2012, 2017).

The other major way through which norms of recognition impact the
politicisation of ethnic identities and inter-group competition is by defining how key resources are redistributed. I use 'means of redistribution' to
refer to the provisions through which recognition norms institutionalise
the allocation of certain resources on an ethnic basis. A redistributive
dimension has been, to various degrees, embedded within political recipes
for recognition. Scholars have gone as far as to identify redistribution as
the most important goal of recognition. In Kymlicka's (2001: 51) words,
'much of the talk of the "politics of recognition" has exaggerated the
degree to which recognition is desired for its own sake and neglected the
extent to which "recognition" really involves underlying issues of the
redistribution of power and resources'. This redistributive component
has acquired particular importance within indigenous rights frameworks,
where land is understood as the *sine qua non* of such rights. Land has
become an integral part of the understanding of indigenous cultural
identity, expressed through indigenous advocacy networks and reflected
in international law (where land and territorial rights are a core part of

Convention 169) (Engle 2010). In many Latin American countries, the influential debate around indigenous rights has shaped agrarian reforms and national land policy since the 1990s. New forms of collective land titles were introduced in agrarian legal frameworks, while the acceleration of the titling process was made possible by the availability of targeted international cooperation funds. Mirroring the impact of the means of recognition on identity boundary-making, the process of mapping and formalising territorial boundaries, which had remained fluid for centuries (Reyes-García et al. 2012), can have unsettling consequences for rural communities. While land is probably the most conflictive issue within recognition reforms, other resource-related issues are permeating many recognition conflicts. Indeed, the recognition agenda often includes other provisions with strong redistributive implications, for example, special taxation regimes or direct transfers of public resources to ethnic groups.

'Means of recognition' and 'means of redistribution' are not discrete mechanisms; their entanglement in conceptual and normative terms is complex and at times very difficult to discern. Furthermore, redistribution has generally been neglected or theoretically and empirically merged in the recognition realm. As McNay (2008: 9) notes, there is a 'tendency ... to allocate recognition struggles to a distinct realm – the lifeworld or culture – thereby disconnecting it from ... the arena of redistribution, the economy or systems'. This is perhaps because the focus has mainly been on 'pre-recognition' struggles that have generally not included explicit distributive claims. Even land, an asset with high redistributive value, has been claimed by indigenous peoples mostly as a function of culture and autonomy (self-determination), rather than as a function of economic redistribution. An argument has been made about the impossibility of separating recognition from redistribution in practice. These processes are so bound together that any search for an origin is irrelevant, the argument goes; the drive to categorise zones or to discern their origin is a drive to create such a distinction (Armstrong 2006). Yet, following Fraser (1995, 2000, 2009), I argue here that, for analytical purposes, the best strategy is to keep these mechanisms separate and identify which component has primacy within the recognition reforms under scrutiny. This is because the two mechanisms of redistribution and recognition can contribute to identifying and explaining different kinds of recognition conflict. Furthermore, while interests and identities might be inextricably linked in practice (Dick 2011), in normative terms, attributing to recognition the 'burden' of redistribution has important and often unexpected

consequences. The conflicts described in this book make these consequences tangible.

Social Communities

I now turn towards the second set of mechanisms that underpin recognition conflicts and that are related to some key characteristics of the social
communities impacted by recognition reforms. As I mentioned in the
Introduction, one of the key innovations of this book within recognition
scholarship is that it adopts a broader sociological approach to recognition, by considering not only the groups that are either claimants or
recipients of recognition but also the social communities in which they
are embedded. These social communities often share similar features, even
across country borders. I identify two such characteristics that, I argue,
increase the likelihood of conflict outcomes from recognition reforms:
social heterogeneity and resource scarcity.

Social heterogeneity characterises social communities in which people
who identify with different collective identities, values and beliefs, and
who (in certain cases) follow different systems of local governance, live
side by side and share the same physical environment in a highly inter-
active mode of social organisation. Social heterogeneity is rooted in both
historical and contemporary processes, as I illustrate in Chapter 3. In the
case of the Andean region, the colonial and even precolonial past of these
countries (and indeed of many countries of the Global South) has left deep
marks on contemporary human landscapes. Until very recently, indigenous peoples had been living at the margins of republican societies, occupying rural and often remote spaces. Here, in different historical periods
(which I describe in Chapters 2 and 3), two alternative modes of social
and political organisation have tended to prevail: indigenous and peasant.
These modes (and their cultural attributes) have in certain cases coexisted
for decades within the same geographical areas, with outcomes that range
from an overlapping and osmotic relationship to a conflictive and mutu-
ally exclusive interaction among social groups. Boundaries between identities can be very flexible and lead to articulation and alliance, or can
become very rigid and trigger social tensions and competition. Oscillation
between conflict and alliance has been taking place since early colonial
times. Traditional forms of indigenous organisation and administration
(e.g. *curacas* and *cabildos*) were maintained throughout the colonial
period. With the creation of independent republics, those institutions
were only partially dismantled. But it was from the mid-twentieth

century, with the creation of peasant unions as ways of organising the rural poor and of providing access to representation and citizenship, that indigenous forms of governance were generally dismantled. In certain cases, peasant unions were created on top of indigenous structures, resulting in hybrids, while in other cases they replaced pre-existing modes of local governance (Rivera Cusicanqui 1993). With the creation of new indigenous organisations since the 1970s and 1980s, indigenous 'counter-reforms' have managed to push out peasant unions in certain areas, while in other cases unions and indigenous organisations ended up coexisting (Fontana 2014a). This is not uncommon in those 'transition areas' around 'demographic fault lines', where a variety of ethnic and peasant communities coexist (often coinciding with the inter-Andean valleys), mainly as a result of old migratory processes (Rivera Cusicanqui 1993).

More recent population dynamics have also had a great impact on socio-cultural heterogeneity. Ongoing migratory processes are constantly reshaping human landscapes. In the Andean region, migration of high-land dwellers towards lowland regions in search of more fertile land has put increasing pressure on already fragile environments (particularly in the Amazon and along the tropical valleys), sometimes generating new tensions with local indigenous inhabitants. Another source of tension comes from endogenous population changes such as the growth of indigenous communities. Changing demographics are placing new pressures on the land in terms of livelihood and community subsistence, as well as on the environment and the conservation of fragile ecosystems. Likewise, they have fuelled growing social tensions not only around new settlements but also in contexts in which different communities have peacefully coexisted for decades.

There is no doubt that the destiny of rural communities has been greatly influenced by external events. But it is also the agency of communities and their capacity to embody broader political processes that have important consequences for the constitution of more or less heterogeneous social landscapes. Conflict is often rooted in the coexistence of opposite attitudes in social groups vis-à-vis normative changes. When people either resist or adjust to change in a homogeneous fashion, conflict between them is rare. It is when certain groups respond positively to external change, while other coexisting groups may be unable or unwilling to adjust, that increased social heterogeneity and potential competition emerge. Indeed, something that recognition scholars tend to ignore is that, in the battle for recognition, different groups can move from very different starting blocks. For new identities to be successful, not only is

34   *Recognition Conflicts*

there the need for a vision and a political strategy, but new identities require a coherent match between new narratives and pre-existent socio-cultural features. In other words, to be successful, it is paramount for the new identities to be embedded in socially accepted cultural repertoires, such as symbols, stories and stereotypes, often pre-existent within the local culture. In this sense, the success of certain ethnic identities cannot be understood without considering the broader history of countries and regions, and the fact that cultural elements belonging to an ethnic tradition were already shared among the population and were part of the local culture. In sum, if culture is not the trigger for ethnic mobilisation, it is certainly a precondition for its success. This also helps explain why the revitalisation of ethnic claims has occurred more smoothly in certain contexts than in others, where indigenous cultural features have been lost or never existed. How different groups are able and willing to mobilise existing cultural markers while other groups cannot access similar repertoires might explain why social heterogeneity is not always a precondition for recognition conflicts, but boundary-making can be activated by the very process of recognition; this, in turn, can fuel new conflict, in a sort of feedback loop mechanism.

The second characteristic of social communities that, I argue, cannot be disregarded when studying recognition conflict is an endemic lack of resources. Resource scarcity is understood here as a property of social communities, rather than of the environment. Indeed, many of the rural poor who are the protagonists of recognition conflicts live in areas with important economic potential. Across the Andes, indigenous peoples inhabit areas that are often extraordinarily rich in terms of biodiversity and both renewable and non-renewable resources. However, rural communities very rarely benefit from the wealth that exists in their territories, and most of them live in extreme poverty, relying on subsistence agriculture and, occasionally, small enterprises and tourism projects. Material and economic conditions of social groups shape both their motives and the possibilities for mobilisation. The more pressing the economic needs, the more likely it is that a group will engage in conflicts to improve its situation. Poverty and economic deprivation – endemic conditions of the vast majority of rural communities in Global South countries – are considered classic triggers of conflict. In addition, if communities have different means of accessing resources, the redistributive implications of recognition reform will have relatively mild effects on intergroup competition, as people will be enjoying comparable levels of well-being and livelihood opportunities. As most of the social communities affected by recognition reforms are rural, land is often the key resource at stake. Indeed, as Albertus (2015: 2) notes, 'land is the chief productive asset for the world's rural poor'. Land tenure insecurity and lack of clarity are very common in developing countries. In many cases, states never possessed the capacity to conduct extensive cadastral studies, and huge parts of their territory are occupied but not legally owned. As a result, security in land tenure and territorial control have been central historical claims not only for indigenous peoples but for other rural dwellers as well, particularly peasants. It has to be noted though that, in extreme situations of marginalisation and poverty, the struggle for survival prevents the creation of the minimal conditions and resources required for mobilisation. In other words, communities that are extremely poor and isolated are often unlikely to mobilise without external support.[3] In sum, conflict often occurs in poor and marginalised areas where, however, people have enough resources and connections to invest in collective struggle.

Varieties of Recognition Conflicts

I propose here a typology of recognition conflicts based on the interactions between the two mechanisms embedded in recognition reforms, which I have termed 'means of recognition' and 'means of redistribution', and the two key characteristics of social communities: social heterogeneity and resource scarcity. These interactions represent, I argue, an effective way of describing different kinds of recognition conflicts while offering a theory for the mechanisms that underpin these conflicts. The four 'ideal types' of conflict are represented in Figure 1.2. To be clear, this typology does not imply rigid boundaries between the mechanisms that operate in each of the four scenarios. These boundaries are fluid, and most conflicts involve a combination of different norm mechanisms and social community characteristics. Indeed, most recognition norms include both means of recognition and means of redistribution, and most social communities where recognition conflict occurs present certain degrees of heterogeneity and economic deprivation. However, to draw these distinctions, I focus on the primacy of a specific pair of mechanisms

---

[3] A telling example is offered by Torres Wong (2018) in her comparative study of the right to prior consultation, where she shows how different outcomes of negotiation processes in the context of natural resources exploitation depend on whether indigenous groups were or were not already mobilised and on their level of internal organisation and external support.

Recognition Norm \ Social Community	Resource Scarcity	Social Heterogeneity
Means of Recognition	*Participation conflicts*	*Access conflicts*
Means of Redistribution	*Social reproduction conflicts*	*Demographic conflicts*

FIGURE 1.2. Varieties of recognition conflicts

in a given scenario. This scenario can sometimes evolve over time, resulting in the transition from one ideal type to another. In other words, different phases of one broader conflict can fit different quadrants of the proposed typology, as I will illustrate in the 'Methods' section. Below I provide a brief overview of each conflict type; I then discuss each of them in detail and with examples in the empirical chapters (Chapters 4–7).

Participation conflicts are conflicts over definitions of inclusion/exclusion in resource-scarce contexts. These conflicts are about who is entitled to recognition in the framework of broader debates on the participation of social groups that have been traditionally marginalised and that experience widespread poverty and precarious livelihoods. The definition of new ethnic subjects becomes very important beyond the social taxonomy dimension, as a way of being included or excluded in key decision-making processes, and is therefore pursued as a strategy to reverse social marginalisation and gain access to power and resources. In Chapter 4, I compare the national debates on the definition of the collective subject that would be entitled to a new participatory mechanism called Free Prior and Informed Consent/Consultation (FPIC) as examples of participation conflicts. Grounded in Convention 169, FPIC has been designed to provide a mechanism to regulate and operationalise the participation of indigenous peoples in any political processes in which their interests are directly affected (Ward 2011). Yet, the strategic importance of the commodity industry has meant that FPIC has often been understood as a way of settling disputes among communities, transnational companies and the state in the framework of hydrocarbon and mineral exploitation projects. Looking at how the national debates on FPIC were framed and how they reshaped the relationships between social actors is illustrative of the tensions embedded in the process of ethnic boundary-making through the redefinition of collective subjects (means of recognition).

Social reproduction conflicts are redistributive conflicts par excellence. They result from the interaction between norms with high redistributive potential and the endemic lack of resources experienced by social communities. As I have already observed, land is a key asset for communities of rural poor, and its implications for redistribution are well known (Albertus 2015). Land has also been one of the key demands of indigenous movements, whose claims emphasise particularly its symbolic and cultural value as essential for their social and cultural reproduction. Without undermining these aspects, I focus here on the redistributive value of land. In contexts of resource scarcity, land becomes the most important good on which communities rely for their subsistence and livelihoods. The redefinition of territorial boundaries and the very process of land titling in highly informal systems of land tenure represent, for some groups, key opportunities to secure and expand land control and, for others, a threat to an already precarious status quo. Land, however, is not the only trigger of social reproduction conflicts. In urban settings, for example, housing policies can have a very significant redistributive effect, similar to that of agrarian reforms in rural areas. As the focus of the book is on rural communities, in Chapter 5 I analyse different cases in which multicultural agrarian reforms are redefining the physical boundaries of ethnic communities and triggering recognition conflicts.

Demographic conflicts are conflicts over redistributive assets (e.g. land) in contexts where increased social heterogeneity as a result of demographic change is putting new pressure on social communities. These conflicts have a lot in common with social reproduction conflicts, but they are related to important changes in local demographics. In Chapter 6, I consider examples of conflicts that are driven by both exogenous demographic changes (incoming migration) and endogenous demographic changes (population growth). Other factors could also fuel this kind of conflict – for example, migration outflows that can shift the balance of power between different coexisting groups, or policies with a high redistributive impact such as taxation systems, subsidies or cash transfers. This might be the case especially in urban settings – where land is not a key asset – or in more developed economies with higher levels of labour formalisation.

Finally, *access conflicts* are conflicts over recognition policies focused on language and cultural rights (i.e. with weak redistributive impact) and affirmative action measures in socially heterogeneous communities. In Chapter 7, I present examples of conflicts resulting from the implementation of education policies, namely affirmative action in higher education and intercultural bilingual education. However, access conflicts can also emerge from the implementation of other policies, such as different kinds of affirmative actions to ensure representation of ethnic groups in public administration or in the workforce. Likewise, they can be triggered by other social provisions with weak redistributive effects, such as health policies. I use empirical examples to illustrate how these disputes not only claim inclusion in a certain measure or policy but also claim exclusion from those very provisions. This is why I call this type of recognition conflicts 'access conflicts' rather than inclusion conflicts.

In the remainder of Chapter 1, I discuss the comparative framework of the study and provide more information on methods and terminology.

WHY PERU, COLOMBIA AND BOLIVIA?

The main reason why the Andes[4] constitutes a particularly interesting terrain in which to study recognition is that, over the last thirty years, efforts in this region have led the world in the implementation of recognition reforms. Not only have Andean countries incorporated ILO Convention 169 within their constitutional frameworks; they have also steadily implemented institutional and policy reforms that give concrete relevance to the international norm. Andean societies have engaged in broader public debates on ethnic diversity, social inclusion and cultural rights, which have shaped innovative proposals for new models of citizenship and development, as I describe in Chapter 2. All in all, relatively similar policies have been adopted in Andean countries for the recognition of indigenous rights, including land distribution, political and community participation, and education reforms. Table 1.1 summarises the main laws and regulations concerning ethnic recognition in Peru, Colombia and Bolivia. Another aspect that these countries have in common is the presence of peasant and indigenous movements active at the local and national levels, maintaining complex and changing relationships among them. In sum, both policy and social features make up an interesting context to explore the effects of the implementation of recognition politics on the social fabric. In the following paragraphs, I briefly illustrate the main steps in the process of implementation of recognition reforms in Colombia, Bolivia and Peru.

---

[4] Understood in this context as a political region (Andean countries) rather than as a geographic space coinciding with the mountain range.

TABLE 1.1. *Recognition reforms in Bolivia, Colombia and Peru*

	Peru	Colombia	Bolivia
ILO Convention 169 ratification	1994	1991	1991
Constitutional reforms	Constitutional Reform (1993) recognised Peru as a multicultural, multi-ethnic and multilingual nation	Constitutional Reform (1991) recognised the multi-ethnic and multicultural nature of Colombia	Constitutional Reform (1994) recognised the pluricultural and multi-ethnic nature of Bolivia Constitutional Reform (2009) declared Bolivia a plurinational state
Land and territorial/ administrative autonomy	Native Communities Law (1978) ruled land tenure of lowland indigenous groups Constitution (1993) established the imprescriptibility and free disposition of communal land, but not the inalienability and indefeasibility recognised by previous constitutions	Constitution (1991) granted some degree of autonomy to indigenous territories Agrarian Law (1994) established the creation and reconstitution of indigenous and Afro-Colombian *resguardos* Decree 2164 (1995) set the administrative procedures for the creation of *resguardos*	Law of Agrarian Reform (1996) introduced indigenous collective land titles (TCOs) Constitution (2009) established autonomous indigenous/peasant territories (AIOC) 11 municipalities opted to become AIOC following a referendum (2009)
Education	Intercultural Bilingual Education (IBE) Law (2002) Decree 006 (2016) approved a sectorial IBE policy	Ethno-education Programme (1985) General Law on Education (1994) included a chapter on ethnic education Decree 2,500 (2010) regulated the administration of local schooling by 'certified territorial entities'	Education Law (1994) mandated the implementation of IBE for indigenous communities and intercultural education for Spanish-speaking communities

(*continued*)

TABLE 1.1. (*continued*)

	Peru	Colombia	Bolivia
Political participation	'Municipal Election Law (1997) introduced the so-called 'Cuota nativa' (15% indigenous candidates for regional and municipal councils)	Constitution (1991) granted two seats in parliament to indigenous peoples	Law of Political Parties, Citizens Associations and Indigenous Peoples (2004) opened the possibility for indigenous peoples to participate in national and local elections as legitimate subjects Electoral Law (2010) established seven indigenous special circumscriptions
Free Prior and Informed Consent/ Consultation (FPIC)	FPIC Law (2011) Decree 001 (2012) ruled on the implementation of FPIC	Decree 1320 (1996) regulated consultations on the exploitation of natural resources in indigenous territories Decree 2957 (2010) regulated consultations with a general scope Decree 1320 (1998) rules FPIC for indigenous and Afro-Colombian communities Law Project on FPIC (2016)	Hydrocarbon Law (2005) introduced the right to consultation and participation for indigenous communities Decree 29033 (2007) regulated FPIC in the hydrocarbon sector Law Project on FPIC (2013) Decree 2298 (2015) regulated FPIC in the hydrocarbon sector

Colombia was one of the first countries to ratify ILO Convention 169 (in August 1991, after Norway and Mexico) and to undergo constitutional reform (1991) that recognised for the first time the country's multiethnic and multicultural society. This new attitude vis-à-vis the indigenous issue opened up a concrete possibility for ethnic groups to strengthen their political participation (through a system of quotas), secure control over their land (in the form of *resguardos*), and access a significant degree of autonomy in the management of resources and service provisions relatively early on compared to the rest of the region. However, the new rights framework for indigenous peoples contributed to widening the gap between ethnic and non-ethnic rural sectors. Indeed, in Colombia indigenous and peasant movements have traditionally developed and organised as political actors following different trajectories, and their goals and interests have rarely found points of convergence. While indigenous communities have often been sources of recruitment for rural guerrilla fighters, indigenous movements have generally maintained a certain detachment from agrarian and redistributive claims, which in turn constitute the main demands of peasant-based insurgent movements like the Revolutionary Armed Forces of Colombia (Fuerzas Armadas Revolucionarias de Colombia, FARC). Both the significant ideological differences, at least among the movements' leaders, as well as the gaps in the systems of legal protection and in their actual implementation, have increased tensions between rural groups and prevented the formation of alliances until very recently.

Like Colombia, Bolivia ratified the ILO Convention very early on (in December 1991) and implemented a constitutional reform in 1994, which recognised the pluricultural and multi-ethnic nature of the country. Article 171 introduced new economic, social and cultural rights for indigenous peoples and, in particular, a new form of collective land tenure (Tierra Comunitaria de Origen, TCO). Initially, TCO was designed with the claims of lowland indigenous groups in mind. Here, indeed, is where most of the cadastral and titling efforts were concentrated during the first ten years, following the approval of the Law of Agrarian Reform in 1996. Yet land claims grew among native and peasant communities in the highlands as well. In the effort to be as inclusive as possible, the 2009 constitution changed the name from TCO to Indigenous Native Peasant Territory (Territorio Indígena Originario Campesino, TIOC) and introduced a new form of Indigenous Native Peasant Autonomy (Autonomía Indígena Originaria Campesina, AIOC). As I discuss in Chapter 2, these changes go beyond semantics and are linked to the attempt to consolidate an inter-rural alliance across different social sectors, ultimately with the political goal of strengthening the popular coalition that supported Evo Morales' election. This coalition, formed in the mid-2000s to back the new political project, managed to partially overcome the tensions and growing competition between indigenous and peasant organisations triggered by the implementation of multicultural politics in the 1990s. After the constitutional approval in 2009, however, this alliance suffered a new crisis, with the peasant unions maintaining a very compact stand in support of Morales and the indigenous and native organisations expressing signs of growing unease with his administration (Fontana 2013b).

In Peru, ethnic recognition came at a slower pace than in Colombia and Bolivia. Convention 169 was ratified in 1994, one year after the constitutional amendment and a few months before the second election of Alberto Fujimori as president. The 1993 constitution recognised Peru as a multicultural, multi-ethnic and multilingual nation and confirmed the legal existence of native and peasant communities as distinct entities. In practice no significant advances, but rather some reversals,[5] were made with respect to pre-existing legislation. In 1974, Peruvian law grounded social groups' differentiation into rigid geographical boundaries, acknowledging an ethnic status only in relation to the inhabitants of the lowlands, while the rural population in the highlands was automatically ascribed to the peasantry. The two groups were also assigned different systems of land use and management: the former being still partially dependent on hunting and gathering, with the latter relying entirely on agriculture. Only very recent discussions on the implementation of a new law on FPIC (approved in 2011) have made advances in bridging the gap between the indigenous and peasant sectors. After a first attempt from certain groups within the government and the business sector to exclude peasants, on the grounds that they would not meet the ethnic criteria required by the ILO Convention, a compromise view prevailed, which argued for a case-by-case evaluation of the ethnic qualities of peasant communities. In response, agrarian organisations have been reframing their discourses and public presence to boost their ethnic credentials. The claims to and mobilisations for the right to FPIC also provided an incentive for the consolidation of a trans-rural alliance, formalised in a Unity Pact, with the

---

[5] Article 89 extended communal autonomy to 'use and free disposal of land', thus rejecting the inalienability and immunity from seizure of communal lands recognised in previous legislation.

aim of improving social movements' coordinated action and influencing policymaking. The results of this effort have been reflected in a more significant, although still marginal, presence of indigenous and agrarian issues in the public agenda, especially during Ollanta Humala's mandate (2011–2016).

As I have briefly illustrated, Bolivia, Peru and Colombia have offered fertile ground for the implementation of recognition politics in the form of indigenous rights, and these reforms have contributed to reshaping the relationships between rural movements in relatively similar ways. In other words, these are cases where, because of similar recognition reforms, I expect to see similar mechanisms at work, and I trace these across different contexts, making sure that they are not linked to a particular legal framework. Yet these countries diverge significantly if we consider other contextual and historical features, and in particular their economies, demographics, political traditions and experiences of protracted political violence (summarised in Table 1.2). As with the similarities, these differences are equally important, as they allow us to situate the implementation of recognition reforms within different political and economic contexts. These contextual variations, in turn, contribute to strengthening the hypothesis of a link between recognition reforms and the emergence of similar patterns of social conflict and inter-group competition across the three countries.

From an economic perspective, the three countries share a unique richness in natural resources, considered both their blessing and curse since colonial times (Galeano 1971). Yet the bases and performances of their economies place them within different economic brackets. Thanks to a steady growth over the last few years that has moved the country up to the group of upper-middle-income countries, Colombia is the biggest and most powerful economy among the three. While oil remains its main export (about 50%), the manufacturing sector is growing, as are the information technology industry and tourism. Peru is chasing Colombia in reducing the gap with the larger regional economies. Although the volume of its economy is smaller, its GDP per capita is very similar to Colombia's and, overall, Peru has fewer people below the poverty line. Metal and mineral exports (especially copper and silver) still account for almost 60 per cent of the country's total exports. Trade and industry are concentrated in Lima, but important flows of agricultural production and exports have improved regional economies as well. Bolivia is the poorest among the three countries and one of the poorest in Latin America. Yet its economic performances have been improving steadily in recent years,

TABLE 1.2. *Contextual features in Bolivia, Colombia and Peru*

	Economic performance/ main export sector	Political orientation	Political stability	Political violence	Ethnic demography (% indigenous population)
Bolivia	Lower-middle income $5,364 (PPP, 2013) Gas	Progressive (with variations)	Relatively unstable	Mild guerrilla conflict (1980s–1990s)	41% (2012)
Colombia	Upper-middle income $13,430 (PPP 2014) Oil	Conservative	Relatively stable	Political violence/guerrilla conflict (1940s–present)	4.4% (2018)
Peru	Upper-middle income $13,735 (PPP, 2014) Minerals	Conservative (with variations)	Relatively unstable	Guerrilla conflict (1980s–2000s)	25% (2017)

thanks to high commodity prices (especially gas, which remains the main driver of exports) and cautious management of state budget reserves. The consistent patterns of growth and poverty reduction notwithstanding, the World Bank still places Bolivia among lower-middle-income countries.

In terms of politics, these countries have different party and political traditions. While Colombia has been firmly anchored to a conservative democratic tradition since the 1940s, over the last half-century, Bolivia and Peru have oscillated between dictatorial regimes and democratic restoration. They have experienced alternation in power of more or less progressive leaders, including populist dictators (such as Barrientos and Velasco) and neoconservative presidents (such as Sánchez de Lozada and Fujimori). A shift in the countries' trajectories occurred in the 2000s, however. In Bolivia, the election of Evo Morales abruptly turned the political rudder towards the left and managed to marginalise and replace traditional political elites. In Peru, changes in political orientation have been patchier and more unstable, with the mandates of progressive leaders such as Alejandro Toledo and Ollanta Humala interrupted by the return to power of conservative governments.

Over the last few decades, the three countries have also experienced different levels of political and civil violence. The more than five decades of civil conflict in Colombia was among the most protracted contemporary wars worldwide. Rooted in the lack of agrarian reform and structural social inequalities, the conflict took the form of a guerrilla war between leftist armed movements (the most well-known of which is the FARC), the state and paramilitary groups. Peace talks held in Cuba between the FARC and the government from 2012 culminated in the signature of a historic agreement on 23 June 2016. It is estimated that more than 220,000 people were killed during the conflict, the majority of them civilians (262,197 according to Colombia's National Centre of Historic Memory). The very nature of this conflict, mainly fought in rural areas, has caused peasant, indigenous and Afro-descendent groups to suffer the most from the war, with their communities often caught in the frontline, forced to relocate or resist the pressure of violent groups without any state protection.

Peru also experienced a phase of intense political violence in the 1980s and 1990s, when the Maoist guerrilla movement known as Shining Path (Sendero Luminoso) launched an internal conflict with the aim of establishing a 'dictatorship of the proletariat' and a 'pure communist state'. Estimates report nearly 70,000 casualties in less than two decades. Although guerrilla groups are still active in a few remote areas of central

Peru, the conflict is considered to have wound down by 2000, when a Truth and Reconciliation Commission was established. According to the Commission's final report, 75 per cent of the people who were either killed or disappeared spoke Quechua as their native language (Comisión de la Verdad y Reconciliación 2003), which indicates the high price paid by rural communities, especially in the central highlands and valleys.

In Bolivia, in contrast, the presence of guerrilla movements has been marginal compared to Peru and Colombia, and the country has not experienced a period of protracted political violence in recent times. After the failed attempt to organise a guerrilla *foco* by Ernesto 'Che' Guevara in the late 1960s, sporadic actions were conducted by other leftist groups during the 1980s and early 1990s, one of which – the Túpac Katari Guerrilla Army (Ejército Guerrillero Túpac Katari) – was of clear indigenous inspiration. All these groups, however, were quickly neutralised following the incarceration of their leaders.

A fourth relevant difference between the three countries lies in their demography and, particularly, in the relative proportion of their ethnic population. With over 49 million people, Colombia is the most populous of the three countries; yet indigenous peoples represent only 4.4 per cent of the overall population (corresponding to just over two million people, according to the 2018 census). The Peruvian population is estimated at 31.2 million people, over 7.5 million of whom are of indigenous origin (according to the 2017 census), which corresponds to 26 per cent of the country's population. Although comparable in size to Colombia and Peru, Bolivia is significantly less populated, with just over 10 million inhabitants, while Bolivian citizens self-identifying as indigenous make up almost half of the total population (41% according to the 2012 census).

Demographics, political contexts and economic performance are all factors that may affect ethnic relations, the level of social conflict and the impact of recognition reforms at the domestic level. Yet this book reveals that across these different national contexts, remarkably similar types of recognition conflicts have been emerging over the last two decades. What these conflicts have in common is their link with relatively similar recognition reforms. The implementation of these reforms has been followed by similar processes of adaptation and resistance on the part of different social actors, which have led to the intensification of social tensions and competition, particularly in rural areas characterised by high social heterogeneity and endemic resource scarcity.

METHODS

This book explores what happens after indigenous rights have been recognised, and yet issues of social justice remain unresolved and manifest in outbreaks of conflict. In order to capture the links between policy reforms and social change, the book moves across different scales, from the international arena of global governance where indigenous rights were first codified; to national arenas of policymaking where legal and policy reforms are debated and approved; and finally to the local spaces where the implementation of those reforms and rights are 'translated' into the discourse and action of social organisations, becoming 'real' and 'tangible' in people's lives. This multi-scale approach, and particularly the focus on the micro-political level, have the advantage of providing an encompassing and empirically grounded understanding of recognition, a concept that has mostly been discussed in a rather normative and abstract sense.

This study takes the individual conflict as the unit of analysis. It inductively builds on cross-national empirical cases to explore under what conditions rural communities have engaged in new competitive and violent behaviours. Cases were identified based on snowball sampling following interviews with key informants at the national level. The initial field research phase in each country led to the identification of national sub-regions where recognition conflicts may be clustered. This approach allowed me to overcome the difficulties of studying protracted, low-intensity conflicts that rarely make headlines in regional newspapers and almost never reach the national level. Preliminary information was gathered on a number of conflict cases in different regions that appeared to present the key conditions for meeting the definition of recognition conflict (namely, involve two or more social groups identified along class/ethnic lines; be linked to claims or implementation of recognition reforms).

Field trips to different conflict locations were instrumental in confirming or dismissing initial information and therefore selecting a subset of conflicts that indeed fell within the 'recognition conflict' definition. While initially this search led me towards land and territorial conflicts, a closer look at local situations unveiled a more complex map of issues at stake, including service provision, local governance and participation, as well as migration and demographic change. The adoption of an iterative approach between empirical findings and theory building allowed me to refine my analytical framework, while at the same time expanding the range of conflicts under consideration. In order to compile my final sample of cases, I therefore prioritised diversity in terms of issue areas (e.g. land, education, participation) among those conflicts that met my definition of recognition conflicts. As a result, I excluded from the sample (and further in-depth analysis) conflicts with very similar characteristics, balancing at the same time as much diversity as possible in terms of mechanisms and fitting into diverse typologies. In order to grasp a broad range of themes and types of recognition conflicts, I also made the decision to include what might appear, at first sight, as very different and diverse kinds of disputes. I consider this diversity illustrative of the multiple shapes and forms that recognition conflicts can take in terms of scale, levels of violence and outcomes. Again, the common denominator in all these conflicts is the existence of tensions *between* social groups *around* recognition reforms. In practice then, recognition conflicts can include a broad range of manifestations, from nationwide political competition to localised violence (or, to use some examples from my case studies, from debates on FPIC and participatory governance to inter-communal violence over land access and territorial control).

It is certainly the case that particular conflicts fit my typology better than others. As I have already highlighted, recognition conflict types ought to be considered as ideal types of conflict rather than faithful representations of observed realities. Moreover, some conflicts span multiple ideal types. This is due to the complexity and inter-connections of the recognition agenda across a range of issues that, at times, tend to converge and overlap in real-life conflicts. I followed the criterion of the primary mechanisms at play in order to allocate conflict cases to different quadrants of the typology. This resulted in unavoidable simplifications and, as would be expected, it proved easier in certain cases than in others. I also made the decision to include an example of a conflict that evolved over time (in San Andrés de Pisimbala, Colombia), shifting across two conflict ideal types. This example is valuable in illustrating how the complexity around recognition conflict typologies unfolds empirically: it shows how the mechanisms I identify in the typology can be intertwined, and how different phases of one conflict can be driven by different mechanisms and therefore ascribed to different quadrants in my typology. Conflict trajectories are often complex, and parties' agendas as well as contextual characteristics can change over time, shifting the very 'nature' of the conflict as a consequence.

It is also important to acknowledge that conflict cases are not uniform in the amount and depth of empirical information they rely upon. Some of them have been the object of extensive ethnographic work (e.g. Apolo and Inzá); others are built on fewer interviews (e.g. San Matías San Carlos); and for a couple of them, I had to rely on secondary sources and key informants without being able to access the locations and field sites (Catatumbo, Los Naranjos). Whenever possible I tried to collect primary data and visit conflict locations. Besides providing crucial sources for my research, these visits allowed me to experience and embed myself within the social and environmental contexts in which the conflicts were taking place. As often happens with qualitative research, these visits offered very valuable insights into aspects of these conflicts that are not directly evident through documents and conversations. Unfortunately, for a few conflicts, this first-hand experience with the space and stakeholders was not possible, either for security reasons, such as in the case of Catatumbo in Colombia, or because the events occurred far back in time, as in the case of Los Naranjos in Peru. For these cases, I relied mainly on secondary sources to reconstruct the events (e.g. existing literature, media and policy reports, Congress proceedings). I also conducted interviews with key informants with in-depth knowledge of the disputes, who had worked with stakeholders directly involved in the conflicts. Despite the limitations derived from uneven access to primary sources and locations, and there-fore the differences in research approach, I consider that all the conflict cases presented in the book add to the analysis, offering key and diverse insights into specific aspects of recognition conflicts.

Empirical qualitative data constitute the backbone of the entire book. This material was collected during multiple field trips across the Andean region between 2009 and 2016 (twenty-four months in total) (Figure 1.3). Field research produced 250 semi-structured interviews,[6] focus group meetings, and participant observation at national and local events. In each country, a first round of interviews was conducted at the national level (generally in the capital cities or other major cities) with government representatives, social organisation leaders and advisors, members of local and international NGOs, officers of international organisations (e.g. the UN) and cooperation agencies (e.g. Danish cooperation agency Danida), academics, and journalists. This initial information was instru-mental in the identification of subnational regional cases in each country.

---

[6] All quotes from interviews and material in other languages are my own translations.

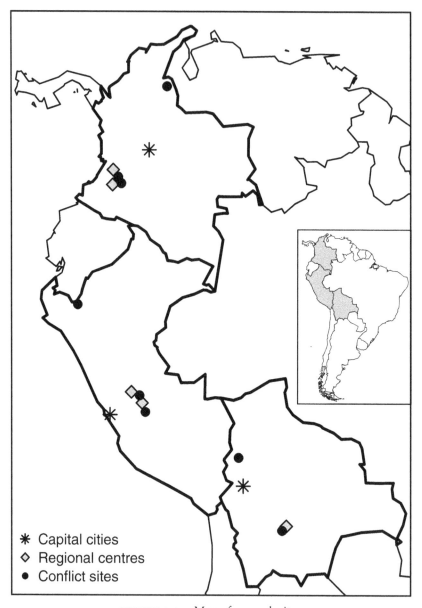

FIGURE 1.3. Map of research sites

Trips to these regions were arranged, first to the local capitals and then to
the communities in conflict. There, I visited local towns and communities
and spoke with key informants, generally within indigenous and peasant
organisations and local administrations (e.g. ombudsman offices, agrarian

tribunals, town councils). I also spoke with community members and ordinary people directly affected by these conflicts. Interviews mainly focused on individual and collective accounts of ongoing or recent conflicts, on how these conflicts changed inter-group relationships, on changes in self-identification and social closure, and on the impact of the conflict on people's daily lives. On a few occasions, interviews followed a general script. Most of the time, I tailored the questions based on the interviewee's role and experience. I also tended to privilege conversation flow over a more rigid structure, as I found this method was bringing up interesting and unexpected elements and was an easier way of interacting with people, especially when they were narrating traumatic experiences.

In Bolivia, I conducted four half-day workshops with community leaders and members (involving between ten and fifteen people each), using participatory techniques such as conflict timelines, maps of actors and brainstorming methods.[7] Workshops were video-recorded, while most interviews were tape-recorded, with the agreement of the interviewees. I also conducted participatory research at community and organisation meetings and national events relevant to the aims of this research (round tables, negotiation spaces, strategic meetings, press conferences, etc.). I conducted all the fieldwork personally, in Spanish, and collected all the material on which this book relies. First-hand empirical data was complemented with extensive review of secondary sources, including international and national reports and legal documents, social organisations' memos and minutes, and newspaper archives. In particular, I relied on hard-copy and online press sources to reconstruct some of the conflict timelines and corroborate interviewees' accounts. In 2015, I visited the ILO headquarters in Geneva, where I conducted interviews with experts on the indigenous rights agenda and Convention 169 in order to gain a better understanding of the origins and implementation of the norm as well as the ILO's strategy in Latin America.

This book relies on qualitative and ethnographic methodologies. The strength of this approach lies in its potential to offer in-depth knowledge of social processes and human agency and, most importantly, its ability to study phenomena that require a localised, micro-perspective and that, as a

---

[7] Timelines are particularly helpful when trying to reconstruct the historical narrative of a given conflict and identify key episodes; participants were also asked to draw maps of actors, indicating the most important actors in the conflict and using a range of simple symbols to visualise the kinds of relationship among different actors; brainstorming was used to identify key associations of ideas and issues at stake for different participants in relation to the conflict.

consequence, tend to escape broader macro-empirical or theoretical analysis. This approach is also the most apt to open pioneer paths of research in terrains that have remained almost completely unexplored and to 'call into question generalisations produced or meanings assigned by other research traditions' (Schatz 2009: 10). This study thus aims to shed light on new forms of ethnic conflict for which no systematic research has been produced to date,[8] as well as to challenge widespread assumptions on the relationship between diversity and equality embedded in theories of recognition.

A NOTE ON CONCEPTS AND TERMINOLOGY

Given the complexity of some of the semantic fields that I engage with throughout the book, a discussion on terminology is in order. One of the key challenges revolves around the definition and operationalisation of collective identities, which are one of the main objects of study. I adopt a broad definition of identity as a shared sense of belonging to a group, and I focus more closely on identities that become dominant references for how individuals perceive themselves as collective subjects. These are, of course, a subset of the multiple identities that an individual can have, and are those that acquire social and political relevance in a particular historical moment. Following constructivist scholarship from a range of social science disciplines, I consider identities as inherently fluid but also more or less resilient to change depending on contextual factors. In other words, identities can be very volatile but can also show a high degree of endurance. The relational dimensions of identity-building in terms of 'limits' and 'boundaries' are crucial to understanding the historical trajectories of collective identities, as well as their political and social role in a given period (Barth 1969; Lamont & Molnár 2002; Tilly 2005; Wimmer 2013). Indeed, boundary mechanisms, especially those institutionalised through hard norms, are sometimes responsible for reducing the potential for permeability or assimilation between different groups, and are the basis for ongoing social and political competition (Lieberman & Singh 2017). From an operational perspective, this non-essentialised conceptualisation of identities means that the only valid and relevant criterion for mapping

---

[8] Despite the fact that only a few cases of inter-communal conflict linked to recognition reform have been documented, it is clear that these conflicts exist beyond the Andean region. Sporadic academic research and newspaper reports describe conflicts involving indigenous, peasant and black communities in Mexico, Brazil, Paraguay and Nicaragua (Mollet 2011; ABC 2015; Boyer 2016; León 2016; Robles 2016).

ethnic belonging is self-identification (i.e. the individual act of identifying oneself as belonging to a particular group).

The book mainly focuses on two collective identities that constitute the most important referents in Andean rural societies: indigenous and peasant. These identities have obvious resonance within the broad categorisation of ethnic and class-based identities. Although indigenous and peasant identities have sometimes been conceptualised as dichotomist and incompatible, this book supports the idea that tensions between them are historically grounded and that their mutual boundaries have been shifting from rigid to more fluid status and vice versa in relatively short time frames, as I discuss in Chapter 3.

'Indigenous peoples' is the term used to refer to contemporary ethnic groups within the globalised discussion on cultural rights, and overwhelmingly so in the Latin American context. Ethnicity in this context is generally understood as a group affiliation defined by common descent and cultural traits (less so by language, religion or physiognomic markers). Contrary to what is commonly thought, 'indigenous' as a self-identification category has a very recent history. Indeed, it was only in the late 1970s that a small group of representatives, mainly from North American and Canadian First Nations, chose to ascribe to it. They borrowed the concept from an abstract normative jargon used since the 1950s by the ILO to identify ethnic minorities, particularly poor workers, in an effort to improve their living conditions. From that moment, the category began to acquire new meanings, not only as a specialised legal term, but as an expression of identity for social actors and in evoking images of exotic realms for lay audiences across the world. Along the way, the category also underwent a process of resignification, whereby the link with tradition was no longer understood as the reason behind marginalisation, but as the root of collective worth and differentiation. This semantic innovation may also be read as a more or less deliberate turn away from 'ethnic' and 'ethnonationalist' discourses. This shift implied a process of depoliticisation and 'depuration' from the old fears evoked by ethnicity for modern liberal thought and democratic projects, only for the new indigenous frame to be repoliticised as a milder, non-violent, non-irredentist version of ethnic mobilisation (Béteille 1998; Niezen 2003; Gutiérrez Chong 2010).

Most Latin American ethnic groups have embraced the transnational language of cultural rights and, especially since the 1990s, have begun to self-identify as indigenous (*indígenas*). There are, however, some exceptions. In the Bolivian context, Aymara and Quechua groups from the highlands prefer terms such as *indio* (indian) or *originario* (native). This choice can be understood as an example of reappropriation by discriminated groups of the colonialist vocabulary in order to create a new narrative of emancipation. In the words of the Bolivian miner leader Domitila Quispe: 'Indian was the name with which they subjugated us; indian will be the name through which we will free ourselves' (cited in Albó 2002: 121). In the case of Peru, the term 'indigenous' has only appeared very recently, while ethnic communities from the Amazon were traditionally referred to as *nativos* (native), in contrast with the 'peasant' highlander – a dichotomy that still persists in public discourse and in the law.

Throughout this book, I use the term 'indigenous' to refer to ethnic-based identities and organisations, in line with most of the scholarship focusing on ethnic issues in Latin America. In contrast with most of this literature, however, I choose not to capitalise the word 'indigenous', since its proper use implying a 'nation-like' identity will put it at a different level compared to other collective identities (e.g. peasant), which would be in contradiction to the theoretical premises of this book. I also refer to the alternative terms that groups and states adopt to describe ethnic identities (e.g. *indio*, *native*) when relevant to the overall argument.

'Peasant' (*campesino* in Spanish) is perhaps a less contested term than 'indigenous', at least from the perspective of social and political actors in Latin America. 'Peasant' is commonly understood as the most important collective identity of those individuals that live in rural areas and practice small-scale agriculture. It is a highly politicised term, however, due to the long-standing history of unionisation and mobilisation of rural sectors under the peasant banner. As with indigenous, peasant semantics also have experienced a process of 'depuration' in recent years. In order to avoid the political connotations embedded in the term 'peasant', particularly since the 1990s, academic scholarship has begun employing the more neutral and technocratic 'smallholder' or 'small-scale farmer' (World Bank 2016). The depoliticisation of peasant sectors, however, is unlikely to be politically neutral, especially if we consider the overlap with the neoliberal turn to be something more than a coincidence. It is also hard not to relate this semantic turn to the steep decline in academic production focused on the peasantry in the past two decades, at least in Latin America. Moreover, and in contrast to the genealogy of the indigenous universe, peasants across the region have not abandoned this term and continue to proudly and overwhelmingly identify with it. I deliberately chose to use the word 'peasant' in line with the semantic choices made by social actors across the Andean region. But I also do so in recognition of the political agency of these sectors, in order to counterbalance both the technocratic efforts to 'wipe out' politics from the rural world and the 'disappearance' of peasants from the academic radar. Indeed, despite the bipartisan predictions that peasants as a social class would become extinct as societies develop, peasant movements have not taken their last breath as yet.

This book focuses on analysing the conflicts between indigenous and peasant groups. It is therefore important to clarify how 'conflict' is understood in this context and particularly with respect to recognition. Drawing from Marxist and Sorelian traditions, scholars have argued that, although social conflict can be disruptive, it can also be a force for social transformation. In the case of recognition conflicts, it can be argued that they constitute an inevitable and temporary phase and are the 'costs' of the adjustment towards a more equal society. In other words, a progressive move often implies pushback from reactionary forces, as well as from actors for whom the status quo is preferable. Furthermore, some may argue that instability is the symptom of a vital society, where the 'rules of the game', including recognition, are subject to debate, negotiation and contestation (Pilapil 2015: 54). It is certainly the case that recognition reforms have been resisted by multiple actors for very different reasons.

Yet I argue that the conflicts presented in this book cannot be understood exclusively as the result of democratic vitality, conservative pushback or temporary adjustment struggles. In fact, they generally become endemic and protracted over time, are not fought against the 'usual suspects' (e.g. elites and big landowners), and mainly occur after reforms have been approved. These conflicts are the manifestation of both struggles for inclusion and struggles for exclusion with respect to recognition reforms. They entail problems with the operationalisation of recognition, but also moral dilemmas around who should be entitled to recognition and differential rights and on what grounds. Contestation in these cases is not the cause but the effect of the dissatisfaction of certain social groups with existing rules. Similarly, a moral argument can be made around the need to make societies less violent and less destructive, and this will come from a deeper understanding of the links between recognition and social justice in practice. From a policy perspective, understanding the causes and dynamics of recognition-related conflicts is a first step towards their solution and towards the establishment of fairer and more peaceful settlements.

Before getting into a more detailed discussion of the different types of recognition conflict, the next two chapters offer an overview of the historical trajectories and institutional frameworks that have shaped Andean politics over the past few decades, which will be helpful in situating recognition reforms and recent changes within the broader processes at play.

2

Citizenship and Development in the Andes

In Latin America, rural communities have historically represented a challenge both for the nation-building process and for countries' development strategies. How should the indigenous population be incorporated into the nation, while moderating the potentially destabilising tensions rooted in persistent ethno-cultural differences? And how can rural households become active contributors to economic development without triggering subversive forces that would threaten the stability of the national economy and its involvement in regional and global markets? To address these questions, since independence Latin American states have adopted a variety of strategies, underpinned by different, and sometimes opposite, visions of citizenship and development. These strategies have had concrete effects in redefining ethnic and class boundaries, shaping at the same time relationships between the state and social groups and among social groups themselves. Since the early twentieth century, citizenship and development regimes have followed somewhat cyclical patterns, oscillating between the dyadic forces of separation and assimilation, social inclusion and differentiation.

This chapter provides a historical background to the rise of identity politics and recognition in Latin America. It does so by establishing a chronology of implementation for four different models of citizenship and development from the early twentieth century to the present: (1) indigenism and *mestizaje* (1920s–1950s); (2) national corporatism (1950s–1970s); (3) neoindigenism and multiculturalism (1980s–1990s); and (4) plurinationalism (2000s–2010s). The historical account draws in particular from the cases of Bolivia, Peru and Colombia. While these countries' trajectories reflect broader regional trends, in-depth analysis of their circumstances will help situate the empirical case studies presented in the subsequent sections of the book.

INDIGENISM AND *MESTIZAJE*

As Lucero (2008: 20) notes, 'States in Latin America have rarely been clear examples of those Weberian ideal-type human communities characterised by clear territorial boundaries and monopolies on the legitimate means of violence'. From the colonial experience, these countries inherited weak institutions under the control of small oligarchies, and fragile economies highly dependent on export markets and the influence of foreign powers (Cardoso & Faletto 1979). Throughout the republican era, the sharp divide between rural and urban areas continued to grow, despite efforts to improve infrastructural and communication networks. Cyclical agricultural booms, technological innovations and intense natural resource exploitation did not provide sustainable solutions to addressing high levels of rural poverty, while the chronically weak presence of the state across countries' peripheries excluded the vast majority of rural inhabitants from political participation and access to public services. The pre-Columbian origins of parts of the rural population also contributed ethnic-based discrimination to other forms of geographic, political and social marginalisation.

Since independence, one of the key challenges for republican governments was managing the great ethno-cultural diversity located within the new national frontiers. This was mainly done through the crystallisation of boundaries of social and political exclusion, often overlapping with ethnic discrimination. From the early republican era to well into the twentieth century, central governments' sovereignty had very limited geographical breadth, cutting off remote and inaccessible areas (sometimes corresponding to the vast majority of the national territories). When peripheral regions managed to escape the control of neo-colonial oligarchies and the *hacienda* system, they rapidly fell under the influence of private enterprises (e.g. mineral, rubber, quinine extraction) based on labour exploitation and rent accumulation, or within the administrative domain of other non-state actors, namely the Catholic Church, local scribes and lawyers. Certain areas, especially in the Andean highlands and the Amazonian jungle, managed to escape this localised and semi-privatised system of 'repressive ventriloquist representation' (Guerrero, cited in Lucero 2008: 51), and communities maintained a certain degree of autonomy as relevant local political units, operating under existing authority and economic structures (Lucero 2008; Cameron 2010).

The rise of Latin American nationalisms rooted in independence struggles did not coincide, therefore, with the affirmation of class-based social movements, but was rather driven by *criollo* elites. Nevertheless, one of the main goals of postcolonial nationalism was to create social and political cohesion through the redefinition of traditionally heterogeneous social and ethnic boundaries. This process took two paths: on one hand, a positive re-evaluation of ethnic identities and contemporary acknowledgement of their underprivileged and marginalised condition (indigenism, or *indigenismo*); on the other, the creation of a new *mestizo* collective identity as a base for nation-building (*mestizaje*). Both these partially overlapping ideological streams became popular in the 1920s among Latin American intellectual elites, and significantly influenced social mobilisation discourses as well as state-led approaches to the ethnic question. What the two ideologies have in common, generally speaking, is a recognition of the inherently discriminatory and racist system that ruled Latin American post-independence societies, the rhetorical celebration of indigenous origins as a source of national identity, and an effort to assimilate indigenous subjects as a precondition for the construction of modern liberal nations. In other words, for the liberal utopia to exist, the old differences between indigenous, *criollo*, *mestizo*[1] and black had to be overcome in favour of a homogeneous national identity (Thomson 2002).

In the first half of the twentieth century, a number of legal reforms inspired by indigenist ideas were implemented in different countries across the region. Mexico in particular constituted a model for the rest of Latin America. Under the leadership of the nationalist general Lázaro Cárdenas and the guidance of the newly created Department of Indigenous Affairs, the indigenous issue was addressed through a broad set of social and economic reforms, including education and land redistribution. The aim of these reforms was the incorporation of indigenous groups into the larger national population on an equal basis. In Peru, the 1921 constitution granted legal recognition to indigenous communities for the first time since independence, while a series of laws and new institutions, such as the Bureau of Indigenous Affairs, were put in place and the first national *indigenista* organisation was founded, the Pro-Indigenous Rights Committee Tawantinsuyo (Comité Pro-Derechos

---

[1] These terms refer respectively to people of full or near full Spanish descent and to people of mixed ancestry.

Indígenas Tawantinsuyo) (de la Cadena 2000; Greene 2009). This started a process of recognition of the central state by rural communities based on a relatively peaceful interaction (Remy 2013). In 1936, the Peruvian Indigenous Communities Statute reaffirmed the prohibition on selling communal land to non-indigenous people and offered protection against property usurpation (Handelman 1975). In Bolivia, politics for homogenising ethnic inclusion were adopted from the 1930s. The 1938 constitution formally granted social rights to indigenous peoples, while the government of Gualberto Villarroel (1943–1946) sponsored the first Indigenous Congress in 1945, which eventually led to the abolition of the system of *pongueaje*[2] (Galindo 2010).

In the same period, however, other countries followed opposing paths, systematically demolishing surviving indigenous institutions. Colombia, for example, approved a Land Act in 1936 which accelerated the process of the dissolution of indigenous collective territories, called *resguardos*,[3] with the argument that they constituted unproductive land and were therefore not contributing to the country's development. Each indigenous family belonging to a *resguardo* was allotted a piece of land according to its size, with a fifteen-year embargo on selling and alienation (Troyan 2015). This process, that in certain cases was welcomed by the indigenous communities themselves as a way to hold on to their land rights in a context of growing pressure provoked by the increase in export crops, certainly contributed to a weakening of local indigenous institutions (*cabildos*). It also illustrates how indigenist ideas remained marginal in the Colombian nation-building process. Indeed, in Colombia, Law 89 of 1890 about 'how to govern savage people' had been the only ruling norm on this matter until the constitutional reform of 1991.

NATIONALIST CORPORATISM

In parallel with the indigenist reforms, the first half of the twentieth century also saw the emergence of the first peasant unions across the region and, more generally, a change in the relationship between the state and the working class (Collier & Collier 1991). Throughout the 1930s,

---

[2] The *pongueaje* is a historical model of agrarian servitude of peasant and indigenous people working within large estates called *haciendas* (Albó 2009).

[3] *Resguardos* are socio-political territorial units of Spanish colonial origin, formed by recognised territories of communities of indigenous descent with inalienable, collective land titles and governed by a special autonomous statute.

important peasant-based mass movements surged in Mexico, El Salvador, Nicaragua, Brazil, Colombia and Bolivia (Petras & Veltmeyer 2001). Peasant mobilisations led to very different outcomes – from violent repression and conservative backlashes (in Cuba, the Dominican Republic, El Salvador and Nicaragua), to more or less substantial agrarian reforms and the consolidation of a new model of state-led rural corporatism (in Mexico, Colombia, Peru and Bolivia). Up until the 1980s, in many Latin American countries corporatism came to represent the solution to the incorporation of popular sectors within nation-building processes.[4] As *mestizaje* with respect to ethnic diversity, corporatism offered a model of incorporation of marginalised social sectors within the state apparatus. Repression was not completely abandoned but was significantly downsized in favour of a strategy of institutionalisation and co-optation of the labour movement. Unions became legitimate actors and began to be mobilised as bases of political support (Collier & Collier 1991). In the countryside, unionisation generally led to the weakening of ethnic-based institutions and identities – a process known as *campesinización* (literally, peasantisation).

The consolidation of a corporatist system followed different and more or less violent trajectories. In the case of Bolivia, it was triggered by a revolutionary outbreak led by the National Revolutionary Movement (Movimiento Nacional Revolucionario, MNR), following six years of continuous social unrest. At the heart of the 1952 Bolivian Revolution was a multi-class coalition mainly formed by workers, miners and peasants, while the revolutionary agenda was a project of national modernisation grounded on three pillars: mine nationalisation, agrarian reform and universal suffrage (Rivera Cusicanqui 1984). A mix of fear of violent escalation and sympathy with the peasant claims, coupled with concerns for decreased agricultural production resulting from rural instability, pushed the MNR to prioritise the agrarian question. With the Agrarian Reform Decree signed on 2 August 1953, the government 'sought to legislate order into the expropriative process' (Kohl 1978: 259). In this context, the institutionalisation of corporatist structures of representation based on peasant unions was understood as the most important measure

---

[4] Incorporation implies a major redefinition of the socio-political arena following the broad and selective inclusion of popular sectors in the polity. It involves a combination of mobilisation of popular claims and implementation of political reforms to channel these claims into new institutional frameworks. The concept was first theorised to describe the process of state-driven corporatisation of labour and peasant movements across Latin American countries in the mid-twentieth century (Collier & Collier 1991; Rossi 2017).

for granting participation and citizenship rights to what was considered an isolated and primitive rural world. The 'peasantisation' of the countryside served the double purpose of class incorporation of marginalised social sectors and ethnic assimilation of indigenous communities into the nation-state (Lucero 2008). The peasantisation campaign was intense and massive, both at the organisational and the symbolic levels. Yet it did not manage to completely homogenise the complex landscape of rural identities. The result was a rather variegated map, with areas where the model was almost perfectly implemented (e.g. the central region of Cochabamba, Gordillo 2000), and others where pre-existent indigenous organisations and new corporatist structures began to coexist in a new symbiotic equilibrium, particularly in many remote highland regions, such as the Norte Potosí (Rivera Cusicanqui 1984).

In Peru, a similar shift towards a corporatist model of social organisation began in the 1960s. In 1968, a decade of social unrest and the rise of peasant and guerrilla movements culminated with the institution of a dictatorial regime under the leadership of General Juan Velasco. His nationalist and reformist programme included a series of social reforms aimed at improving the conditions of marginalised sectors, and in particular radical agrarian reform pushing for massive land redistribution from landowners to poor peasants, along with education reform based on decentralisation and bilingual education. A process of peasantisation was also part of Velasco's modernisation plan, though with slightly different characteristics from the one taking place in neighbouring Bolivia. Land was not handed over to communities but to newly created rural enterprises, called Agricultural Societies of Social Interest (Sociedades Agrícolas de Interés Social), which were granted twenty years to pay back the state for the assigned land, animals and equipment. The government's modernisation project implied the conversion of 'backward Indians (superstitious and lazy almost by definition) into modern peasants (effective and dynamic entrepreneurs, commercially-oriented farmers)' (Nuitjen & Lorenzo 2009: 26). Velasco formally renamed indigenous communities peasant communities, in an effort to abandon what he considered unacceptable racist habits and prejudices (Greene 2006), while the 'Day of the Indian' was converted to the 'Day of the Peasant' to emphasise this identity shift (Seligmann 1995; Remy 2013).

Beyond semantics, this change had practical implications in the restructuring of land tenure and rural labour relations. Traditional authorities were undermined by a new form of bureaucracy, which privileged educated, Spanish-speaking intermediaries, and long-standing cohabiting dynamics between communities were suddenly broken by the redefinition of new territorial boundaries (Seligmann 1995). The shift towards class-based categories, however, only applied to highland communities. Lowland peoples were formally organised into 'native communities' with the Law of Native Communities and Agrarian Development of the Jungle approved in 1974 (Greene 2005). As we shall see, in the subsequent decades the legal crystallisation of the distinction between lowland and highland communities (or what Remy (2013) calls 'colonial' vs 'frontier' indigenous) would contribute to shaping different paths of collective struggle and self-identification in a more radical fashion compared to other Latin American countries with similar geographic and demographic features.

As with Peru and Bolivia, Colombia also experienced a rise in rural unrest during the first half of the twentieth century. Here, however, social conflict degenerated into political violence and eventually led to a decade of bloody civil war known as La Violencia (1948–1957). Although the war was largely fought by peasants in rural areas, it should not be confused with a class war. It was rather a conflict in which peasants were 'fighting for the interests of others', identifying it as 'the last, and the most important, of the clientelist wars in Colombia' (Zamosc 1986: 18). In the aftermath of the war, the National Front (a new political coalition of Liberal and Conservative parties based on the agreement of power rotation for a period of four presidential terms) saw agrarian reform as a necessary concession in order to manage the still unstable and potentially explosive peasant question. The Agrarian Social Reform Law was approved in 1961, implementing redistributive measures (although with quite convenient terms for landowners), promotion of peasant coopera-tives and colonisation movements, peasantry reconstruction in *minifundia* areas, and better service provision to rural areas. These ambitious goals, however, failed to trigger structural change and resolved into weak palliative measures aimed at containing social unrest.

The election of the progressive liberal leader Carlos Lleras Restrepo in 1966 had a more significant impact on peasant political participation. Lleras Restrepo turned towards the countryside as his electoral basin and prioritised the agrarian question as a way of restraining the unsustainable urban exodus. In order to put pressure on conservative sectors still resisting any serious attempt at agrarian reform, he embarked on an effort to strengthen and mobilise the peasantry at the national scale through a massive participatory project. As a result of this project and in order to foster the implementation of a reformist agenda, in 1967 the creation of a

National Association of Peasant Users (Asociación Nacional de Usuarios Campesinos, ANUC) was sponsored by the state as a way of providing a controlled framework for the expression of peasant interests as a class. The ANUC's relationship with the state was therefore characterised by a high degree of dependency at both formal and informal levels, at least until 1970, when the organisation began to radicalise, organising autonomous land occupation and adopting a more combative and antagonising agenda via-à-vis the government. In contrast with Bolivia and Peru, however, the corporatist organisation of a peasant movement in Colombia was never explicitly understood as a process of peasantisation of indigenous groups. This can be linked to demographic factors (indigenous peoples account for a much smaller percentage of the total population than in other Andean countries), as well as to the already strong debilitation of indigenous institutions through the dismantling of the *resguardo* system in the first half of the twentieth century, which effectively weakened, if not dissolved, indigenous communities in most parts of the country. Yet, as we shall see, Colombia was one of the first countries to experience an awakening of a new type of indigenous mobilisation beginning in the early 1970s, in a fashion that would gain popularity across the region in the subsequent decades.

NEOINDIGENISM AND MULTICULTURALISM

Corporatist regimes set up by nationalist governments profoundly reshaped the relationship between rural communities and the state, as well as local institutions and collective identities. The corporatist model of social incorporation did not survive, however, the democratisation wave that swept the region in the early 1980s. In this context, a different sensibility towards cultural and ethnic issues began to develop, which emphasised the need to recognise indigenous peoples as distinct members of society, to value their cultural distinctiveness and to protect their rights as ethnic minorities. Neoindigenism, as this position came to be known (Ibarra 1999; Paz et al. 2004; Canessa 2006), partially revitalised early twentieth-century ideas about ethnic diversity, while at the same time being grounded in a harsh critique of the indigenist integrationist approach as paternalist and assimilationist. The state, neoindigenism postulated, should still play an active role vis-à-vis indigenous populations by guaranteeing, in virtue of their ethnic distinction, specific rights in the framework of a pluricultural model of citizenship (Pallares 2002).

This new approach to the 'ethnic question' can be traced back to the proposal of a small group of anthropologists and activists during a meeting in Barbados in 1972. In the following decade, it would become influential in the discourse of both national politics and social movements. This popularity was favoured by the surprisingly low level of antagonism with which neoindigenism was regarded by the neoliberal orthodoxy that controlled Latin American political economies in the 1980s and 1990s (Hale 2005). It was in this context that, not only was ILO Convention 169 widely ratified across the region, but some form of multicultural reform was implemented in most Latin American countries. This ranged from the renegotiation of national constitutions to formalise the 'pluricultural character' of national societies (what Donna Lee Van Cott (2000) calls 'multicultural constitutionalism'), to the implementation of a new generation of legal reforms and policy measures recognising indigenous peoples as bearers of specific rights, including the right to culture, language and education, as well as some form of administrative autonomy, land and territorial control, and political participation. Among the most important legal reforms were new agrarian laws granting collective land rights to indigenous communities and decentralisation measures offering indigenous leaders concrete and unprecedented opportunities for political participation (Cameron 2010; Faguet 2012). Although, in most cases, these reforms had more rhetorical than real implications, they opened the way for the rise of ethnic recognition and cultural rights claims in national politics (as Rousseau and Dargent (2019) illustrate in the case of education reforms in Peru).

Multicultural reforms were strongly encouraged and in certain cases sponsored by international actors – in particular the World Bank, the Inter-American Development Bank, and different UN agencies and NGOs – anxious to link the new democratisation and 'good governance' paradigms with their economic development agendas (Andolina et al. 2009). At the local level, international actors also played an important role in funding and implementing development programmes, which attempted to build on what were considered 'the positive qualities of indigenous cultures and societies – such as their sense of ethnic identity, close attachment to ancestral land, and capacity to mobilise labour, capital, and other resources for shared goals – to promote local employment and growth' (Uquillas & van Nieuwkoop 2003: 1). For the first time, international development agencies began to allocate specific resources to ethnic communities in order to support different kinds of development interventions, from small agricultural projects to tenure regularisation, cultural heritage activities and institutional strengthening. Since the 1990s, 'ethnodevelopment' or 'development-with-identity', as these interventions came to be known, have become new buzzwords for international development cooperation.

Ethnodevelopment and multicultural reforms were particularly widespread in the Andean region. In Colombia in the late 1980s a decisive push was given to the reconstitution of indigenous *resguardos* (with about 13,000 hectares titled between 1986 and 1989). In 1991, Colombia was one of the first countries to reform its constitution to incorporate multi-ethnic and pluricultural principles, and grant political, legal and cultural recognition to indigenous and Afro-Colombian minorities. Bolivia revised its constitution in 1994, and implemented administrative decentralisation in 1995 as well as an agrarian reform in 1996 that gave collective land rights to indigenous peoples (Native Communal Lands, Tierras Comunitarias de Origen, TCOs). Under Alberto Fujimori's government (1990–2000), Peru reformed its constitution in 1993, including a tepid recognition of the state's cultural plurality and the right to customary legal jurisdiction – already recognised by law – while weakening, in fact, land and community rights. Peasant and indigenous movements were also greatly debilitated in this phase, particularly through the clientelist apparatus and Fujimori's pervasive patronage politics (Remy 2014). A more serious attempt to institutionalise multiculturalism based on the Colombian model was pursued by president Toledo in the early 2000s with the creation of the Development Institute for Andean, Indigenous, Amazonian and Afro-Peruvian Peoples (Instituto Nacional de Desarrollo de Pueblos Andinos Amazónicos Afroperuanos INDEPA) and a new attempt to reform the constitution (Greene 2005). Although no major constitutional change was achieved, the Peruvian Congress approved two laws in 2002 and 2003 that ruled on the establishment of an indigenous legal jurisdiction.

While the programmatic coincidence of neoliberalism and multiculturalism has been well documented, discerning its consequences in reshaping the relationship between state and ethnic and rural movements is complex. The neoliberal era and the process of legal and institutional reform coincided with the multiplication of indigenous organisations and movements across Latin America and the parallel decline of peasant unions as forms of collective organisation in rural areas. But there is no agreement on whether these changes were the underlying trigger of multicultural reforms (Pallares 2002) or the outcome of those reforms (Andolina et al. 2009). Critical perspectives highlight how the alliance between neoliberalism and multiculturalism responded to the strategic need of Latin American governments to move away from class politics and find a new way of conceiving the relationship between marginalised social sectors and the state, which was compatible with their goals of economic growth and market-driven development. Charles Hale (2005), for example, points out how the progressive reforms brought about by these governments – including language and educational policy, anti-discrimination legislation, devolution of power to local administrations, and increased indigenous political participation, among others – in fact had disempowering consequences for social struggle. In practice, neoliberal multiculturalism, Hale argues, had the major limitation of setting criteria to discriminate between acceptable and unacceptable rights and claims, and, even worse, put constraints on the spaces, modes and identities of socio-political struggle. Following this logic, far from being the result of indigenous empowerment, multiculturalism represented a threat to the autonomy of ethnic movements, depriving indigenous peoples of 'their potentially hegemonic status and their capacity to affect the state', and transforming them into a 'multicultural adornment for neoliberalism' (Rivera Cusicanqui 2012: 99).

While agreeing with these critical analyses, Kymlicka also considers that the relationship between the state and social actors in shaping models of citizenship and participation is more dynamic and less unidirectional than is sometimes postulated: 'Just as neoliberalism sought to transform the structure of ethnic relations, so too members of ethnic groups have drawn upon the social resources generated by their ethnic identities and relations to contest neoliberalism'. In this sense, 'some ethnic groups have managed to resist aspects of the neoliberal project or even to turn neoliberal reforms to their advantage' (Kymlicka 2013: 100). Furthermore, in many cases, the agency of new indigenous movements clearly went beyond resistance and took the form of adaptive and symbiotic strategies. As Laurie et al. (2005) show, highly organised indigenous movements have been engaging in transnational development networks and local development initiatives, actively contributing to the shaping of development politics. This was made possible by the increasing professionalisation of an indigenous elite of development experts, emerging from the rank and file of the social movements themselves.

If, on one hand, the strengthening of ethnic-based rights and the weakening of socio-economic rights under neoliberalism encouraged the politicisation of ethnic cleavages (Yashar 1998), on the other, they pushed peasant movements and corporatist networks to the margins of the political arena. Reforms unrelated to recognition, particularly in relation to the electoral system and territorial governance, created new mechanisms for political access that, in turn, have been used by ethnic groups to claim recognition (Rousseau & Dargent 2019). Decentralisation processes sponsored by neoliberal governments offered indigenous leaders the opportunity to engage in the political game and develop administrative experience, which would prove crucial for their ascent to national politics in the following decade (Cameron 2010). These new political actors have been critical forces behind the left parties and coalitions that have been elected into power across the region since the early 2000s (Levitsky & Roberts 2011).

TOWARDS A PLURINATIONAL CITIZENSHIP?

In the 2000s, the election of leftist governments throughout Latin America[5] marked what some authors have called a 'post-neoliberal turn' (Grugel & Riggirozzi 2012). This has been described as a shift away from the dominance of the market in the economy in policy and everyday lives, towards more socially progressive political economies. The role of the state was reinforced and new social policies were put in place in order to target structural problems of poverty and inequality (Levitsky & Roberts 2011). The rise of a 'pink tide' of leftist governments coincided with the popularisation of a new paradigm in national discussions on citizenship and state-building. The idea of plurinationality or plurinationalism, albeit not new (de la Cadena 2000; Pallares 2002; Lucero 2008), became increasingly popular, at first in the discourse of social leaders and intellectuals. As a concept, multiculturalism started to be considered ill-equipped to capture the complexity of ethnic relationships and citizenship regimes. While multiculturalism is focused on the improvement of social competition through tolerance, plurinationalism emphasises interaction among diversities. In general, the plurinational paradigm was perceived as better able to accommodate the material and political dimensions of ethnic claims, especially in regard to political and administrative autonomy and territorial control (Pallares 2002; Gutiérrez Chong 2010).

In Ecuador and Bolivia, plurinational ideas promoted by social actors were incorporated into the agendas of the leftist governments elected in the mid-2000s, and eventually crystallised in new constitutions, which

---

[5] Presidents running on leftist platforms were elected between 1998 and 2011 in eleven Latin American countries, which meant that by 2011 two-thirds of the regional population was represented by left-wing governments (Roberts 2012).

formally replaced the geopolitical and administrative paradigm of the unitary republic with one of a plurinational state (Gustafson 2009; Fontana 2014c). The constitutional texts do not include a definition of plurinationality, but some ideas can be drawn from the proposals and preparatory documents put forward by indigenous organisations during the constitutional negotiations. Below, two definitions are presented, the first by the Confederation of Indigenous Nationalities of Ecuador (Confederación de Nacionalidades Indígenas del Ecuador, CONAIE), and the second by the Bolivian Pact of Unity and Commitment (Pacto de Unidad y Compromiso), an umbrella organisation of indigenous and peasant movements:

Plurinationality is a system of government and a model of political, economic and socio-cultural organization, which advocates for justice, individual and collective freedoms, respect, reciprocity, solidarity, equitable development of the whole Ecuadorian society and all its regions and cultures, based on the legal-political and cultural recognition of all Nationalities and Indigenous Peoples that form Ecuador. (CONAIE 2007: 17)

[The Plurinational State is] a model of political organization for the decolonization of our nations and peoples, reaffirming, restoring and strengthening our territorial autonomy. Legal principles of juridical pluralism, unity, complementarity, reciprocity, equality, solidarity and the moral and ethical principle to end all forms of corruption are fundamental for the construction and consolidation of the Plurinational State. (OSAL 2007: 167)

As these examples illustrate, at the very core of the concept of plurinationality, the idea of 'indigenous people' is coupled with the even more radical and evocative concept of the 'nation'. This change mirrors the latest discourse of indigenous movements in the region, which are increasingly resorting to indigenous nationalist discourses to fight their political battles. As Perreault and Green (2013: 51) note about the Bolivian case, however, the new constitution attempts to interpret 'indigenous differences (and nationalism) not as a threat to the Bolivian nation but, rather, as a founding principle' based on pluralism and mutual recognition. In Bolivia, following constitutional approval, the new plurinational model has been shaped through an ongoing process of institutional and legal reform. This includes the creation of territorially autonomous regimes that can be formed without the need to have been part of other pre-existing political-administrative divisions, but rather on the bases of ethno-cultural features; the recognition of community justice as parallel and coexistent with ordinary justice; and the consolidation of a system of collective land titling following ethnic-based criteria.

More broadly, in the framework of the new left's social and political reforms across Latin America, plurinationalism took the form of a political project able to mobilise traditionally marginalised social sectors, in particular indigenous peoples, albeit with important differences in outcomes, as illustrated by Gutiérrez Chong (2010) in the cases of Ecuador, Bolivia and Mexico. In a phase characterised by high social tensions and deep reshaping of long-standing political settlements, leftist governments started looking for opportunities to consolidate an alliance among their constituencies, that is, those popular sectors that had been particularly hit, divided and debilitated by a decade of neoliberal reforms. In this sense, plurinationalism can be understood, following Rossi (2017), as a key component of a 'second wave of social incorporation' that spread across Latin America from the early 2000s, in reaction to the cycle of continental mobilisation against neoliberal disincorporation.

In Bolivia, the election of the coca-growers' union leader Evo Morales as president in 2005 shifted the focal point of national politics towards the rural world, and the new government soon confronted the challenge of keeping in place the fragile trans-rural alliance formed by peasant and indigenous sectors (the Pacto de Unidad) that brought it to power. The pragmatic solution found in the framework of the Constitutional Assembly was the formalisation of a new trifold category, the 'indigenous native peasant',[6] which was widely used to describe a new collective citizen entitled to a new set of plurinational rights. The concept, mentioned more than a hundred times within the constitution, is used as if it refers to a clearly existing entity. Empirically, however, it is hard to identify such a sociological aggregate. Indeed, native movements, indigenous groups and peasant unions in Bolivia continue to exist as separate organisations, and despite a phase of alliance and collaboration, in recent years their respective agendas and changing political alliances have brought them back to opposite fronts, as I will describe later (Fontana 2013a; 2014c).

So far, plurinational ideas have had limited impact outside Bolivia and Ecuador. Peruvian indigenous movements have only very recently started to make use of the idea of the 'nation' as a way of strengthening their sense of identity and belonging to a specific ethnic group, distinct from others within the country and from the state. Ethno-nationalist discourses

---

[6] 'An *indígena originario campesino* nation or people is each and every human collectivity that shares cultural identity, language, historical tradition, territorial institutions and view of the world, and whose existence is previous to the Spanish colonial invasion' (Art. 30).

have been mobilised, particularly in the context of socio-environmental conflicts with foreign companies and the government around mining exploitation (e.g. Las Bambas).[7] At the same time, both ruling elites and civil society have been showing a higher degree of permeability to ethnic and cultural demands with respect to the past (Remy 2014). However, debates on rights and citizenship at the national level have not incorporated the idea of plurinationality. In Peru, these discussions have been much more lukewarm than in neighbouring countries, both because the turn to the left with the election of Ollanta Humala in 2011 had very limited impact in reshaping broader political equilibria and was not sustained over time (the election of Pedro Pablo Kuczynski in 2016 saw the government return to the right), and because the presence of social movements in the country's national arena remains weak and relatively marginal compared to Latin American standards.

If Peru was somehow under the influence of the constitutional and political changes happening in Ecuador and Bolivia, Colombian politics have firmly remained within the conservative tradition until the 2022 presidential election and the country has not experienced any significant reformist process since the 1991 constitution. The rural question, however, has regained centrality in public debate in recent years, when a new attempt to negotiate with the FARC was launched by President Santos. The first point of the peace agreement, signed by the government and the guerrilla group on 23 June 2016, includes plans for a new integral agrarian development policy, aimed at providing solutions for structural issues such as land access, infrastructure, social development and food security. It might, however, be too soon to assess the concrete implications of this historic breakthrough in terms of legal reforms and institutional arrangements for the countryside.

---

[7] This conflict started in 2014 when local communities in the Apurímac region in the central Peruvian highlands began to mobilise against the mining megaproject of Las Bambas. Residents were concerned with the environmental impact of exploitation and connected infrastructural developments. Some communities also protested in order to be included in the influence zone of the project. Following the escalation of violence that led to the death of three people, in 2015 President Ollanta Humala declared a state of emergency for the affected districts. Negotiation tables were set up and then suspended in 2017, while a new state of emergency decree was issued in April 2018, despite the opposition of local leaders. This conflict is also discussed in Chapter 7.

3

Class and Ethnic Shifts

In the previous chapter, I briefly illustrated the changes in citizenship and development models institutionalised by Latin American governments from the early twentieth century up to the present day. These transformations have shaped the very identities of social actors, and their modes of interaction with the state and between themselves. How have patterns of collective self-identification changed over time and how have scholars made sense of these processes? In this chapter, I focus on changes in collective identities through a critical assessment of the narratives used to describe the alternations between class and ethnicity as referents for social organisation. Indeed, as Yashar (2005) has famously demonstrated in the Latin American context, different kinds of citizenship regimes diffuse and then activate different identity cleavages. A review of the abundant literature on rural movements in Latin America clearly shows how scholarly production has been greatly influenced by intellectual fashions and political ideologies, often in a cyclical way. As a result, the same aspects of reality have been glorified in certain periods and neglected in others, and most narratives of social change have oscillated between either dichotomous or homogenising interpretations of collective identities. Here, I consciously try to remedy this imbalance as I analyse the political roles, forms of organisation and social relevance of both indigenous and peasant movements since the 1950s.

In the first part of the chapter, I offer an alternative framework for understanding rural movements based on the concept of 'articulation' (and 'disarticulation'). I identify four main historical phases in this regard: (1) hierarchical articulation (class over ethnicity); (2) hierarchical articulation (ethnicity over class); (3) organisational disarticulation; and

(4) pragmatic articulation.[1] The aim is to provide a narrative of Andean socio-political history over the last seventy years, taking rural movements as its main subject. The value of this effort rests in highlighting the interdependence and fluidity of ethnic and class identities, as well as the influence of broader socio-political processes. This will be instrumental to understanding more recent changes in collective identities and their relationship to recognition conflict, discussed as part of specific case studies in the subsequent chapters. As in the previous chapter, my analysis focuses on empirical and historical cases within the Andean countries, in order to illustrate the shifts in collective identities and social mobilisation patterns.

TOWARDS A NEW UNDERSTANDING OF ETHNIC AND CLASS RELATIONSHIPS

Rural actors in Latin America have provided a rich terrain for social sciences research for almost a century. The narratives of social change used to describe and interpret processes of social mobilisation and identity building have generally tended to focus on certain aspects of reality, often under the influence of intellectual fashions and political ideologies. Reviewing the abundant literature on rural movements in Latin America, it is clear how quite different theoretical lenses have been employed to make sense of paradigmatic shifts.

After the indigenist phase in the early twentieth century, when, for the first time, interest in ethnic groups overcame narrow anthropological and cultural lenses, scholarly attention was generally catalysed by the peasant world. Following a turn away from classic Marxism, leftist intellectuals became increasingly interested in the peasantry as a force of change in pre-industrial societies. In this phase, ethnic categories either vanished or were subsumed within class categories. Peasant studies generated an important tradition in the region that proliferated until the 1980s, with rare exceptions up to the 2000s. Over the last thirty years, however, a sharp turn 'from class to identity' occurred, reflecting both the rise of new ethnic movements as well as the broader intellectual trends around identity politics and recognition described in my introduction. While peasant movements have still been active, although greatly debilitated, they almost completely disappear from the academic literature – which was absorbed by the exciting developments in the ethnic camp. In this phase,

---

[1] This is an elaboration of Fontana (2014a).

subaltern and postcolonial perspectives developed mainly by Asian scholars became very popular theoretical frameworks for the study of Latin American indigenous movements, producing countless books, essays and articles.

In sum, the history of the rural movements in Latin America can be reduced to a double shift: 'from indians to peasants and back to indians'. This is of course an uncouth simplification. But it concisely illustrates the different phases that mainstream narratives on rural movements have gone through, mirroring overall the historical transitions experienced by those movements. Yet what is puzzling looking at the literature on social movements is the relative ease with which entire groups and categories have appeared and disappeared from both political and analytical narratives. If the wave of national revolutions confined the ethnic dimension of rural communities to the background, since the 1980s we witness the steady decline of studies focusing on social movements other than indigenous ones. Also, in the latter phase, the differences between ethnic and class identities, which were completely absent from earlier debates, suddenly became epistemologically relevant. In this context, the relationship between class and ethnicity is generally reframed following three main models. The first stresses the incompatibility of indigenous and peasant identities, either ontologically or in political terms. The second assumes the historical primacy of indigenous over peasant identities, where the latter would represent a sort of externally imposed 'false consciousness', which is now in the process of dissolution to reveal the underlying indigenous identity.[2] The third position adopts a 'double consciousness' explanation, where both ethnicity and class would be equal and contemporary sources of grievances and identity.[3] Yet, like the narratives on peasants in earlier periods, the problem with these approaches is that they tend to crystallise ethnic and class identities in either dichotomous or perfectly overlapping categories.

I propose here an alternative way of understanding the relationship between class and ethnicity based on the concepts of 'articulation' and 'disarticulation'. I consider the collective and political dimension of identities and narratives, leaving aside questions about systems of beliefs and

---

[2] This is basically the reverse argument of the Marxist understanding of ethnicity as false consciousness.

[3] What this perspective fails to explain is that grievances and identities, even if potentially compatible in theory, can collide in practice.

individual identity formation, which can be better captured by social psychology tools rather than through sociological and political analysis.

Firstly, I argue that social and identity relationships can be better understood by placing real actors in historical contexts, and by embedding sociological analysis within a historical perspective able to mitigate narratives of social exceptionalism. Processes of identity construction and redefinition of group boundaries do not occur in a vacuum. As I will show throughout this chapter, in different historical moments, ethnic and class categories have come to play more or less significant roles as engines of political struggle and inspiration for the creation of 'imagined communities' (Anderson 1991). In different periods, ethnicity and class have been able to affirm themselves as more or less legitimate and effective sources of meaning and collective identification. Identity shifts have also closely mirrored broader changes in the institutional arrangements and citizenship regimes described in Chapter 1. Factors exogenous to the social groups themselves are therefore crucial to explaining why certain identities are more successful in providing collective frameworks for self-identification and social mobilisation than others. These factors include institutional arrangements but also support from external actors, as well as the lifecycle of mainstream collective narratives. Indeed, paraphrasing Greene's (2009) concept of customisation as a form of articulation, a project of articulation is constrained by the politics of articulation in which it is enmeshed.

Secondly, while ethnic and class features can be considered compatible in theory (a person can at the same time be engaged in small-scale agriculture and be a member of an indigenous group), in practice it has often been the case that political circumstances have led to their articulation as opposing identities and made them incompatible or competing alternatives. Whether the focus has been placed on either the first or second part of this statement, conclusions have been drawn about the absolute dichotomy or perfect overlap between class and ethnic identity. In fact, I argue that the interaction between ethnicity and class can be better explained as a contingent process of articulation (or disarticulation).

Stuart Hall (1996: 141–42) defined articulation as:

the form of the connection that can make a unity of two different elements, under certain conditions. It is a linkage, which is not necessary, determined, absolute and essential for all time. You have to ask, under what circumstances can a connection be forged or made? The so-called 'unity' of a discourse is, really, the articulation of different, distinct elements which can be rearticulated in different ways because they have no necessary 'belongingness'. The 'unity' which matters is a linkage between the articulated discourse and the social forces with which it can, under certain historical conditions, but need not necessarily, be connected.[4]

Following this definition and as a clarifying premise, the focus in this context is not on the authenticity of identity, or on its anchorage to a given set of objective referents (e.g. language, culture, dress, traditions), but on its functionality in terms of articulation, that is, its ability to generate a sense of self-identification shared within a given social collectivity. More specifically, I define the articulation of identity as the process of compatibilisation and mutual interdependence between two or more identities, often in a functional way with respect to a particular political and historical context. Articulation and disarticulation between peasant and indigenous identities are thus defined in terms of alliance and conflict within both the space of ideas and world visions (ideologies and discourses), and the space of action, decisions and projects (politics). As we shall see, this articulation/disarticulation dynamic is reflected in how the ideal types 'indigenous' and 'peasant' occupy symbolic spaces and engage in struggle around purity and authenticity in the framework of horizontal struggles for recognition.

The identity shifts that occurred in the Andes over the last century can be described as an oscillation between phases of articulation and disarticulation between class and ethnicity, which have had direct effects in swinging intra-rural relationships across phases of alliance and conflict. To summarise these phases, the relationship between ethnicity and class can be divided into four main moments (Table 3.1): (1) Indigenism brought ethnicity to the forefront for the first time, in what can be defined as a *hierarchical articulation* with class identities (*ethnicity over class*). This movement, however, remained the prerogative of intellectual elites and, while it generated important literature and artistic production, it did not manage to influence concrete forms of social and political organisation. (2) From the 1950s, national corporatism overturned the terms of the *hierarchical articulation* (*class over ethnicity*), still looking at a unified rural subject, whose indigenous features were however overshadowed by their 'class consciousness' through a process of massive peasantisation. (3) Beginning in the 1980s, the fracture between peasant and indigenous identities reopened with the rise of neoindigenism. The latter catalysed the claims of indigenous peoples, distancing itself from peasant unions and

---

[4] The concept has also been used by other scholars to describe ethnic identity formations, including James Clifford (2001), Tania M. Li (2000), María Elena García (2005), Antonio Lucero (2008) and Marisol de la Cadena (2010).

TABLE 3.1. *Class and ethnic shifts: time frames, phases and social actors*

Time frame	Citizenship models	Articulation / disarticulation	Key social actors		
			Bolivia	Colombia	Peru
1930s–1950s	Indigenism	Hierarchical articulation (ethnicity over class)			
1950s–1970s	National corporatism	Hierarchical articulation (class over ethnicity)	CSUTCB	ANUC	CAN
1980s–1990s	Neoindigenism/ multiculturalism	Organisational disarticulation	CIDOB CONAMAQ	CRIC ONIC	AIDESEP CONACAMI
2000s–2010s	Plurinationalism	Pragmatic articulation	Pacto de Unidad y Compromiso	Cumbre Agraria Campesina, Étnica y Popular	Pacto de Unidad de Organizaciones Indígenas del Perú

inaugurating a phase of *organisational disarticulation*, strengthened throughout the 1990s by the wave of neoliberal reforms. Rural movements reorganised around a multi-polar system with two main poles: the peasant union and the native/indigenous movement. (4) In recent years, the sealing of new trans-rural alliances and the consolidation of shared platforms for political negotiation opened a phase of *pragmatic articulation* based on the increasing resort to ethnicity as a discursive tactic and on practical commitments to a broader agenda of social reforms. In the remainder of this chapter, I analyse these different phases, relying in particular on historical accounts from the Andean region.

FROM 'INDIANS' TO 'PEASANTS'

For a long time in Latin America ethnicity was considered a relatively marginal and weak category for social and political organising (Yashar 2005). As in most postcolonial societies, Latin American states had been ruled by political oligarchies of *criollo* or *mestizo* origins. Under these regimes, indigenous peoples (descendants of pre-Columbian populations) were subordinated and marginalised. Discrimination was perhaps less institutionalised than in colonial times,[5] but nevertheless extremely effective in preventing social mobility. As we have seen in Chapter 2, the indigenist ideology in the early twentieth century engaged for the first time with the idea of these groups' social and political agency as part of the broader national community. This focus on ethnicity played a critical role in positioning the issue within broader intellectual debates, particularly among Latin American Marxists. While classic Marxism remained generally unsympathetic to ethnic-based claims and maintained a sceptical position even towards the revolutionary potential of the peasantry (Brass 2000),[6] in the Andes, Marxists encountered a double challenge: understanding non-industrialised countries, whose core still gravitated around the rural world, and making sense of postcolonial societies, whose

---

[5] During Spanish colonial rule, two separate administrative divisions existed: a 'Republic of Indians' (*República de Indios*) and a 'Republic of Spanish' (*República de Españoles*). This arrangement was meant to keep strict status and class boundaries based on racial criteria (Ogburn 2008).

[6] Under the influence of this pessimistic view of peasants as lacking power for social change, early rural movements have often been depicted as 'parochial and defensive "reactors"' to exogenous pressures with quite limited political horizons (Stern 1987: 5) or as 'pre-political people who have not yet found ... specific language in which to express their aspirations about the world' (Hobsbawm 1959: 2).

construction of a national identity was still dealing with important ethno-cultural differences grounded in pre-Columbian times.

It was precisely from the observation of these tensions, as well as from the influence of early twentieth century indigenism, that José Carlos Mariátegui, one of the most influential Latin American intellectuals of the past century, drew inspiration to elaborate an original perspective on the rural world. He linked the study of the problem of rural wretchedness with that of national identity, establishing a connection between the agrarian relations of production and the struggle for self-determination (Stein 1984). In practice, he argued, there is no fundamental difference between 'indians' and 'peasants', who together constitute the bulk of the exploited and racially discriminated rural population. But, while no distinction is made between ethnic and class identities, for Mariátegui the 'indian problem' is 'not racial but social and economic' (Mariátegui 1969: 45, cited in Stein 1984: 18). Moreover, while the strengthening of rural communities would facilitate the transition towards socialism, the Peruvian intellectual still claimed that revolutionary forces had to develop among the urban working class rather than among pre-capitalist rural formations.

The coincidence between ethnic and peasant identities postulated by Mariátegui in the case of Peru has been shared by many peasantry scholars throughout the twentieth century, especially in those countries featuring considerable ethno-cultural diversity (e.g. Bolivia, Guatemala, Mexico). On one hand, it was genuinely believed that there was no way of discerning the primacy of one identity over the other (besides the fact that the distinction between indigenous and peasants was probably considered too muddied to be analytically useful), or a perfect overlap was assumed; on the other, questions around identity and class relationships were not considered central in the first place. Between the 1950s and the 1970s, in fact, efforts were instead concentrated on testing the actual revolutionary potential of the peasantry as a main ally of either populist or socialist forces fighting against the established order. At the same time, normative perspectives on the rural question were still clearly dominated by the primacy of class-based discrimination and socio-economic injustice to which the ethnic issue represented a corollary.

In general, studies that refer to this period tend to assimilate class and ethnicity as characteristics of the same social group, while the issues of identity and self-identification did not seem central – neither for scholars nor for social actors themselves. In his longitudinal ethnography of the town of Quinua in the Peruvian highlands begun in 1966, for example,

Mitchell (1991: 2) writes that 'peasants speak Quechua, chew coca leaves and dress in what is offhandedly described as "Indian" clothing', and goes on to describe their traditional authority system (*varayoc*) and *corvé* labour practices of Inca origin without raising questions about their cultural identity or ethnicity.

This tendency to privilege class over ethnic categories reflected the period of political apogee experienced by peasant movements between the 1950s and 1960s across the Andean region. As we have seen, they not only assumed key political roles in the framework of the new wave of regime change and civil unrest, but also received formal support and consideration from the new governments in power. In Bolivia, peasant unions exerted powerful influence during the 1952 National Revolution and the first nationwide peasant union – the National Confederation of Peasant Workers of Bolivia (Confederación Nacional de Trabajadores Campesinos de Bolivia, CNTCB) – was created in 1953. The early phase of the revolution was marked by land seizures and increased violence between peasants and landowners, while in a later phase power struggles developed mainly between peasant communities competing for hegemony over key rural areas, especially in the inter-Andean valleys (Dandler 1969; 1984). Here the growing opposition to the *hacienda* system constituted fertile ground for unions to take root, while in other regions of the highlands where the economy gravitated around mining exploitation, the peasant movement made its first appearance only years later, and indigenous authorities managed to preserve their influence and role in local governance (Rivera Cusicanqui 1984). The empowerment of peasant movements resulting from the National Revolution consolidated them as key political forces in Bolivia during the following decades, when the peasantry became an important ally of dictatorial regimes. Indeed, the corporatist system survived the MNR government and was converted into the central pillar of General Barrientos' military regime (1964–1969). Until the mid-1970s, this alliance was formalised in the so-called Military-Peasant Pact (Pacto Militar-Campesino), used by the state to exert control over the rural world and prevent the potentially destabilising growth of communist influences.

The Bolivian Revolution of 1952 caused shockwaves that were felt in neighbouring countries and across Latin America. Although Peru did not experience such radical transformations, in the late 1950s successful land invasions were carried out in the highlands and valleys, and peasant unions gained strength in different regions. These became the main forms of political organisation and social mobilisation for those groups that were subjugated to the *hacienda* as well as for communities that maintained a certain independence but whose lands were usurped by the colony. As in Bolivia, the governance transition from indigenous community to peasant union was in general relatively smooth, as it was mainly conceived as a strategic move to gain recognition from the state and access to legal representation in the juridical battle to recover ancestral land (Remy 2014). The Peasant Confederation of Peru (Confederación Campesina del Perú, CCP), founded in 1947 and for a long time the major peasant organisation in the country, played an important role in this phase, mobilising rural communities and organising land seizures. A first significant attempt by leftist forces was also made to scale up local insurrections in the Cuzco province into a national revolutionary movement. Fearing nationwide unrest and Cuban-inspired communist subversion, the government response consisted of large-scale eviction campaigns and bloody repression. At the same time, however, the awareness grew among Peruvian elites that some form of land redistribution was needed to avoid greater instability. Repression, in fact, did not stop land seizures, which, by the end of 1963, were widespread across most highland departments (Handelman 1975). As part of the agrarian reform launched by General Velasco in an effort to control a very unstable countryside, another nationwide peasant organisation – the National Agrarian Confederation (Confederación Nacional Agraria, CNA) – was founded in 1974 with government support. The government's co-option strategy was successful in deradicalising the highland peasants (Handelman 1975) – at least until the rise of the Marxist guerrilla movement of Sendero Luminoso in the 1980s – and in diluting ethnic identities and institutions into class-based categories and modes of organisation. The latter process had longer-term effects in Peru compared to other similarly diverse countries such as Mexico and Bolivia, where, as we will see, the indigenous issue came back into the national agenda two decades earlier than in Peru.

In the mid-twentieth century, Colombia experienced a much more dramatic political transition than any other country in the region, which brought the peasantry and the agrarian question to the core of national politics. In the early 1950s, widespread political violence became a way of forcefully settling old and new land disputes, while the first peasant strongholds for self-defence began to organise with the support of the Communist Party. Most of this peasant resistance was, however, neutralised relatively early on and, by 1957, only a few of these groups were still active. One of the key components of the pacification efforts by the

National Front was the introduction of mildly reformist policies. The fragmentation and internal divisions of the peasantry as a result of the political opposition during La Violencia prevented any effective pressure for more radical change and led to a progressive weakening of existing peasant organisations. According to Ministry of Labour estimates, only 89 of the 567 registered peasant unions were still active in 1965 (Zamosc 1986: 37).

Even more so than in Bolivia and Peru, the restoration of a nationwide peasant movement was a top-down endeavour in Colombia. In 1966, the National Association of Peasant Users (Asociación Nacional de Usuarios Campesinos, ANUC) was created by presidential decree as a key ally in the implementation of agrarian policies and as a 'direct corporatist bridge between the peasantry and the state' (Zamosc 1986: 52). A large-scale campaign to set up local and regional organisations was conducted under the coordination of the Ministry of Agriculture. Despite the ANUC's dependency on the state and its para-official status, in practice its creation contributed to a strengthening of organisational networks and new leadership cadres from below. This offered the opportunity for a progressive emancipation of the peasant movement from state control, until the rupture provoked by both the election of a hostile government and the rise of a radical autonomist faction within the ANUC in the early 1970s. The following decade would be characterised by a new radicalisation of land struggles and growing repression by the government, with the sudden reversal of any reformist efforts in agrarian politics.

THE PEASANT CRISIS

The years between the 1950s and the 1970s saw the consolidation of peasant movements as political actors across the region. Interestingly, the strengthening of rural corporatism was, in this period, a common strategy of both revolutionary and conservative governments. The former saw in the mobilised peasantry a key ally in the effort to trigger social unrest, as well as in the process of economic modernisation; while the latter advanced ideas of the peasants as bulwarks against the spread of socialism and as guarantors of political and social stability (Brass 2000). In this phase, the ethnic heterogeneity that characterised peasant communities was considered irrelevant and removed from the equation through a narrative and institutional shift that emphasised the need to ground citizenship on corporatist/classist rather than ethnic bases.

Yet this golden age for the Latin American peasantry did not last, and the 1970s and 1980s generally marked a phase of decline for peasant movements. This crisis can be attributed to a number of factors, including downturns in countries' economic performance, rising tensions and ideological fractures within the peasantry itself, and the progressive deterioration of the system of political alliances that had characterised the previous decades. In Bolivia, in the mid-1970s, a new wave of brutally repressed social unrest against General Banzer's regime ended the political alliance stipulated through the Military-Peasant Pact. At the same time, a schism arose within the peasant movement: in 1971, Jenaro Flores was elected head of the CNTCB, embodying a new intellectual current called Katarismo (after the eighteenth-century indigenous leader Túpac Katari), which questioned the assimilationist model of the *mestizaje* and stressed the need to acknowledge two coexisting forms of oppression of the rural sectors, based on both class and race (Rivera Cusicanqui 1987). Following one of its prominent ideologists, Fausto Reinaga, Kataristas saw the 'peasant' as a Western construct that did not apply to Bolivian reality, where the rural inhabitants were mostly of indigenous origin and, therefore, not a class but 'a race, a people, an oppressed Nation' (Reinaga, cited in Engle 2010: 61). During 1979, in the midst of a period of great instability which saw the alternation of military coups and electoral rounds, a new peasant organisation – the Unified Confederation of Peasant Workers of Bolivia (Confederación Unica de Trabajadores Campesinos de Bolivia, CSUTCB) – was founded under a Katarista leadership. The CSUTCB stood in opposition to government-sponsored peasant unions and immediately replaced the CNTCB, becoming the headquarters for practically the whole Bolivian peasantry. In the following years, a women's branch was created, called the National Federation of Peasant Women Bartolina Sisa (Federación Nacional de Mujeres Campesinas Bartolina Sisa, or Bartolinas), named after Túpac Katari's wife and comrade.

The internal tensions within the peasant movement meant it was ill-prepared to deal with the aggressive neoliberal economic policies implemented throughout the 1980s and 1990s. During this period, parties attempted to exert more direct influence on organisations' internal politics, which resulted in increased fragmentation rooted in personal rivalries and ideological differences (Ticona 2000; Van Cott 2005a). In the 1990s, a new current represented by the coca-grower (*cocalero*) sectors of the Cochabamba valleys gained strength within the peasantry and managed to organise into a national political actor. Under the leadership of Evo

Morales, the *cocaleros* seized control not only of the CSUTCB, marginal-
ising the Kataristas, but, a decade later, of the Bolivian state with the
victory of Morales in the 2005 presidential election.

The trajectory of the Bolivian peasant movement in this latest phase is
quite exceptional in its ideological inspirations and political outcomes, in
particular in how the peasant organisation was able to return reinvigorated from a moment of deep crisis. In Peru and Colombia, by contrast, the
progressive weakening of rural actors led to their political marginalisation. In the 1980s in Peru, the Belaúnde government withdrew efforts
from agrarian reform, with the effect of limiting the political influence of
peasant organisations, and in particular of the CNA. Perhaps more than
any other trade union and social movement in the country, the peasantry
had seen its mobilisation capacity greatly reduced by a phase of economic
recession and hyperinflation, as well as by the militarisation and violence
following the proliferation of the rural-based Maoist guerrilla movement
Sendero Luminoso.[7] Any manifestation of dissent during this phase,
particularly in rural areas, was considered evidence of support for the
guerrilla groups and therefore severely repressed. Under this scenario, it
was relatively easy for President Fujimori to use patronage and clientelism, coupled with an aggressive military strategy, to defeat Sendero
Luminoso, in order to reduce opposition to the government and find new
alliances and loyal constituencies in the rural world (Remy 2014). As a
result, 'organizations such as the CCP and CNA found themselves
largely eclipsed, no longer able to articulate the interests of peasants and
small-scale producers and officially ignored as valid intermediaries'
(Crabtree 2003: 149).

In Colombia, the capitulation of the ANUC, the main organised peasant movement of the twentieth century, also occurred relatively quickly
and followed a similar path. The organisation, which had managed to
gain some autonomy and legitimacy by leading land struggles in the early
1970s, was hit by economic and social changes (including increased
urban migration, the boom of the marijuana industry and the formation
of a rural proletariat). Its capacity to respond to those changes was
hindered by its bureaucratic style of vertical leadership and the progressive detachment of the central organisation from regional demands. The
last land struggles coordinated by the ANUC took place in 1977 and

---

[7] In her essay *Conflicto y cambios en la sociedad rural* (2014), Marisa Remy offers some
insights into the complexity that characterised the relationship between Sendero Luminoso
and peasant and indigenous movements in the Peruvian highlands.

1978, but they were rather limited in number and scope. A failed attempt
to launch a peasant party was additional evidence of the inability of the
ANUC to retain the confidence of the peasantry. By the 1980s, the
bureaucratic residue of the ANUC was eventually co-opted by the state,
while some leftist fringes tried to coordinate a unified opposition with
limited success due to disconnection with the grassroots and internal
ideological differences (Zamosc 1986). It was not until the mid-1990s
and the wave of protests against the fumigation of illegal crops that the
Colombian peasantry re-entered the political arena, with the creation of a
number of regional peasant associations and two national organisations:
the National Association for Agricultural Salvation (Asociación Nacional
por la Salvación Agropecuaria) and the National Peasant Council
(Consejo Nacional Campesino). These organisations led some important
initiatives, such as the national agrarian strike, and actively worked to
reposition the agrarian question within the national debate.

FROM 'PEASANTS' TO 'INDIANS'

The crisis and reconfiguration of peasant movements across the region
coincided with the rise of a new generation of social movements with
strong ethnic inclinations. On one side, the weakening of the peasantry
was interpreted as evidence that 'class as an axis of political mobilisation
had lost much of its power' (Lucero 2008: 88), and even more so in the
context of a wave of neoliberal reforms, economic austerity and conservative politics. On the other side, the vacuum left by the retreat of peasant
organisations and new attention being paid to the ethnic question by
international and academic elites (especially anthropologists and development cooperation agents) opened new spaces for cultural and identity-
based claims.

Given the novelty represented by the indigenous rise, it is not surprising
that culture and identity suddenly became central concerns for activists,
scholars and practitioners alike. Ethnic differences could no longer be
ignored nor reduced to class differences. Although they may greatly
overlap in practice, they began to be perceived as 'qualitatively different'
(Orlove & Custred 1980: 167). This differentiation had two interpretative implications on the understanding of the rural poor as political
actors: on one hand, the rural poor went from being perceived as reactionary to being the progressive vanguards of social change; on the other,
the material differences that were used as traditional markers of social
boundaries were assimilated into cultural and identity cleavages, blurring

the distinctions between poverty, class and ethnicity. As a result, self-identification progressively became a relevant criterion for the establishment of social cleavages. As Cameron (2010: 5) puts it, 'being a peasant in the 21st century has more to do with self-identification based on community ties than on [an] objective definition linked to means of production'.

With perhaps the sole exception of Katarismo, which, at least in its early years, found a way of incorporating anti-racist and ethnic recognition claims within the agenda of the main Bolivian peasant movement (Rivera Cusicanqui 1984), most indigenous organisations developed independently from existing peasant unions. In fact, they often began to compete with them for influence over the same grassroots and for control of overlapping political spaces. It is not by chance that early indigenous organisations were often constituted among lowland communities, where the peasant unions' influence had traditionally been weaker.

Bolivia, Peru and Colombia all saw the rise of new indigenous movements between the 1970s and the 1990s, following relatively similar trajectories. In Bolivia in 1980, the German anthropologist Jürgen Riester, with other colleagues, founded the NGO Support for the Indigenous Peasant of the Bolivian East (Apoyo Para el Campesino Indígena del Oriente Boliviano, APCOB). APCOB received funds from the Danish cooperation Danida, the NGO HIVOS, Oxfam America and Cultural Survival, to bring about long-term projects that linked development programmes with institutional strengthening of indigenous communities. From that moment, lowland indigenous groups started to be politically structured and, in 1982, the Centre of Indigenous Peoples of the Bolivian East (Central Indígena del Oriente Boliviano, CIDOB) was founded – later renamed the Confederation of Indigenous Peoples of Bolivia (Confederación de Pueblos Indígenas de Bolivia). This organisation became one of the main social actors of the lowlands and played a key role in national politics. It proposed an innovative project of state reform and put forward for the first time an agenda for the implementation of indigenous rights (Lacroix 2011).

In the highlands, similar experiences of symbiosis between academic and cooperation sectors stemmed out of ethnodevelopment projects (Andolina et al. 2005).[8] The most important was the Workshop of Oral

---

[8] Guillaume Boccara and Paola Bolados studied similar processes in Chile, focusing in particular on ethnodevelopment policies implemented by state or para-state institutions (ethnogovernment), with the aim of strengthening partnerships with indigenous communities to hold them accountable, following the World Bank's motto to 'help those helping

Andean History (Taller de Historia Oral Andiana), created in 1983 in La Paz with the support of Oxfam America. This project developed research on the indianist movement between 1869 and 1950, with the aim of strengthening indigenous history, culture and identity in the highlands (Choque & Mamani 2003). The results served as a discursive basis for the legitimation of a movement of 'reconstruction of the *ayllus*'.[9] The consolidation of a highland-based indigenous organisation, however, took much longer than in the lowlands, mainly due to the resistance of peasant unions across the region. In March 1997 in Ch'allapata, the National Council of Ayllus and Markas of the Qullasuyu (Consejo Nacional de Ayllus y Markas del Qullasuyu, CONAMAQ) was founded and consecrated as the 'national authority of the Aymaras, Quechuas and Urus' (Choque & Mamani 2003: 166). In its early days, this organisation made great efforts to differentiate itself from its natural 'competitor' – the CSUTCB – though an ethnic-based discourse that emphasised the 'genuineness' of this movement as an expression of an 'original' Andean peoples' identity (Albó 2008: 161). The key concept in this sense was 'nativeness' (*originarios*), which allowed CONAMAQ not only to distance itself from the peasants (*campesinos*), but also from the indigenous peoples of the eastern lowlands (*indígenas*) – and thus to build its own identity boundaries.

   In Peru, the Native Communities Law of 1974 gave a first impulse towards the creation of ethnic and zonal federations. But it was the increasing support of outside groups, including Catholic and Protestant missions, NGOs, environmentalists and anthropologists that, in the early 1980s, allowed Amazonian peoples to create an umbrella organisation – the Interethnic Association for the Development of the Peruvian Rainforest (Asociación Interétnica de Desarrollo de la Selva Peruana, AIDESEP) – which sought to represent them nationally and internationally (Peeler 2003; Greene 2005). During the following years,

---

themselves' (Boccara and Bolados 2010: 653). This and other works by Boccara aim to describe ethnodevelopmentism as the juncture between capitalism, neoliberalism and cultural diversity (Boccara 2014).

[9] The *ayllu* is a form of extended familial community originally from the Andean region, which works the land in a collective in the framework of a commonly owned territory. In its origin, the *ayllu* was a territorial unity that gathered a lineage of related families, belonging to segmented and dual hierarchies, with different geographical scales and complexity (Albó & Barrios 2006; for an in-depth analysis of the debate around the definition of the *ayllu* see Wightman 1990). Nowadays, there exists considerable variance in the form and meaning of the *ayllu*, generally defining groups based on kinship and virilocality with their own system of land management (McNeish 2002).

other nationwide and regional organisations were created to represent Peruvian indigenous peoples, including the Union of Aymara Communities (Unión de Comunidades Aymaras, UNCA) in 1985, representing indigenous communities of the southern highlands; and, in 1995, the National Organisation of Andean and Amazonian Indigenous Women of Peru (Organización Nacional de Mujeres Indígenas Andinas y Amazónicas del Perú, ONAMIAP), which focused on gender issues.

As in Bolivia, the development of an ethnic discourse and institutional apparatus in the highlands took longer than in the lowlands. In fact, scholars have often argued that ethnicity has still not managed to influence self-perception and political discourse among Peruvian Andean people, despite similarities in the demographic and linguistic structures with Bolivia and other neighbouring countries. Peru is therefore often considered an outlier with respect to the ethnic question (Gelles 2002). Instead of adopting ethnicity as a political tool, Peruvian highland communities have continued to resort to other non-indigenous ideologies and rural identities (Greene 2005; Remy 2014). Since the 2000s, however, something has begun to change, at least in the political discourse of some highland social movements, if not in their popular forms of self-identification. A somewhat atypical organisation called National Confederation of Communities Adversely Affected by Mining (Confederación Nacional de Comunidades del Perú Afectadas por la Minería, CONACAMI) – founded in 1999 to deal with the social impact of extractive industry in mostly Quechua communities – started to place emphasis on ethnicity in its discourse. It became what has been described as 'the most coherent and influential indigenous highland organisation to come along in a long while' (García 2005: 59). Even after the sudden decline of CONACAMI, traditional peasant organisations such as the CNA and the CCP have increasingly turned towards identity as a way of justifying rights and participation claims, although these recent developments are still not very well documented in the literature.

In contrast with Peru and Bolivia, Colombia's nurturing environment for the rise of indigenous movements has not been the Amazon, but rather the Western Andean valleys. In 1971 – a decade earlier than in neighbouring countries – the Regional Indigenous Council of the Cauca (Consejo Regional Indígena del Cauca, CRIC) was founded (Troyan 2008). The organisation drew inspiration from the early twentieth-century ethnic mobilisation led by Manuel Quintín Lame in this region, and took advantage of a relatively favourable attitude towards ethnic-based claims adopted by the central government in order to diminish the power of class-based movements. Despite its name, in this early phase the

CRIC raised very similar claims about land access and redistribution to those of peasant movements. However, the ANUC's insensitivity towards the cultural specificities of ethnic struggles and its 'big stick' policy vis-à-vis the CRIC (Zamosc 1986), as well as the government's hostility to class discourse and inter-group alliances, had the effect of strengthening the organisation's ethnic identity, as it attempted to survive political competition and physical repression (Troyan 2008). At the same time, the CRIC began to consolidate an alliance with other indigenous groups that were organising across the country, particularly in the Amazonian regions. This alliance was eventually sealed with the foundation, in 1982, of the National Indigenous Organisation of Colombia (Organización Nacional Indígena de Colombia, ONIC). The ONIC remains the most important indigenous organisation in Colombia, although over the subsequent decades other regional indigenous organisations were created, namely the Organisation of Indigenous Peoples of the Colombia Amazon (Organización de los Pueblos Indígenas de la Amazonía Colombiana), founded in 1995, and the Indigenous Confederation Tayrona (Confederación Indígena Tayrona), founded in 1983.

'FROM THE STREET TO THE PALACE'[10]

The rise of new indigenous movements during the 1980s and 1990s triggered mixed responses from peasant organisations. While in certain cases the unions 'rebranded' under an ethnic banner, other peasant organisations perceived indigenous groups as direct competitors in the 'battle' for resources and power. Despite these tensions, at the national level efforts were made by both peasant and indigenous organisations to form political coalitions and seal strategic alliances, either to get their voices heard by unsympathetic governments or to access the electoral competition through a common platform. Particularly under neoliberal governments, these inter-rural coalitions were key to fuelling sustained mobilisation and social unrest, which in certain cases represented turning points in long-standing historical trajectories (Lapegna 2016). Such experiences of political resistance improved the level of coordination of social actors and granted national and sometimes international visibility. In some cases, the strength gained in the mobilisation phase served as the

---

[10] Stefanoni (2006).

basis for the launch of political initiatives and the transition towards more formalised political platforms.

Bolivia is probably the country where this transition 'from the street to the palace' (Stefanoni 2006) has generated the most outstanding process of social and political change. The popular uprisings in the early 2000s against the implementation of economic privatisation and liberalisation measures by the neoliberal government of Gonzalo Sánchez de Lozada (the so-called Water and Gas Wars), offered the opportunity for greater coordination among different social sectors. In September 2004, the main peasant and indigenous organisations signed the Pact of Unity and Commitment (Pacto de Unidad y Compromiso), formalising their common reformist agenda, which included demands for agrarian reform, land redistribution, hydrocarbon nationalisation and (primarily) the rewriting of the 1967 constitution through a Constitutional Assembly (Valencia García & Égido Zurita 2010). The Pact also became the main social platform for Evo Morales' presidential campaign. After his historic election in 2005, the Pact joined the pro-government grassroots alliance called National Coalition for Change (Coalición Nacional para el Cambio) and played a key role in fighting right-wing opposition within the Constitutional Assembly. The composition of the Pact of Unity has varied over time, but since 2006 it has generally consisted of five nationwide organisations: CSUTCB, Bartolinas, the Syndicalist Confederation of Intercultural Communities of Bolivia (Confederación Sindical de Comunidades Interculturales de Bolivia, CSCIB), CIDOB and CONAMAQ. However, in recent years, and particularly after the 2011 conflict between the government and the lowland indigenous organisations of the Indigenous Territory and National Park Isiboro Sécure (Territorio Indígena and Parque Nacional Isiboro Sécure, TIPNIS), the Pact has experienced a period of crisis and internal fragmentation. Because of leadership divergence over the TIPNIS conflict,[11] the two main indigenous organisations – CIDOB and CONAMAQ – split into an opposition group and a pro-government group. Morales' efforts to reconstitute the Pact involved only pro-government sectors, worsening the internal crisis of the indigenous organisations even further and compromising the initial spirit of the Pact in regard to the consolidation of an inclusive and equal peasant-indigenous alliance.

[11] This is a conflict over the construction of a road that would cut across a national park and indigenous territory. A more detailed description of this conflict can be found in Chapter 4.

In a similar fashion, the early 2000s marked a significant turn towards greater inclusion of social forces within the Peruvian political arena. After the collapse of Fujimori's regime, an independent candidate of Quechua origins, Alejandro Toledo, became president. Relying on his poor beginnings, Toledo was able to mobilise the rural masses around ethnic banners and neo-Inca symbolism. His electoral success encouraged Andean and Amazonian movements, for a long time separated by their either peasant or native affiliations, to unite their causes and revitalise the Permanent Coordinator of the Indigenous Peoples of Peru (Coordinadora Permanente de los Pueblos Indígenas del Perú) – a joint umbrella organisation first established in 1997 (Van Cott 2005a). A political alliance was consolidated around a proposal for constitutional reform that addressed collective rights claims. During the press conference to present the proposal in October 2004, the leaders of peasant unions and native organisations publicly affirmed a shared identity as *pueblos indígenas* (Greene 2005). Likewise, over the following years, CONACAMI, the newly formed organisation representing mining-affected highland communities, began to pair its environmentalist agenda with a new emphasis on indigenous rights and recognition. Oxfam America and other NGOs played an important role in this process, facilitating meetings with other prominent indigenous organisations in the region (e.g. the Confederation of Peoples of Kichwa Nationality, Confederación de Kichwa del Ecuador; CONAMAQ). However, the transnationalised language of indigeneity was received with scepticism by Peruvian local leaders and grassroots (Lucero 2013), and CONACAMI's example was not immediately followed by more traditional peasant organisations such as the CCP and the CNA. After a difficult period for Peruvian social movements coinciding with the government of Alan García and his declared opposition to rural communities as hindrances to economic development, a new attempt to revitalise an indigenous-peasant alliance was made in 2011, with the constitution of a Unity Pact of Peruvian Indigenous Organisations (Pacto de Unidad de Organizaciones Indígenas del Perú). The alliance's main goals were strengthening indigenous movements, formulating joint proposals, and providing an interface between social organisations and the state. The Pact was formed by the CNA, the CCP, ONAMIAP, UNCA, the National Federation of Peasant Artisan Indigenous Native Salaried Women of Peru (Federación Nacional de Mujeres Campesinas Artesanas Indígenas Nativas y Asalariadas del Perú) and the Unified National Organisation of Peasant Rounds

(Central Única Nacional de Rondas Campesinas). Neither AIDESEP nor CONACAMI, the two souls of the Peruvian indigenous movements, joined the Pact – although for very different reasons. Over the years, AIDESEP had managed to consolidate its reputation as the main Peruvian indigenous organisation and most likely, in its own calculations, the advantages of a common platform would not compensate for potential losses in visibility and independence. CONACAMI, on its side, was shackled by infighting and a legitimacy crisis that eventually relegated the organisation to the margins of public debate. It should also be noted that, despite the similarities with the Bolivian case, the Peruvian Unity Pact has not played a comparable role in shaping national politics, due in part to the structural weaknesses of Peruvian movements and to the difficulty of identifying political allies and interlocutors.

In Colombia, the last two decades have also opened a new phase in the relationship between indigenous and peasant movements, and have seen greater participation of rural movements in national politics. Indigenous and peasant sectors followed different trajectories throughout the 1990s: the indigenous movement came out reinvigorated from the 1991 constitutional reform and gained access for the first time to the national political arena. The peasant movement, in contrast, was as debilitated as ever, without institutional or social recognition and still trying to challenge national politics through social mobilisation. In other words, as the indigenous organisations found a more institutionalised position within the state, peasant unions were relegated to an antagonistic role via a very debilitated social platform. The approval of a new agrarian law (Law 160) in 1994 sent an encouraging signal to the peasants, which, however, faded quickly once the reluctance of the government to take any concrete steps towards its implementation became clear. The peasant movement had to conduct massive mobilisation across the country, and particularly in the coca production regions of Putumayo, Caquetá, Cauca, Sur de Bolívar and Guaviare, in order to press the government to undertake negotiations, which led to an agreement around the creation of four Peasant Reserve Zones (Zonas de Researva Campesina, ZRCs). Instituted by Law 160, these are specific areas with a mixed system of individual and collective land management under the authority of an elected committee. They are protected from land grabs, entitled to receive special rural development benefits and primarily devoted to small-scale farming.

Unsurprisingly, the creation of the ZRCs generated significant resistance, especially from agribusiness sectors (Fajardo 2000). As a result, further demands for the creation of other ZRCs and the formalisation of self-declared zones (more than thirty across the country) put forward by the National Committee for the Promotion of Peasant Reserve Areas (Comité Nacional de Impulso de Zonas de Reserva Campesina) were denied by the government. A national dialogue around this issue stagnated until 2012, when the ZRCs were included in the first point of the peace negotiation agenda with the FARC. The constitution of the ZRC, which has been one of the leading proposals of the Colombia peasant movement in recent years, has never received official support from indigenous sectors, mainly because of concerns over territorial overlapping with their *resguardos*.

In recent years, however, indigenous and peasant organisations have managed to articulate a new kind of alliance centred on the agrarian question. In 2013, a nationwide agrarian strike (*paro agrario*) mobilised peasant, indigenous and other popular sectors around an agenda of demands which included: the implementation of measures against the agriculture and livestock crisis; claims for land access; recognition of peasant territories; respect for the political and social rights of rural populations; peace and social justice. A negotiation table with the government was set up and, in March 2014, the Peasant Ethnic and Popular Agrarian Summit (Cumbre Agraria Campesina Étnica y Popular) was launched to improve coordination efforts among the various rural sectors.[12] Yet unresolved internal differences around key issues persisted. While peasant and political organisations such as the Patriotic March and the Peoples' Congress were in favour of the launch of a Constitutional Assembly as a result of the peace agreements and in line with the FARC proposal, indigenous peoples and Afro-descendants feared it constituted a threat to the recognition of collective rights gained in the 1991 constitution, and were therefore supporting the referendum option proposed by the government. Ethnic organisations have also been sceptical with respect to the entitlement of peasant communities to differentiated collective rights, such as some form of free prior and informed consultation on natural resource exploitation and development projects; and they have

---

[12] The Summit included political organisations such as the Patriotic March (Marcha Patriótica) and the Peoples' Congress (Congreso de los Pubelos), peasant organisations such as ANZORC and the Table of Interlocution and Agreement (Mesa de Interlocución y Acuerdos), ethnic organisations such as the Process of Black Communities (Proceso de Comunidades Negras), and the ONIC.

generally been resistant to the creation of ZRCs, especially those bordering their territories. These disagreements notwithstanding, the Cumbre has been considered 'one of the most important political movements in the post-conflict scenario' (Bermúdez 2014) and has been able to reach an almost unprecedented degree of articulation across different rural sectors. Its role and political potential beyond the initial conjuncture became clear when a second national rural strike was enacted in June 2016, to express frustrations around the stagnation of negotiations with the government. This strike lasted twelve days and concluded with some preliminary agreements and a commitment to engage in more effective dialogue. The signing of a historic peace accord with the FARC in 2016 also opened encouraging new pathways for Colombia and its as-yet unresolved agrarian question.

The trajectories of the relationship between peasant and indigenous movements in the Andes over the last two decades and the alternation, and sometimes coexistence, of conflict and alliance are a useful reminder of the complexity that characterises social dynamics. In general, at the national level, this latest phase has been characterised by an unprecedented number of new indigenous and peasant organisations struggling to gain political relevance. Alliances have often emerged by sharing spaces and agendas of protest, particularly in efforts to challenge the dominant neoliberal order (Lapegna 2016). Contentious politics from the street have been key coagulators of social pacts that have then resulted in the constitution of durable platforms, instrumental in engaging either in political negotiations or directly in the electoral game. At the same time, the sustainability of these platforms and alliances over time, and especially beyond moments of crisis or social effervescence, has been one of the main challenges for rural movements. This has been reflected in a trend towards the demobilisation of social movements across the region following the rise of leftist governments in the 2000s (Lapegna 2013).

This downturn in political momentum is coupled with the long-standing coexistence of divergent and often competing goals among indigenous and peasant sectors. While these movements are generally aligned behind classic rural fights for land redistribution, expansion of social benefits, agricultural subsidies and political participation, their interests often diverge over the nature and magnitude of economic and development interventions, the preferable type of land tenure, the degree of institutional autonomy, and priority-setting criteria. These competing interests become more visible and tangible at the local level. Here, the alliances between indigenous and peasant sectors have been weak or never materialised and, locally, organisational relationships have rather become more conflictive in recent years. In the remainder of the book, I analyse these new conflict trends across different rural sectors. Applying the theoretical framework that I outlined in Chapter 1, the following chapters discuss in detail empirical cases that illustrate different types of recognition conflicts.

4

Recognition for Whom?

In this chapter, I compare national debates around the definition of the collective subject that should be granted access to a new participatory mechanism for development and resource governance called Free Prior and Informed Consent/Consultation (FPIC). This is an interesting case, I argue, around which to discuss a type of recognition conflict that I call participation conflict. These conflicts result from the implementation of means of recognition (through categorisation exercises) in contexts where opportunities to control new strategic resources are pursued by traditionally marginalised social actors. Regulated by ILO Convention 169 and included in most Latin American legal frameworks since the 1990s, in recent years, FPIC has suddenly catalysed the attention of both governments and social movements. FPIC aims at achieving more effective bottom-up participation by establishing an obligation to consult – or obtain the consent of – indigenous peoples before large development projects and legal reforms that would affect them can proceed. Given its relevance for natural resource governance, interest in FPIC initiatives has been growing, particularly in the framework of political economy models that increasingly rely on commodity exploitation to sustain economic growth and welfare investments. The Andean region has been pioneering the implementation of FPIC worldwide. Here is where the most advanced legislation and institutionalisation processes in regard to FPIC have developed over the past decade. However, these advances have not occurred without tensions. Heated disputes on the definition of the collective subject that should be granted this new right have led to very different outcomes in Bolivia, Colombia and Peru. Some crucial knots in this discussion have revolved around how to operationalise the distinction between ethnic and non-ethnic communities and, notably, whether or not peasant communities should be entitled to FPIC. This represents, therefore, a telling example of an ethnic boundary-making exercise (a classic 'means of recognition') with important implications for groups' self-perception and mutual relationships. The different answers offered by the three countries to the subject question not only have important implications in terms of the inclusion and exclusion of considerable parts of the rural population from new mechanisms of participatory governance; they also reflect the models of citizenship and development that these countries are committed to building through the redefinition of identity articulation/disarticulation processes and delimitation of social boundaries.[1]

RESOURCE GOVERNANCE AND THE FRONTIERS OF ETHNIC PARTICIPATION

In Latin America, the rise of new institutionalised forms of direct participation constitutes one of the main features of the most recent wave of democratisation (Cameron et al. 2012). After the representation crisis in the framework of the transition from authoritarian to democratic regimes, as well as the failure of market-oriented policies, participatory governance and democratic decentralisation became the main tools in the effort to reduce the gap between state and civil society, and to manage conflict and social grievances (Faguet 2013; 2014). What is peculiar in the Latin American case is that the neoliberal approach to participation was driven by a multicultural agenda rather than by a more inclusive version of the liberal citizenship model. In the effort to disentangle the empirical overlapping of ethnic belonging and extreme poverty, neoliberal multiculturalism engineered special programmes to 'target indigenous poverty', initially through top-down initiatives and then through more participatory approaches (Eversole et al. 2005). One of the main effects of these programmes, not entirely expected by their creators, was the political strengthening of indigenous movements, as well as the deepening of ethnic cleavages. In this sense, indigenous claims to collective rights and forms of territorial autonomy raised what Deborah Yashar (1999: 285) calls a new 'postliberal challenge': they question the univocal correspondence between individuals and citizens and claim the recognition of

---

[1] This chapter draws inspiration and some empirical material on the Bolivian case from Fontana and Grugel (2016).

differentiated sets of rights and institutions according to ethnically defined citizenship boundaries.

Participatory resource and environmental governance became one of the most strategic and conflictive policy areas even beyond neoliberalism. In the 2000s, the election of leftist governments throughout Latin America marked a post-neoliberal turn (Grugel & Riggirozzi 2012), characterised by a new commitment to welfare investments and wealth redistribution. In this phase, however, economic and social development has mainly been sustained by revenues from commodity exports, taking advantage of the high value of natural resources in international markets (Bebbington & Humphreys Bebbington 2011). Neoextractivism, as Gudynas (2012) has called this economic model, underpins contemporary development politics across Latin America, particularly in the Andean region. Peru's unprecedented economic growth (8.8% just after the recession of 2009) has been supported mainly by mineral extraction, with the country becoming the largest global producer of silver, the second-largest source of copper and zinc, and Latin America's largest source of gold and lead (Hoffman & Grigera 2013). Likewise, more than 70 per cent of the Peruvian Amazon has been parcelled into hydrocarbon blocks (Bebbington 2009). Bolivia holds 35 per cent of the world's lithium, has the third-largest gas reserves in South America and 55 per cent of its territory is considered to be of potential hydrocarbon interest (Bebbington 2009; Hoffman & Grigera 2013). While Colombia is the only Andean country where the political right has managed to solidly remain in power in the midst of the pink tide that swept Latin America, austerity measures (instead of welfare expansion) were equally accompanied by heavy reliance on commodity exports. Colombia is the world's fourth-largest coal exporter and Latin America's fourth-largest oil producer. It also possesses significant reserves of minerals such as nickel, gold, silver, platinum and emeralds. In order to boost what Colombia's former president Santos called the 'mining locomotive' (*locomotora minera*), by the end of 2012, over one-third of Colombia's land was either issued in mining titles, requested in concessions or destined for mining through national plans (Weitzner 2017).

The recent boom in natural resource exploitation has meant a sudden expansion of affected and potentially affected areas, with the map of concessions increasingly overlapping with natural protected areas, indigenous territories and communal land alike (O'Rourke & Connolly 2003). In Peru alone, it has been estimated that over half of the country's rural communities have been affected by mining activities

(Williams & Bebbington 2008). In this context, rural populations across the Andes and the Amazon have been confronted with new challenges – as well as opportunities – following the arrival of state and international companies intending to initiate extractive projects on their lands. On one hand, concrete opportunities in terms of jobs and improved access to services and infrastructures have been flourishing, opening up new economic scenarios for remote and inaccessible regions that had been systemically excluded from national development processes. On the other, the negative externalities of exploitation activities are associated with environmental degradation and destabilisation of traditional livelihoods, governance mechanisms and cultural systems. The increased economic value of land has also provided incentives for community leaders and members to pay closer attention to property rights issues, generating expectations and demands for greater tenure security. Ultimately, the changes that these processes have introduced in the relationship of local communities with the state, private companies and neighbouring communities have often been characterised by increased tensions over the control of natural resources and development processes (Li 2015; Merino Acuña 2015; Haslam & Tanimoune 2016; Torres Wong 2018). In this chapter, I will add to the abundant literature on socio-environmental conflict in Latin America by focusing in particular on the horizontal dimension of these conflicts. I will show how resource governance has become a battleground centred around the redefinition of identity cleavages. In other words, participatory mechanisms embedded in the international indigenous rights framework have introduced new 'means of recognition' that have crafted juridical collective subjects entitled to new rights. This in turn has resulted in narrative shifts and new epistemologies of inclusion/exclusion, self/otherness and articulation/disarticulation. The redefinition of identity boundaries among extremely poor and marginalised social communities, combined with growing extractive pressure, is at the root of new social grievances.

FROM PARTICIPATION TO CONFLICT

According to the Environmental Justice Organizations, Liabilities and Trade (EJOLT) project, of 342 'environmental justice conflicts' recently registered across South America, 197 are located in the Andean countries of Bolivia, Colombia, Ecuador, Peru and Venezuela (EJOLT 2015, cited in Siegel 2016: 10). In Peru alone in October 2016, the Ombudsman's Office reported 212 social disputes on file, of which 149 related to environmental concerns, including 97 related to mining and 23 to hydro-carbon activities specifically (Defensoria del Pueblo 2016). The escalation of some of these conflicts into deadly outbreaks of violence has put them on the radar of the international media and transformed them into tipping points in the relationship between governments and social organisations. Well-known cases include protests against the Belo Monte dam and other hydropower developments in Brazil, the conflict around an infrastructural project in the Indigenous Territory and National Park Isiboro Sécure (Territorio Indígena y Parque Nacional Isiboro Sécure, TIPNIS) in Bolivia, and the so-called Baguazo, a series of bloody confrontations between Peruvian police forces and indigenous peoples protesting against the government's decision to open a vast area of the Peruvian Amazon to development and exploitation.

In both Peru and Bolivia, one of the major outcomes of these outbreaks of violence faced by the state and social (mainly indigenous) organisations was the rise of claims for FPIC that quickly made their way into national debates. Rooted in international human rights law, the FPIC mechanism is designed to regulate the participation of indigenous peoples in decision-making and political processes that might directly affect their interests (Ward 2011). While this right has been included in these countries' legal frameworks since the 1990s with the ratification of ILO Convention 169, in practice it remained a *lettera morta* until indigenous protests suddenly brought it to the forefront of their agendas in the late 2000s.

A number of factors contribute to explaining why FPIC has become a highly strategic issue in recent years. In the Andean region, this demand generally emerged in the context of economic bonanza and the high value of natural resources, increasing tensions between social and political actors around new territorial demarcations and a growing reliance on commodity exports in order to sustain economic growth and welfare expansion plans. It is not surprising that, in this context, FPIC became one of the most important mechanisms within national debates on recognition as well as a key tool for addressing distributive issues and the widespread lack of resources for poor rural communities.

The advantages of linking the recognition agenda with natural resource management have been highlighted by recent evidence empha-sising how indigenous knowledge and practices are key allies against deforestation, climate change and environmental degradation. Recent studies by the World Resources Institute and the Rights and Resources Initiative show how tenure-secure indigenous forestlands have lower rates of deforestation, higher ecosystem-service benefits, and better conservation and carbon mitigation outcomes (Rights and Resources Initiative 2015b; Vergara et al. 2016). A prerequisite for these outcomes is reliance on traditional indigenous knowledge systems (Mistry & Berardi 2016). This positive evidence, alongside a discourse that pictures indigenous peoples as protectors of 'Mother Earth', has been used by indigenous activists and their allies to advocate for the recognition of new rights and the strengthening of participatory mechanisms in decision-making processes in relation to development initiatives and natural resource management. In practice, however, the operationalisation of these new rights, including FPIC, entails complex political processes and new challenges for the participatory agenda. One crucial issue, seldom explored in the literature on FPIC and socio-environmental conflict, has revolved around the identification of which groups should be entitled to consultation.

FPIC: WHO HAS THE RIGHT?

FPIC is a relatively new concept in law and jurisprudence. According to indigenous rights advocates, it is rooted in the principle of self-determination, as recognised by Common Article 1 of both the International Covenant on Civil and Political Rights and the International Covenant on Economic, Social and Cultural Rights. However, within international human rights jurisprudence, FPIC is rather based on property and cultural rights and the right to not be discriminated against (Ward 2011).

While there is no single internationally agreed definition of FPIC, nor a one-size-fits-all mechanism for its implementation (Schilling-Vacaflor & Flemmer 2013; UN-REDD 2013), references to the need to consult or to obtain consent from indigenous peoples are found in all the main human rights instruments on indigenous rights. Article 6 of Convention 169 states that:

Governments shall consult the peoples concerned, through appropriate proced-ures and in particular through their representative institutions, whenever consider-ation is being given to legislative or administrative measures, which may affect them directly. ... The consultations carried out in application of this Convention shall be undertaken, in good faith and in a form appropriate to the circumstances, with the objective of achieving agreement or consent to the proposed measures.

An ILO handbook on C.169 published in 2013 attempts to clarify some of the controversial issues raised by the Convention and clearly places emphasis on the right of indigenous peoples *to be consulted*. However, it does not suggest that consent is necessary, nor does it invest indigenous peoples with veto power: 'Convention No. 169 does not provide indigenous peoples with a veto right, as obtaining the agreement or consent is the purpose of engaging in the consultation process, and is not an independent requirement' (ILO 2013: 16). The United Nations Declaration on the Rights of Indigenous Peoples (2007), meanwhile, explicitly calls for *consent*, and sets out the circumstances in which this is required, namely: relocation of a population (Art. 10); impact on culture and intellectual property (Art. 12); adoption and implementation of legislative or administrative measures (Art. 19); exploitation of lands, territories and natural resources (Art. 27); disposal of hazardous waste (Art. 29); and development planning (Art. 30). In addition, the Cartagena Protocol on Bio-Safety (2000) to the Convention on Biological Diversity seeks to attach FPIC to the transboundary movement, transit, handling and use of all living organisms (EMRIP 2011). In short, FPIC is now talked about in connection with a very broad set of issues, though thus far it has been applied mainly in relation to natural resource exploitation.

Because it is so recent, FPIC is international law-in-the-making and, as such, there is some confusion about the value and purpose of consultation, the nature of consent, and the arenas in which it is required (Fontana & Grugel 2016). Still, despite its legal ambiguities, FPIC is increasingly being put to use. The United Nations Programme on Reducing Emissions from Deforestation and Forest Degradation (UN-REDD) recognised FPIC as a key instrument for sustainability (UN-REDD 2013; Sunderlin et al. 2014). FPIC experiments have been introduced in a number of countries, including Suriname, Guyana, Tanzania, Malaysia, the Philippines, Indonesia and Australia. But it is in Latin America above all – and especially Bolivia, Peru and Colombia – where attempts to use FPIC to institutionalise participatory development governance are most advanced. These three countries are among the few to include FPIC in their constitutions and to articulate formalised standards and mechanisms for its implementation. Despite these similarities, however, the ways in which the discussion on FPIC has been framed across these countries show noticeable differences, which are reflected in the legal and procedural measures for its implementation. One of the most relevant – and contentious – concerns the subject of consultation, or who should be entitled to FPIC.

This issue goes beyond a purely legal dimension; it broadly refers to the identification of individuals or social groups who are entitled to moral consideration, that is, those who deserve recognition and hold rights

(Sikor et al. 2014; Martin et al. 2016) – in other words, the 'means of recognition' embedded in FPIC. The identification of who should be entitled to FPIC has been a crucial issue of contention and debate in all Latin American countries that have taken steps towards the implementation of this right. The FPIC subject issue is particularly problematic in countries, such as those in the Andean region, in which, as I have shown in previous chapters, ethnic identity boundaries are often blurred and volatile and characterised by cyclical phases of articulation/disarticulation of different rural identities. As the examples of Peru, Colombia and Bolivia illustrate, governments have made very different decisions in this regard, adopting either strict or loose definitions of ethno-cultural belonging, with important consequences for how different social groups have been able to access FPIC. These tensions are grounded in different and competing claims by indigenous and peasant movements, which illustrate a type of recognition conflict that emerges at the intersection between recognition norm-making and resource governance. I call this type of conflict participation conflict. In the following sections, I discuss three different outcomes in terms of the definition of juridical subjects entitled to FPIC, and analyse the configuration of social and political forces behind each of these cases.

The Inclusive Approach to Consultation in Bolivia: The 'Indigenous Native Peasant' Subject

Despite the early recognition of the social, cultural and economic rights of indigenous peoples by the Bolivian state with the constitutional reform of 1995 (Art. 171), the duty to conduct consultations (exclusively in the hydrocarbon sector) was for the first time introduced in the legislation only a decade later, in 2005. FPIC was then included in the new constitution approved by referendum in 2009. Although binding consent for all resource-related activities was mandatory in preliminary drafts (Bascopé Sanjinés 2010), the final version of the constitution only grants the right to consultation in relation to the exploitation of non-renewable natural resources (Art. 30). Between February 2007 and December 2013, forty consultation processes were concluded, mainly in the gas sector (Flemmer & Schilling-Vacaflor 2016). But it was in the aftermath of the 2011 political crisis, following one of the worst social conflicts in recent years, that the need to regulate FPIC became an unavoidable priority for the Bolivian government (Fontana & Grugel 2016).

In 2011, Morales' administration announced a plan to construct a road through the TIPNIS as part of a Brazilian-led network of mega-projects aimed at generating development throughout the continent. The announcement triggered mass mobilisation by lowland indigenous peoples, who, supported by environmental NGOs and urban activists, set off on a protest march to La Paz. Indigenous communities argued that the designation of TIPNIS as a park and an indigenous territory should protect it from mega-development projects, and meant they had the right to be consulted. Tensions then developed between the indigenous groups and the peasant and coca-growers' unions (mainly Aymara and Quechua settlers), who saw the road as a way of expanding the agrarian frontier (Webber 2011; Perrier Bruslé 2012; McNeish 2013). The conflict generated international attention, which pushed the government into holding a consultation, the outcome of which favoured building the road. The consultation has not resolved the conflict: the indigenous communities, who demanded consultation in the first place, felt betrayed and refused to participate, while the outcome was questioned by an independent assessment led by the Catholic Church and by the TIPNIS indigenous communities themselves (Comisión Interinstitucional de la Iglesia Católica et al. 2012; Sub-central TIPNIS Comisión de Recorrido 2012).

It is not by chance that a national debate around an FPIC Law began as a result of the TIPNIS conflict, when it became clear to both the government and social organisations that having a national regulatory framework in place would be of crucial importance. The final version of the draft law regulating FPIC (August 2013), before being submitted for parliamentary approval, took twelve months of talks between the government and the main rural organisations – indigenous (CIDOB and the Guaraní People Assembly, Asamblea del Pueblo Guaraní APG), native (CONAMAQ) and peasant (CSUTCB, its female branch, Bartolinas, and CSCIB) – at moments when these organisations were experiencing high levels of conflict and internal fragmentation.[2]

It is not surprising that the government found it difficult to manage the competing demands that were articulated, for, in the end, at the heart of

---

[2] At the time of the negotiations, CONAMAQ was yet to be formally split into two branches, while CIDOB's separation occurred during those months. In the latest phase of the talks, the government was therefore in dialogue mainly with the *oficialista* branch closer to the executive. See also Chapter 3.

the conflicts over the FPIC Law was the question of who has the right to be consulted, with the implication that some groups have more rights than others. Article 17 of the first FPIC draft law prepared by the government stated that 'indigenous native nations and peoples of the TCOs (i.e. with titled land)' should be the subject of FPIC, while 'indigenous native peasant peoples, intercultural communities and Afro-Bolivians' are entitled to a more generic and less demanding public consultation – which, in fact, according to the constitution, should be a right for all Bolivians (working document, Ministerio de Gobierno 2012). But this proposal provoked a massive stand-off between the government and social organisations, since it meant some would have more voice than others. The peasant leaders argued that they had the same right to FPIC as indigenous/native groups. As the Secretary of International Affairs of the CSUTCB told me:

> There is no understanding between indigenous and peasants. The indigenous representatives say: 'We have the right to consultation, as "indigenous native peasants", because we have TCOs, but the peasants don't. They have no right to consultation because they have no [collective] land, no TCO, they have individual lands'. . . . But we want to be considered *equal* to the indigenous brothers. That is, if a road or something is going through a peasant community, we are entitled to be consulted. (Interview, La Paz, August 2013)

Indigenous organisations, meanwhile, would only agree to the inclusion of the indigenous/native peoples and nations, as the 'true' subjects to benefit from consultation, thereby excluding all other rural groups (APG and CONAMAQ's draft law proposals 2012). Indigenous leaders repeatedly appealed to international agreements on this matter, claiming that peasant organisations do not meet the criteria of 'authenticity', 'nativeness' or 'pre-colonial existence':

> C.169 . . . clearly says that indigenous native people must have historical continuity, and the peasants have no historical continuity. Those international standards must be taken into account in the discussion about consultation. (Interview with CONAMAQ leader, La Paz, July 2013)

In the new plurinational Bolivia, however, excluding the 'peasant' would actually be unconstitutional. Indeed, as I discussed in Chapter 2, the category 'native indigenous peasant' (*indígena originario campesino*), negotiated during the Constitutional Assembly, became one of the main pivots for the institutionalisation of plurinational citizenship and served as the basis for crafting a new legal subject entitled to collective rights (Fontana 2014c). However, at the moment of operationalising those rights, disagreements around this category exploded.[3] Indigenous organisations tried to guarantee for themselves exclusive access to new rights, which would have important consequences on their development as organisations vis-à-vis the state and other rural groups.

Yet, from the outset, the state also tried to limit access to FPIC for the peasant sector. This, however, was mainly driven by pragmatism rather than by political or ideological goals: the inclusion of 'peasants' as subjects implies a drastic widening of the population for whom, and of the territorial demarcations in which, the consultation ought to take place. This would generate more 'constraints' for the state in the processes of decision making on strategic resources and infrastructural development. Moreover, depending on the boundaries crystallised in the norm, the balance of forces at the local level might vary significantly. The TIPNIS conflict is indeed an example of how the inclusion of peasant organisations in the consultation might have led to a different outcome.

The TIPNIS is also an interesting case for illustrating another aspect of the 'subject problem'. Independently of which social groups would be entitled to this right, another operational issue should be addressed concerning who in practice will be consulted: whether it is the communities, the traditional authorities (e.g. *jilakatas* or *capitanes*, union secretaries), the 'people' (e.g. Guaraní, Mojeño, Yurakaré, Mozeten, Uru Chipaya) or the leaders of the social organisations (e.g. CIDOB, CONAMAQ, CSUTCB, CSCIB). In the TIPNIS, the government consulted each community without considering the broad organisations they belonged to (whether indigenous or peasant), which led to the accusation that they were jeopardising the indigenous movement. In fact, the result of the consultation (in favour of the road construction) might have been quite different if indigenous authorities were consulted through their social organisations, rather than at the community level.

On this matter, international law refers to a legitimate representative, which is the one that should be consulted, while the Bolivian constitution provides that 'within the native indigenous peasant peoples and nations, the consultation will be carried out with respect given to their own norms and procedures' (Art. 352); this is mirrored by the FPIC draft law. However, these definitions remain vague and are not instrumental for the concrete determination of a standardised consultation protocol. A first problem is how to define the level of governance in line with the scale of

---

[3] Similar discussions have emerged around issues such as the establishment of ethnic autonomy regimes and ethnic quotas in Parliament and local administrations.

the potential impact (whether local, regional or national) and what kind of organisation should be consulted at those different levels. For example, a conflict of interest might arise between communities (indigenous or peasant), social organisations and the indigenous people on what would be the appropriate authority to be consulted. The lack of clarity on this matter can potentially undermine social groups' claims and rights, allowing the government to select the level to be consulted and increasing the chances of turning the outcome in its favour. Indeed, indigenous peoples and NGOs involved in past consultations have denounced the efforts of the state for being prejudicial to indigenous movements, preventing alliances and cohesive action between communities and their organisations (Bascopé Sanjinés 2010; Pellegrini & Ribera Arismendi 2012). A second problem concerns how to define whether the designated authorities are legitimate and representative. This might be done through previous accreditation in a national register of recognised 'traditional organisations', but even this precaution will not necessarily guarantee that local authorities are acting in the name and representing the interests and opinions of all, or at least of the majority, of the local inhabitants.

Despite the initial apparent willingness of the government to make FPIC the object of genuine negotiation with social parties, over a decade from the historic entry of the TIPNIS march into La Paz in October 2011 and from the formal handing over of the FPIC draft law to President Morales, the draft remains sitting in a drawer, unlikely to be opened anytime soon. Meanwhile, in March 2015, Morales' Government issued a Supreme Decree (2298) establishing new parameters for consultations with affected communities and introducing stricter deadlines and methods for carrying out consultations. If, on one hand, the Bolivian government seemed to acknowledge the need to regulate FPIC in an inclusive way, therefore maximising the potential impact of this participatory mechanism for different communities and social organisations (both indigenous and peasant), on the other hand, more recent developments suggest that it is adopting a top-down approach that threatens to jeopardise the efforts made to reach an agreement on the draft law through social participation.

The Bureaucratic Approach to Consultation in Peru: Assessing 'Objective Indigeneity' in Rural Communities

Peru ratified ILO Convention 169 in 1993. That same year, a new constitution was approved that restricted communities' collective ownership rights to the surface of their land, while a new Hydrocarbon Law concentrated all decision making about subsurface resources in the hands of the state, including activities on indigenous titled land (Coxshall 2010; Orta-Martínez & Finer 2010). These radical neoliberal reforms by the Fujimori government were clearly incompatible with the protection of indigenous rights. Nor did the return to democracy in 2000 immediately contribute to relaunching the recognition agenda, which continued to be perceived as a threat to economic development for another decade.

As in the case of Bolivia, in Peru the discussion on indigenous participation and rights also abruptly re-emerged when tensions between the state and the indigenous movement escalated into a nationwide conflict. In 2009, the approval of a series of decrees allowing private companies access to the Amazon for development and resource exploitation, in compliance with the free trade agreement between Peru and the United States, triggered a wave of protests by indigenous organisations in the lowland regions of five departments. The bloodiest episode in this dispute occurred in Bagua, in the northern Peruvian Amazon, where thirty-four people were killed and hundreds more injured during an attempt by security forces to break down an indigenous blockade (Hughes 2010; Merino Acuña 2015). This peak in the violence shocked Peruvian and international public opinion and forced the government into negotiations with indigenous organisations to clarify responsibilities, but also to discuss a broader agenda of indigenous rights, including FPIC. In this context, the two main lowland indigenous organisations (AIDESEP and CONAP) took the lead in drafting an FPIC law proposal. The draft was then circulated among Andean peasant organisations, which generally welcomed the text, placing particular emphasis on the need to adopt a broad definition of 'indigenous peoples', which should include peasant communities. The proposal was then submitted for Congress approval and, after a heated discussion that led to the reformulation or elimination of the most controversial articles, an FPIC Law was eventually passed in August 2011. This norm introduced a bureaucratic and formalist approach to the issue, listing specific 'objective' criteria for the identification of indigenous peoples, including:

(1) Direct descent from the original populations of the national territory. (2) Lifestyles and spiritual and historical links with the territory that they traditionally use or occupy. (3) Particular social institutions and customs. (4) Cultural patterns and way of life different from those of other sectors of the national population. (Art. 7)

Additionally, a subjective criterion related to 'the consciousness of the collective group [that they] have an indigenous or native identity' should also be considered. In practice, this means that the state – namely a special unit within the Ministry of Culture[4] – is in charge of conducting a case-by-case evaluation of communities' compliance with the above criteria. As the Director of Indigenous Politics within the Vice-Ministry of Interculturality explained to me, 'we send a team to the area of impact of the administrative measure, it produces an ethnography, and now, *with hard, in-depth data*, you can see if it is indeed an indigenous people or not' (interview, Lima, March 2016). The results of this empirically grounded evaluation are used to advise the institutions in charge of organising the consultation (i.e. the state entity responsible for the specific issue area to be consulted; e.g. the Ministry of Hydrocarbons for consult-ation on hydrocarbon projects) about which communities should be consulted.

This rather bureaucratic process reflected the need to find a comprom-ise answer to the question of whether peasants should or should not be consulted. Indeed, in the case of Peru, peasant communities are not a priori included (as in Bolivia) nor excluded (as in Colombia) from con-sultation. Their ethnic belonging is assessed on a case-by-case basis and, through this process, peasant communities can be found to be also – but not always – indigenous. This solution was, however, considered too narrow by the peasant organisations, which continued advocating for the inclusion of all peasant communities, arguing that identity categories are often misleading and any state-led decision would be arbitrary:

We did not decide to change our name. It was the state that changed our name [through the peasantisation process in the 1950s[5]]. For this reason, we demand that all peasant communities ... are recognised as [rights] holders under Convention 169. If the state reserves the discretion to decide who is and who is not [entitled to consultation], this seems to us arbitrary. (Interview, former Secretary of the CCP, Lima, March 2016)

Nor was the formulation satisfactory for President García, who vetoed the law, asking for a greater emphasis on 'national interest' and for the complete exclusion of peasant communities. These objections led to the eruption of new protests and only managed to postpone the promulgation of the FPIC Law by a few months. In September 2011, Peru's newly

---

[4] This unit is also in charge of compiling a database of indigenous peoples, which represents the first systematic attempt to capture ethnic demographics by the Peruvian state.
[5] See Chapter 2.

elected president, Ollanta Humala, signed the FPIC Law (No. 29785) as one of his first official acts and opened a consultation on its regulating norm (Schilling-Vacaflor & Flemmer 2013). This consultation signalled the willingness of the government to enter into dialogue with social organisations, but also brought up some unresolved issues around FPIC. On the subject problem, President Humala himself made some quite controversial declarations that triggered strong reactions and yet synthesised widespread opinions among Peruvians:

> There have been some problems in defining which communities are native and which are not. Because here – with such informality – everyone wants to be consulted, because that can give them a certain bargaining power. ... First, on the coast, where 60% of the population is [living], there are basically no native communities due to the process of migration .... In the highlands, most are agrarian communities, a product of the Agrarian Reform, etc. More than anything, native communities occur in jungle areas. (Cited in Remy 2013: 6)

In other words, even among the more progressive sectors of Peruvian society, doubts persist about the existence of indigenous peoples in the highlands as well as about the appropriateness of consulting communities beyond Amazonian groups. This opinion is generally grounded in two sets of arguments: the first focuses on the fact that peasant communities are more 'developed' and in closer contact with the rest of the country (as a former Vice-Minister of Interculturality articulated to me: 'if they are already developed, they are not indigenous any more' (interview, Cambridge, MA, October 2016); the second stresses how peasant communities generally do not self-identify as indigenous. This, however, has a historical explanation in the peasantisation campaigns conducted by the Velasco government (see Chapters 2 and 3) and the strengthening of negative and racist connotations attached to the term 'indigenous' – as mentioned by the leader of the CCP and documented in multiple academic works (de la Cadena 2000, 2008; Remy 2013, 2014).

In general, the historical trajectory of Peruvian highland communities is not very different from their Bolivian counterparts – as I discussed in Chapter 3. But if in Bolivia the process of disarticulation and revitalisation of indigenous identities began in the 1990s, in Peru it was only after 2010 that an ethnic turn emerged among the peasantry. On one hand, the tragic episode of the Baguazo had the effect of widening solidarity towards Amazonian communities from other social sectors, including peasant organisations. Indeed, this conflict marked a turning point in the relationships between Peruvian rural movements, which have historically been quite weak and fragmented (see Van Cott 2005a; Yashar 2005), fostering a new alliance between native and peasant organisations under a common 'indigenous' banner. On the other hand, in the early phase of the post-Baguazo negotiations, peasant organisations began to perceive that they were losing out, as new emphasis was placed on the indigenous rights agenda and the government was primarily engaging with native organisations. They therefore started to adopt a new ethnic discourse in the effort to gain a seat at the negotiating table (interview with the coordinator of the working group on indigenous peoples, Vice-Ministry of Interculturality, Lima, April 2016). In the words of a peasant leader:

> In Peru, we are living in a period of implementation of the 169 Convention, so this context emphasises in a clearer way the issue of identity. This process offers an excellent window of opportunity to redefine concepts …. For example, in Peru, the term 'indigenous' was used by the colonisers to discriminate. Therefore, for the peasant the indigenous denomination is pejorative and we normally do not use it. But this Convention and its implementation forces us to reconceptualise the notion of 'indigenous' also for peasants. (Interview with former Secretary of the CCP, Lima, April 2016)

In the first instance, this strategy was effective in shaping the discussion on the Forestry and Wildlife Law, where the involvement of the CNA and the CCP allowed non-indigenous rural populations to obtain forest harvest rights (Soria Dall'Orso 2015).

Peasant organisations, however, did not manage to wield as much impact in the FPIC discussion. Nonetheless, since its implementation, they have been adopting a pragmatic strategy to ensure the right to consultation for peasant communities, which consists of a long-term process to revitalise ethnic identities among rural inhabitants.

> In the CCP, we are trying to emphasise the work-stream on identity, seeking visibility for the peasant community not only as a space for agrarian production, but mainly as an expression of a native people that have culture, that have territory, that have a social organisation based on ancestral values such as the *ayllu*. (Interview with former Secretary of the CCP, Lima, April 2016)

The ethnic turn has been stronger in highland communities affected by mining operations. In these contexts, local leaders quickly realised that ethnicity could become an effective mobilisation discourse to fight socio-environmental conflicts. A telling example is the conflict around the Las Bambas mining project in the Apurímac Department, already mentioned, in which forty-seven peasant communities opposing exploitation mobilised under the new ethnic banner of the Chanka-Yanahuara (or Yanawara) Nation.[6] In March 2016, fifty leaders from the region undertook a long march to Lima and went on a month-long hunger strike to denounce the social and environmental damages caused by mining activities as well as their exclusion from the ongoing negotiations. In their statements, they made clear reference to the violation of Convention 169 and their claim for ancestral rights to their communal lands (Asociación Unión de Comunidades Campesinas de Influencia Directa e Indirecta Afectadas por el Proyecto Minero Las Bambas, UCCAMBA 2016).

It is still too early to assess how effective the turn towards ethnicity will be in fighting socio-environmental conflicts in Peru. Perhaps, in the near future, the Chanka-Yanawara Nation will be added to the official list of Peruvian indigenous peoples compiled by the Vice-Ministry of Interculturality, and these communities will secure new rights, including FPIC. For now, peasant organisations have managed at least to gain some international support to foster their 'process of self-recognition as native indigenous' from cooperation actors – including the Ford Foundation – particularly in mining-affected communities (interview with President of the CNA, Lima, April 2016). Yet it is not easy to overturn the reluctance of rural inhabitants to adopt ethnic categories, and peasant leaders had been working hard so that some initial changes could be reflected in the 2017 national census when, for the first time, a question on ethnic self-identification was included (interview with President of the CNA, Lima, April 2016).

Perhaps because the ethnic turn among the peasants is still very recent and relatively weak, it has not generated strong reactions from Peruvian indigenous organisations. A certain degree of scepticism permeates indigenous leaders' opinions about this process, and some have doubts about how deep these changes can go beyond discourse: 'Now they say they are indigenous, but they are not indigenous. The discourse has changed. The discourse before was about peasant farmers' (interview with AIDESEP leader and Vice-Ministry of Interculturality consultant, Lima, April 2016). Moreover, indigenous organisations only partially embraced a shared platform of claims and the most powerful indigenous organisation – AIDESEP, representing over 350,000 indigenous people living in

---

[6] The Chanka was an ethnic group that occupied the Andahuaylas region (Department of Apurímac, Peru), reaching the peak of its expansion around AD 1400 (Bauer & Kellett 2010).

the Peruvian Amazon (Hughes 2010) – opted for a stand-alone strategy, by, for example, declining the invitation to join the Unity Pact. As a consequence, social organisations could not attend the five national consultations conducted between 2013 and 2016 under a single platform.[7] National divisions are in certain cases reflected at the local level, where disagreements have emerged when different organisations claimed consultation rights as representatives of the same grassroots communities. These tensions arose particularly in those contexts in which social organisations (e.g. AIDESEP and CONAP) had conflictive goals in terms of consultation outcomes (e.g. were more or less prone to sign off on the state or private companies' offers).

Despite the inevitable complexity that any consultation process entails, Peru has made important progress in implementing FPIC. According to the Ministry of Culture's website, by 2018, thirty-two consultation processes had been completed or were in progress, twelve of which were in peasant communities. In practice, Peruvian movements managed to overcome resistance to include all peasant communities, although the bureaucratic approach to assessing indigeneity may in practice lengthen consultation procedures and fail to work as a preventive mechanism to address the exponential increase of socio-environmental conflicts in the highland regions.

The Dualistic Approach in Colombia: Towards a Peasant FPIC?

Colombia has made the greatest progress in institutionalising FPIC and in conducting consultations. The first consultations started soon after the ratification of Convention 169 in 1991 and the approval of Colombia's first multicultural constitution.[8] Between 2003 and 2015, approximately 800 processes were concluded or begun, with a total of about 6,000 communities involved, according to a chief division officer of the FPIC

---

[7] Up to 2016, five FPIC processes took place at the national level. Apart from the already mentioned FPIC regulating norm and the Forestry and Wildlife Law and its regulating norm, consultations were conducted on intercultural health and education policies and on the so-called Law of Indigenous Languages.

[8] Even though the term 'prior consultation' does not appear in the constitution, Article 330 states: 'The exploitation of natural resources in indigenous territories shall be without prejudice to the cultural, social and economic integrity of indigenous communities. In decisions taken regarding this exploitation, the Government shall encourage the participation of representatives of the respective communities'.

Unit of the Ministry of Interior (interview, Bogotá, November 2015). This ministry is in charge of coordinating consultations, and since 2011 its FPIC unit occupies four floors of a government building in downtown Bogotá and employs 130 people.

Despite this solid institutional apparatus, Colombia still lacks a coherent regulatory framework on FPIC. Two decrees have been issued on this matter – Decree 1320 (1996) and Decree 2957 (2010) – which respectively regulate consultations on the exploitation of natural resources in indigenous territories and consultations with a general scope. The presidency has also produced some guidelines for FPIC implementation, which, among other issues, regulate which situations require consultation and what are the main steps and how the process should be funded, as well as providing an inter-ministerial coordination protocol that defines responsibilities and duties. This body of norms is, however, partially conflicting and was repeatedly contested by the Colombian Constitutional Court (Parra 2016). Indeed, the Court has been developing the region's richest jurisprudence on FPIC, playing a particularly active role in regulating national FPIC implementation (Rodríguez-Garavito 2011; Parra 2016). In particular, the Court has emphasised the need to consult, not only on practical measures, but also in regard to laws and even international treaties that may affect indigenous peoples (Newman & Ortega Pineda 2016).

The Colombian Constitutional Court has also introduced some important innovations concerning the FPIC subject, recognising the fundamental right to consultation not only for indigenous peoples but also for other national minorities, namely Afro-descendants (including *raizales* from the Archipelago of San Andrés, Providencia and Santa Catalina, and *palenqueros*, a small community of the Caribbean region speaking a language derived from West African dialects) and Roma people. In this sense, Colombia represents a unique case, as some of these groups (that are also present in other countries) have not managed to secure access to FPIC anywhere else in the region. In a recent judgment (SU-217 of 2017), the Court has also defined the criteria that should be used to identify 'differentiated ethnic communities', including an objective dimension related to their characteristics (e.g. language, religion, rituals), as well as a subjective dimension defined through self-recognition (Urrutia Valenzuela 2017). These recommendations were incorporated into the FPIC Law proposal elaborated by the Ministry of Interior in 2012 that, since 2016, is in the process of consulting with the 232 ethnic groups' representatives within the

National Consultation Space (Espacio Nacional de Consulta).[9] Article 5 on the subject of FPIC states that:

> Prior consultation processes ... will be applied to indigenous communities, Roma communities, and black, *raizal* and *palanquera* communities that meet the following requirements: (1) have an ancestral relationship with the territory; (2) have their own community life with mechanisms of autonomous government; (3) self-recognise as belonging to a constitutionally recognized ethnic group; (4) possess a cultural and historical identity clearly differentiated in their uses and customs.

These criteria closely reflect the ILO standards that are also included in other countries' legislation, such as the Peruvian FPIC Law. The procedures also look quite similar: as in Peru, in Colombia a case-by-case analysis to assess the presence of ethnic communities in a given area ought to be conducted. Yet, unlike Peru, there is no flexibility around peasant communities, which are therefore always excluded from FPIC. Peasants can instead access another form of public consultation, which is less demanding and is restricted to the evaluation of environmental impact on the territory they occupy (Milano & Sanhueza 2016; Dietz 2019).

Colombian peasant communities have, however, been greatly affected by socio-economic changes and development projects, the impact of which goes beyond the environment, often undermining peasant institutions and their capacity to 'pursue an active transformation towards desired futures' (Feola 2017: 126). Moreover, as I have described in previous chapters, it is common for peasant communities to live side-by-side with indigenous *resguardos*, and therefore to be exposed to similar challenges. After a decade of exponential growth in the number of consultations, it is not completely surprising that resentments have been mounting among the peasantry about their exclusion from these participatory spaces.

It is not only that peasant organisations feel unprotected vis-à-vis the boom in infrastructural projects and growing investment in commodity exploitation; they also consider that denying them access to FPIC constitutes discrimination against them on a weak juridical basis. Indeed, their exclusion from FPIC is grounded on a narrow interpretation of the peasant subject as a *mestizo* with no clear ethnic and cultural identity. Yet, as I described in Chapter 3, peasant organisations have begun to contest this idea and strongly claim their kinship to a unique and

---

[9] Information retrieved from the Ministerio del Interior website, http://www.mininterior.gov.co/mision/direccion-de-consulta-previa/procesos-de-consulta-previa, accessed 5 August 2018.

differentiated culture, with its own mode of production, norms and living conditions, clearly distinct from the majority of Colombian society. This distinctiveness would make peasants equally as entitled to special rights as other cultural minorities, including the right to FPIC. Such ideas have recently gained traction among peasant leaders, and a proposal for a peasant FPIC was put together by a legal expert and advisor of peasant organisations. According to this proposal, the exclusion of peasants from minority rights is unconstitutional and violates Convention169:

> There is no constitutional section where it can validly be inferred that these spaces of participation are 'exclusive patrimony' of indigenous communities, because in fact, they are applicable to all ethnic peoples and communities and, therefore, we add, to the peasantry that shows specific identity traits .... Both culturally and economically, peasant communities in Colombia comply with the requirement of differentiating themselves from the dominant national block under the terms of ... Convention 169. ... If prior consultation and participation is not extended to include the peasantry as a differentiated community, this will generate an unjustified legal and material discrimination by denying peasants their status as a collective subject to exercise their rights. (Quesada Tovar 2013: 83–85)

Peasant cultural distinctiveness and identity is one criterion that would justify peasant communities' access to ethnic rights. The other is the engagement of peasant organisations in the constitution of collective territorialities (such as ZRCs). Strengthening the link between a collective peasant identity and a given territory is indeed another way of converging towards the ethnic rights framework:

> Peasant political, cultural and economic proposal is reflected in the social production of space .... The community that initiates the process of constitution [of a ZRC] identifies itself as peasant and links its identity and life project to that territory ..., generating a self-recognition as peasants of a specific region. (Quesada Tovar 2013: 74–75)

Critically, the proposal for a peasant FPIC is understood as 'one mechanism of defence of peasant territories against powerful interests that make them vulnerable' (interview with a leader of the National Association of the Peasant Reserve Zones, Asociación Nacional de Zonas de Reserva Campesina, ANZORC, Bogotá, November 2016), such as those linked to the exploitation of natural resources or the realisation of development projects by the state or private companies. Likewise, the institutionalisation of a peasant FPIC would also open up spaces for the participation of marginalised communities and for them to voice their concerns, as well as serve as a tool for conflict resolution. This was the spirit that inspired a pilot consultation organised by the peasant movement in the Catatumbo region, in the Norte de Santander Department. Here, over the past few years, tensions have been mounting between peasant and indigenous communities around conflicting territorial claims, not dissimilar to the cases in the Cauca and elsewhere described in Chapters 5 and 6.

Since 2009, the local peasant organisation – the Peasant Association of the Catatumbo (Asociación Campesina del Catatumbo, ASCAMCAT) – has been developing a proposal for the constitution of a ZRC in the area. The proposal was made public in 2011 and shared with authorities of the Barí (or Motilón-Barí) indigenous people. But in 2012, the two existing indigenous *resguardos* claimed an extension of their territories that overlaps with the land included in the ZRC. The contested area is inhabited by both indigenous and peasant communities and also partially overlaps with a forest reserve. While the indigenous authorities' claim is grounded on ancestrality arguments and requires the relocation of non-indigenous settlers, local peasants point out that their communities were constituted in the mid-twentieth century (although they do not have property titles) and they are therefore not ready to abandon their land. As a result, the Barí people are opposing the constitution of a ZRC, which was, however, de facto declared by ASCAMCAT. The situation has been aggravated by the presence of private companies involved in hydrocarbon exploitation and agribusiness, as well as by the frightening levels of violence by paramilitary and guerrilla actors, which has decimated many communities and forced hundreds to flee.

In an effort to find a solution to the territorial dispute, an 'autonomous peasant consultation' was conducted among peasant communities about a proposal to constitute an intercultural territory that would include the contested areas inhabited by both peasants and indigenous communities (interview with leader of ANZORC, Bogotá, November 2016). The consultation also opened a dialogue through the creation of an Intercultural Table (Mesa Intercultural) that facilitated an agreement around the exclusion from the ZRC of the territory claimed by the Barí people, despite the presence of peasant communities (interviews with a leader of ANZORC and an ASCAMCAT consultant, Bogotá, November 2015).

The Catatumbo conflict was also at the centre of a recent claim of unconstitutionality against the law that regulates the creation of ZRCs (Law 160 of 1994). The claim was filed in 2014 by Edward Álvarez, an economist and advisor to indigenous organisations, and supported by some of the most important Colombian indigenous organisations (Negrete 2014). In one of its statements during the hearing, the ONIC summarised the widespread feeling towards ZRCs by indigenous groups as follows:

The constitution of ZRCs represents a threat to the ancestral property of the indigenous peoples, since in the areas for which the creation of the ZRC is claimed, there are territories traditionally occupied by them and even recognised collective [land] titles. ... Conflicts between peasants and indigenous peoples have already begun to arise for this reason, as between the peasants of Catatumbo region and the Motilón Bari *resguardo*. (Colombian Constitutional Court 2015)

Indeed, the Catatumbo conflict was specifically brought to the attention of the Court as an example of how the constitution of ZRCs is fuelling violent territorial conflicts between indigenous people and peasants. This would demonstrate the incompatibility of these groups' territorial models, whose coexistence would 'violate the indigenous right to autonomy' (Colombian Constitutional Court 2015). In the 2015 sentencing, the Court acknowledged the obligation to conduct consultations when the constitution of a ZRC affects ethnic communities. Nonetheless, it did stress the legitimacy of the constitution of the ZRC, therefore rejecting the unconstitutionality petition. This ruling will perhaps provide some leverage for the peasants' efforts to constitute ZRCs, even if we are still far from a national debate on whether peasants should also be entitled to some form of FPIC. At the same time, the sentence illustrates the ongoing tensions around new territorial projects similar to those that I describe in the next chapter, and the aspirations as well as the resistance of social actors in their struggle for participation and autonomy.

THE POLITICS OF EXCLUSION IN PARTICIPATORY GOVERNANCE

Since countries have begun to undertake serious attempts to implement and regulate FPIC, a rapidly growing academic literature on this topic has emerged. Scholars have generally been quite critical of this participatory tool, and pessimistic about its potential to foster bottom-up participation in resource and development governance. Empirical studies, particularly from the Andean region, have highlighted the limits of FPIC as a mechanism for conflict mitigation or resolution and as a truly open and bottom-up participatory space. As Flemmer and Schilling-Vacaflor (2016: 812) note:

prior consultation is frequently understood as a tool for conflict prevention and resolution. It is expected that taking into account the fears and needs of local populations, finding joint solutions and complementing expert knowledge with the insights of affected groups will bring about more democratic, peaceful and sustainable solutions. But this expectation has not yet been empirically proven, especially because instances of meaningful participation in Latin America's resource governance are scarce, while reports of absent or flawed prior consultations abound.

In practice, FPIC most frequently operates as an 'invited space' dominated by the state, rather than as a space co-created with indigenous peoples, thereby reinforcing existing power relationships (Schilling-Vacaflor & Flemmer 2013; Perreault 2015; Flemmer & Schilling-Vacaflor 2016). In justifying these claims, scholars have mostly focused on implementation, studying the procedures, impact and outcomes of specific consultation processes. In particular, they have shown how, despite the fact that consultations generally end with the approval of extractive projects, this does not imply that genuine participation rights were upheld, nor that the impact of extraction projects was mitigated.

In this chapter, I have focused on a different aspect of FPIC that has generally gone unnoticed and yet, I argue, is crucial to assessing the participatory scope of FPIC, as well as its implications for broader discussions of recognition. This research also complements critical studies of FPIC by offering hints as to how problems in implementation might be rooted in the very way the norm is designed within international law and operationalised at the national level. As I have illustrated, the different responses to the 'subject question' offered by Bolivia, Peru and Colombia are the outcomes of complex (and contentious) negotiations, which reflect not only the contingent balance of power between different social and political forces, but also their understanding of collective rights and their visions concerning ethnic boundary-making as the redefinition of rules for inclusion and exclusion. What is at stake here is a moral paradigm as well as a procedural approach to defining who holds rights and deserves recognition. In this sense, the tensions between groups' visions and claims for inclusion (and exclusion) are the manifestation of participation conflicts around norm-making. This is a compelling example of how means of recognition are embedded in norms and policies through the contentious process of the crystallisation of identity boundaries in order to identify new collective subjects for rights.

The 'subject problem' cannot be understood without considering the great complexity of the historical circumstances that shape ethnicity in postcolonial countries. While this complexity has been overlooked in international law-making, 'indigenous people' is proving to be a 'tricky' category both from a sociological and normative perspective (Eversole et al. 2005). One of the most prevalent definitions of 'indigenous people' was given by the UN Sub-commission on the Prevention of Discrimination of Minorities in 1986; it identified common and distinctive traits as the fact of being original inhabitants of a land later colonised by others, representing distinct and marginalised sectors of society, and holding unique ethnic identities and cultures. Although this definition might seem reasonably detailed, its operationalisation can, as I have shown, follow a number of different pathways and interpretations, leading to very different outcomes in terms of the articulation or disarticulation of collective identities. At the two edges are the maximalist and minimalist approaches that I described in this book's introduction. According to the former, all populations that pre-existed colonisation ought to be considered indigenous. This would include, for example, Inca descendants (Quechua) in the Andes. A minimalist approach, by contrast, considers only those sparse and traditionally nomadic groups that previously occupied those territories (e.g. some Amazonian peoples in South America). Whether countries have opted for one or the other has been greatly influenced by national (geo)politics and by the prevailing vision of society in different time periods, as I described in Chapter 2. The discussions around the FPIC subject can be understood as the latest development in the remaking of ethnic boundaries and articulation/disarticulation processes in these countries.

In the Andean region, countries have undertaken significantly different approaches to FPIC. In Bolivia, a maximalist (and inclusive) strategy has prevailed in recent years, as a result of the constitutional negotiations of the late 2000s. For reasons linked to the balance of power within Evo Morales' social bases, as well as to avoid some of the problems related to the delineation of 'objective' criteria for identifying indigenous peoples in a context characterised by high ethnic volatility and politicisation, self-identification has progressively been adopted as a reasonably robust alternative, and the 'peasant' category has eventually been drawn into the ethnic camp. Colombia tends to lean towards the opposite (minimalist) edge of the spectrum, although the inclusion of Afro-descendants and Roma people reveals an effort to grant collective rights to minorities whose ethnic belonging is at least debated and often denied in other countries. Yet peasants remain excluded from this framework, although new claims from these sectors have opened a debate in this direction. Finally, Peru is a middle case, where the drawing of identity boundaries and access to rights have been delegated to a highly bureaucratic process, which privileges 'objective' criteria over self-identification. As a result, peasants are not a priori excluded, nor automatically included, but their participation is conditional upon a state decision about their ethnic belonging on a case-by-case basis.

These strategies not only reveal different ideological inspirations and political dynamics; they also have huge concrete implications. The most obvious is that they define inclusion or exclusion from new spaces of participation (however limited, invited and conflictive they might be) and delimit recognition of important sectors of these countries' societies. The inclusion of the peasantry in Bolivia means that communities from the vast Andean region, the majority of whom belong to a peasant union, have the right to be consulted. By contrast, the narrow focus of Colombian FPIC has resulted in the exclusion of approximately seven million people (*El Espectador* 2012). In Peru, the inclusion of peasants opens up the possibility of consultation for more than 6,000 communities (about 1.5 million households), tripling the numbers compared to the sole inclusion of the approximately 1,400 native communities (Instituto Nacional de Estadistica e Informatica 2014). These variations in numbers make it easy to realise why states have been reluctant to adopt an inclusive approach to FPIC, given the procedural and financial implications of having to deal with potentially very high numbers of consultations – besides the fact that FPIC is generally seen as a deterrent for private investment, given the monetary and institutional costs of negotiating with local communities.

But FPIC debates have also had implications beyond the state and private companies. In particular, the process of tracing collective identity boundaries through recognition norm-making has contributed to redefining relationships among social actors. In general, the need to face common threats and political resistance has encouraged the creation of shared platforms, as in the cases of Peru and Bolivia (with the Pactos de Unidad), while in Colombia this convergence is still at a very early stage. Interestingly, peasant movements have, in all three countries, embraced an ethnic turn – at least in their discourse. Yet the new emphasis on culture, identity and territory has not automatically enabled them to access new rights or participation spaces. Constraints have come from the indigenous movements themselves, which have generally been reluctant to 'share' what they perceive to be the achievements of their own struggle. In all three countries, these movements have shown conservative attitudes towards potential changes to already established ethnic boundaries. But, more importantly, limitations are embedded in the ethnic rights framework itself.

While FPIC is meant to offer partial redress for profound historical marginalisation, in so doing it embeds a powerful exclusionary ontology and potentially violates the notion of equal citizenship (Abelson et al. 2003). Prioritising the voices of excluded groups over those of others can of course be justified democratically. In this specific case, arguments might be based on the fact that indigenous peoples' livelihood and culture are more dependent on their relationship to their territories and customary land management than other communities – and such arguments might well be persuasive. But the force of these arguments depends on those groups formally recognised as indigenous being uniquely vulnerable; and in the case of the Andean region, it is hard to make this argument. As Goodland (2004: 69) asks: 'Why is it that the rural poor can be displaced against their will, but other peoples cannot? Can development have a double standard and advocate democracy for some, but autocracy for the rest?'

Besides the theoretical and operational complexities of justifying different configurations of ethnic boundaries corresponding to differentiated access to rights, there is at least a need to acknowledge the widespread demand for participation and social control over critical development interventions. This demand does not come only from indigenous sectors, but is shared across rural communities increasingly affected by development and resource exploitation initiatives. Indeed, disputes around 'means of recognition' (in this case the definition of the FPIC subject) cannot be understood without considering the endemic lack of resources and access to basic services with which rural communities are confronted. The relationship between socio-economic deprivation and FPIC is evident in the fact that, in practice, FPIC tends to be used as a bargaining chip to obtain economic returns, often at the expense of environmental and territorial rights (Torres Wong 2018). Indeed, what Pauline Peters (2004: 285) has written in reference to Africa perfectly describes the Latin American scenario: 'As competition increases over resources, the costs and benefits of being excluded as compared with being included in definitions of belonging (to a lineage, village, ethnic or religious group) mount'.

Participation conflicts are not only manifested in the framework of national debates on FPIC. They have emerged powerfully across the region in a growing number of self-organised consultations and referenda promoted by environmental justice movements (usually with the support of local governments) and conducted outside of the FPIC framework.

In recent years, sixty-eight such participation exercises have taken place in Argentina, Guatemala, Colombia and Peru (de Castro et al. 2016). These examples of bottom-up participation, as well as the attempts of peasant movements to access FPIC, should inspire a broader discussion on the need to strive for 'more equitable spaces of engagement' (Martin et al. 2016: 260) and for a more inclusive way of understanding recognition. This should be an understanding that does not strengthen protectionist and sectarian attitudes, but rather encourages broader access to rights and participation.

5

The Physical Boundaries of Identity

As we saw in the previous chapter, demands over common resources can reveal new dynamics of the articulation/disarticulation of identities and can result in the consolidation of new ethnic boundaries. In this chapter, I focus on the consequences of identity boundary-making for physical spaces. I argue that the endemic lack of resources in contexts where recognition reforms with important redistributive components (what I have called 'means of redistribution') are implemented is behind the rise of perhaps the most common among the types of recognition conflict I identify in this book: social reproduction conflicts.

In the first part of the chapter, I analyse recent changes in agrarian politics in Andean countries to illustrate how new forms of collective land tenure have increased territorial autonomy for indigenous peoples and accelerated the titling process since the 1990s. Multicultural agrarian reforms, however, have also triggered resentment and a feeling of injustice in non-indigenous communities that, while facing similar conditions of poverty and precarious livelihoods, are still struggling to secure tenure over their land. In some instances, conflicts have been escalating following radical strategies put in place by indigenous groups to regain control over ancestral territories through occupation of peasant land. I draw on two cases of conflicts between peasant and indigenous groups in Bolivia and Colombia to discuss the linkages between land politics and identity changes. For each of these countries, I describe one paradigmatic case in which identities have evolved into increasingly salient tools in social conflicts, impacting the way people self-identify and reshaping the very nature of land struggles in the Andes.

MULTICULTURAL AGRARIAN REFORMS

Although agrarian reforms in Latin America have been 'frequently enacted and rarely enforced' (Handelman 1975: 247), and have often failed to meet the expectations of rural communities, the alternation of different land tenure regimes has generally trickled down to the local level and palpably affected social relationships. If, after the agrarian reforms of the 1950s and 1960s, the central axis of conflict was the redistribution of *hacienda* land and big *latifundia* among former *peones*,[1] the new generation of multicultural reforms implemented since the 1990s has had a great impact in reshaping horizontal relationships among communities of rural poor.

The shift in governmental recognition towards ethnic land rights profoundly influenced the way in which new land regimes were designed, allowing for the introduction of specific forms of collective land tenure, and favouring the recognition of new customary norms. In concrete terms, the process began by mapping territories claimed by indigenous peoples to facilitate the issuing of new collective property titles in favour of officially 'recognised' ethnic groups. The emphasis on property titles ('propertisation', Coombes et al. 2012) as the new solution for the 'indigenous question' reflected the neoliberal belief – most prominently advocated by the World Bank and other multilateral and bilateral donors – that economic development benefits from the clarification and protection of property rights (Adelman 1975). Despite its neoliberal inspiration, the new framework generated minimal social resistance and indigenous movements quickly transitioned towards a discourse centred on land titling and tenure formalisation (Wainwright & Bryan 2009). In this context, indigenous 'reterritorialisation' was often conceived in terms of restitution. Placing emphasis on the 'temporal aspect of land' (Fay & James 2009: 6), multicultural reforms promised to restore the territory of specific groups that had been historically dispossessed. This process entailed the formalisation of a new set of ownership rights, which were, however, grounded on an old (pre-colonial or colonial) social order.

As illustrated in Chapter 1, Bolivia, Colombia and Peru have demonstrated a commitment to indigenous rights through the ratification of

---

[1] *Latifundio* was a semifeudal institution consisting of a very extensive parcel of privately owned land, which relied mainly on unfree or wage labour by low-skilled exploited workers (*peón*). In Latin America the *latifundio* was introduced by Iberian settlers and was widely perpetuated in the *hacienda* system.

international agreements and by reforming their own constitutions. In this context, collective land tenure and redistribution (or restitution) became central to the implementation of indigenous rights (Roldán Ortiga 2004). Although all three countries implemented some kind of multicultural agrarian reform over the past thirty years, these adjustments were made at different paces and through a variety of policy instruments. Variation should be noted in particular around land access requirements.

Among the three countries, Peru has experienced the most discontinuous implementation of indigenous land rights. Since the titling process was first initiated in the 1970s, significant delays have been experienced. Pressing indigenous claims did not manage to completely overcome two key limitations of the legislation in place (the Law of Native Communities of 1974): the narrow definition of collective property titles for communal land rather than indigenous territories, and the retention of state control over natural resources. As has been the case across the region, land titling in Peru has primarily been funded through international cooperation programmes such as the IDB-sponsored Special Land Titling and Cadastre Project (Proyecto Especial de Registro y Titulación de Tierra; Stock 2005). In its first two phases, the project prioritised the coastal and Andean regions, with 83 per cent of properties registered on the coast and 53 per cent in the highlands.[2] A third phase, renamed PTRT3, started in 2015 with a specific focus on the Amazon and fewer highland properties.[3] This has aggravated an already unequal situation in which a clear legal distinction between native and peasant communities, applied respectively to lowlands and highlands, has prevented Quechua and Aymara communities from claiming collective land titles (and indigenous rights). This trend has recently been challenged by Andean movements in an effort to halt mining exploitation.

Differences between lowlands and highlands are also relevant in the case of Bolivia, although, unlike Peru, they have not been firmly

---

[2] Information retrieved from Inter-American Development Bank website, http://www.iadb.org/en/projects/project,1303.html?id=PE-L1026, accessed 18 February 2018.

[3] AIDESEP, on behalf of sixty-four indigenous peoples and 1,809 native communities of the Peruvian Amazon, submitted a complaint to the Independent Consultation and Investigation Mechanism claiming that the Project's prioritisation of individual titling would exacerbate the insecurity of land ownership as native communities: 'The prioritization and sequence of investment in titling does not adequately consider the risks of conflict following the consolidation of colonisers' plots and the incentives for more migration to the edge of the rainforest with consequent pressure on indigenous lands' (AIDESEP 2015: 4).

crystallised in a legal framework. In 1996, the Law of the National Institute of Agrarian Reform (Instituto Nacional de Reformal Agraria, INRA) instituted a ten-year period for cadastral mapping (*saneamiento*), in order to regularise property rights throughout the country. Claims for collective land titles (TCOs) were also given priority by the state, thanks to both the availability of international funding (particularly from the Danish cooperation Danida), as well as to the relatively easy process of boundary mapping. Between 1996 and 2010, many indigenous groups, formally recognised with certification from the Vice-Ministry of Indigenous Issues and Native Peoples (Vice-Ministerio de Asuntos Indígenas y Pueblos Originarios, VAIPO), successfully obtained their collective land titles. In their original form, TCOs were not created for peasant communities, although they did not exclude highland groups by definition. Highland communities, therefore, could follow two different strategies: maintain their affiliation to peasant unions and claim collective or individual land titles, or reconstitute an ancestral *ayllu* to form a TCO. Despite its relative flexibility, especially compared to Peru, the multicultural agrarian reform in Bolivia triggered new tensions between rural organisations and generated a feeling of discrimination amongst the peasantry. As I described in Chapter 3, in order to remedy peasant marginalisation and consolidate an inter-rural alliance to support the Movement Towards Socialism (Movimiento al Socialismo) government, the 2009 constitution replaced the TCO with the Native Indigenous Peasant Territory (Territorio Indígena Originario Campesino, TIOC). The inclusion of the word 'peasant' justified unions' claims without them needing to 'rebrand' into indigenous organisations.

The pan-rural approach that has recently prevailed in Bolivia, however, is quite exceptional. In Colombia, peasant and indigenous groups still receive very different treatment. Although, in the mid-1990s, a law introduced the possibility for peasant communities to constitute collective territories called Peasant Reserve Zones (Zonas de Reserva Campesina, ZRCs), in practice their creation has been incredibly slow and contested. In contrast, following the constitutional reform of 1991, indigenous peoples were formally granted control over many *resguardos*,[4] whose total area covers about a third of the country's territory (Hoffman

---

[4] In fact, the constitution integrated the old *resguardos* into inalienable Indigenous Territorial Entities (Entidades Territoriales Indígenas, ETIs) with high degrees of administrative autonomy and control over their natural resources (including the subsoil) (Van Cott 2000). Yet, more than twenty years later, ETIs still lack clear juridical regulation.

2000). *Resguardos* are governed by an elected council, the *cabildo*, with significant control over legal, financial and administrative matters; they have a land tenure regime in which families are assigned usufruct but not ownership rights. *Resguardos* often host the non-indigenous population as well, who can own private property with the agreement of the *cabildo* (Stock 2005). Since 1996, Afro-Colombians have also been entitled to collective land and a World Bank-funded project has been instrumental to titling their territories. In this respect, Colombia constitutes an important exception compared to the rest of the region, where Afro-descendants are generally not entitled to collective rights (Paschel 2016).

This brief overview of multicultural land reforms since the 1990s demonstrates the important progress made by Andean governments in the recognition of indigenous rights to land. Yet, as might be expected, the translation of new rights into practice has not always been smooth. In particular, the implementation of these reforms (or the post-recognition phase) was followed by a rise in new conflicts between and within communities, and it has also underpinned a shift towards a greater emphasis on culture and ethnicity in collective narratives on identity. In the following sections, I illustrate how the implementation of multicul-tural agrarian laws (as key expressions of the 'means of redistribution' embedded in recognition reforms), and the redefinition of rural identity boundaries driven by attempts to access strategic resources by social communities confronting extreme poverty, have fuelled social reproduc-tion conflict in the cases of Bolivia and Colombia. Although single con-flicts inevitably possess unique characteristics, the underpinning dynamics reflect broader trends visible across the region.

CAMPESINOS NATIVOS AND INDÍGENAS ORIGINARIOS IN BOLIVIA[5]

In Bolivia, agrarian struggles have typically involved indigenous commu-nities or landless peasants and big landowners in the fertile lowlands (Villanueva 2004). However, most recently land conflict has shifted to the western highlands and valleys, confronting rural movements them-selves, and has become predominantly inter-communal (Bottazzi & Rist 2012). What the chief of the INRA's Conciliation and Conflict Management Unit told me in one of my first interviews for this project

---

[5] This section is based on Fontana (2014b).

was illuminating, and contributed to a change of direction in my early research on land conflict:

Nowadays, the greatest land conflicts in Bolivia are between native communities and peasant unions. These conflicts are more intense than the conflicts between communities and big landowners, since ... there are no clear and defined criteria to resolve them. Both ideological and economic problems are at stake, which, however, are never openly admitted. (Interview, La Paz, May 2010)

Indeed, as my fieldwork would later reveal, beyond formal tenure claims, a variety of factors fuel these inter-communal conflicts, such as organisational differences, natural resource control, and power and identity issues that are connected to the land as a productive and social good.

Although Bolivia has among the lowest population densities in the world (10 per km^2), land scarcity provoked by several factors such as population growth, highly fragmented tenures (*minifundio*) and loss of soil fertility has been a constant issue for rural communities. This is coupled with a highly unequal distribution of land among families and social groups. According to INRA data (2006), 91 per cent of the land is in the hands of large landowners, while 71 per cent of the population control only 9 per cent of the land. Land scarcity and unequal distribution are certainly among the main drivers of social tensions around land tenure within rural social communities. However, the land conflicts that followed the implementation of multicultural reforms present new features that make them hard to explain as simply yet another manifestation of the long history of land struggles in Latin America. In particular, they appear to be closely tied to changes in the regulatory framework, namely the collectivist policy implemented over the past twenty-five years – including the prioritisation of TCO titling and the funding received through international cooperation agencies – which has created tensions between rural organisations and a sense of discrimination amongst the peasantry. A political environment that became more responsive to indigenous claims encouraged social groups to increasingly resort to cultural and ethnic repertoires to frame their demands. Ethnicity acquired more weight in local politics and started to catalyse new and old claims about land as the most valuable asset for the rural poor. This is relatively obvious in the case of indigenous organisations but is also surprisingly true in the case of peasant unions.

On one hand, two of the main indigenous/native organisations in Bolivia – CIDOB and CONAMAQ – started to claim the titling of their territories as TCOs. To cement their claims, they relied on an ethno-identitarian narrative driven by a recent process of cultural recovery:

The natives want the titling of their territory to directly guarantee access to natural resources and to restore our territory and traditional collective life. We all have our own functions within our principles of rotation, complementarily and reciprocity in our *ayllus*. (Interview with a CONAMAQ advisor, La Paz, August 2010)

On the other hand, peasants affiliated with CSUTCB prefer individual land titles or, in some cases, communal titles. However, they oppose the TCO and consider it an unfair and irrational way of allocating land. The classist dimension is central in peasant discourse. The emphasis on the peasant mode of production is, however, coupled with a sort of syndical-ist native primordialism.

Blood and the surname that runs through the blood of each and every one that lives in the CSUTCB area is peasant, before indigenous. Peasants, whether farmers, stockbreeders, fishers, llama shepherds – we are identified as peasants. [We] are from different cultures and languages, but before being 'indigenous' [we] identify as native peasants. (Interview with the CSUTCB's Secretary of Land and Territory, La Paz, August 2010)

In Bolivia and elsewhere in the region, the revitalisation of indigenous issues and a generalised process of ethnicisation of rural politics cannot be understood without considering the role of external actors. Indeed, the economic and ideological basis of this change lies, at least in part, in the actions of international cooperation agencies and some anthropologists, who financed and supported new indigenous and native movements (Andolina et al. 2005; Rodríguez-Carmona 2009). In Bolivia, one of the most important interventions was Danida's programme 'Support to the Rights of Indigenous Peoples', which developed over fifteen years from 1995 to 2010. While the programme was intended as an effort to bring the indigenous issue into the mainstream of public policy design, in practice its most significant impact was the drastic increase in funding allocated to the titling of indigenous land. In internal documents, Danida portrays the programme as an exemplary experience of international cooperation. For example, in a programme pamphlet's prologue, the former Bolivian Minister of Autonomies Carlos Romero wrote that:

among the various contextual factors that have been favourable to the TCO titling process, the support of the Danish cooperation is to be considered fundamental, and to such an extent that, we could argue, it has been the most important external strategic ally of indigenous peoples. (Danida & International Work Group for Indigenous Affairs IWGIA 2010)

A similarly enthusiastic opinion was shared by a Danish embassy officer who was in charge of the programme for four years:

Personally, I think that this programme has been one of the most successful I have ever seen, because it was well formulated and it had very interesting results. The Danish cooperation has been supporting the process that the country is living through, also according to state authorities. In terms of titling, eleven million hectares were titled, which correspond to 70 or 80% of what has been titled so far to indigenous peoples.[6] It was not only a titling process but an empowerment process for indigenous peoples. (Interview with a Project Manager of Danida, La Paz, June 2011)

Clearly, the effects on identity-building and the positive discrimination criteria introduced in favour of ethnic groups were not only well known, but explicitly incentivised by the programme, as demonstrated by the following considerations:

The increasing problem of territorial titling implied the need to analyse indigenous peoples' identity. Throughout the clearing process, the involvement of indigenous peoples was strong. Identity and empowerment of their identity, and a sense of pride for being indigenous, were evident …. They would tell me: 'Before it was impossible for us to negotiate with a mayor or with a businessman. Now we sit as equals'. In the process, their identity has been strengthened. We worked on the land issue, but this is closely tied to the cultural identity issue as well. (Interview with a Project Manager of Danida, La Paz, June 2011)

However, a former officer of the VAIPO expressed a different and more critical opinion of the role of international actors in the context of the Bolivian multicultural agrarian reform:

There are cooperation agencies that expressly supported exclusively indigenous peoples, and not the peasant sector, because they thought that, from the 169 ILO Convention, the logic of indigenous peoples was different and that it had been made invisible. This fact has contributed to the resurgence of certain identities and to the empowerment of others. … In fact, distortions introduced by international cooperation funds generated conflicts, as … there are cooperation agencies that only sponsor indigenous, and not peasant [groups]. (Interview, La Paz, August 2010)

Tensions and competition between peasant and indigenous organisations have increased, following the efforts of indigenous groups to expand and consolidate their grassroots. New indigenous organisations have often attempted to gain the support of local communities, affirming themselves

---

[6] According to the systematisation document of the programme, during the first ten years of implementation, international funding covered 67 per cent of the total costs of the TCOs' titling process. Moreover, until December 2009, 135 TCOs with a total extension of more than eleven million hectares were titled thanks to the support of Danida (Danida & IWGIA 2010: 74).

as valid and effective social brokers vis-à-vis the state by, for example, starting to compete in local electoral politics. They replaced, in other words, the main functions performed locally by peasant unions. In certain cases, indigenous leaders organised 'conversion campaigns' to persuade people to join their organisation. This is how a former advisor of CONAMAQ described the 'native proselytism':

There are leaders who enter the peasant territories to convince people. They go and put native authorities where once there was the peasant union .... For many leaders of CONAMAQ, reconstitution means controlling the peasant communities that, before, were part of their ancestral territories. This is exactly the root of the ideological and political conflicts that exist in the local space. The members of the peasant federation do not want to be reconverted into indigenous. (Interview with an officer of the Ministry of Autonomies and former advisor of CONAMAQ, La Paz, June 2010)

In some cases, the initial situation was quite clear in terms of identity and cultural features, such as in many areas of the highlands where Quechua and Aymara people preserved their language, culture and traditional governance structures, although sometimes adapting to the union system. In other areas, where indigenous groups were smaller and more vulnerable to external shocks, many of the local cultural, linguistic and ethnic identity traits were lost. Here, identity revitalisation was more complex, leading in certain cases to reindigenisation or ethnogenesis processes. Similar phenomena have been documented across Latin America following the rise of identity politics (French 2009; Jackson 2019). Although a great part of the Latin American indigenous movement has relied on reinventing tradition and cultivating discourses on ethnic authenticity, ethnogenesis specifically refers to those cases where the creation of an ethnic identity has only marginally relied on pre-existing cultural, physiognomic and linguistic markers. These markers have almost entirely been shaped based on a conscious exploration of a more or less remote historical past and mythology. The rise of new identities has become an object of long-standing controversy over authenticity and legitimacy and, in certain contexts, it is directly linked to land claims and the implementation of multicultural agrarian reforms. In Bolivia this is the case in the Apolo municipality.

Ethnogenesis and Territorial Conflicts in Apolo

Apolo is a remote municipality in the north-west of Bolivia, nested between highly eroded hills descending into the Amazon rainforest. The main town square is surrounded by a few dirt roads and brick buildings, including the church, the school and the town hall. Rural communities in the vicinity are formed by small adobe houses in a landscape of poor pastures, coca and corn fields. Despite the tropical climate, land here is not ideal for agriculture and most fresh fruit and vegetables are imported and sold in the town market. Poverty levels are very high even for rural Bolivia.[7] The precarious condition of the only, mostly dirt road connecting the region to the highlands and from there to La Paz means that the movement of goods and people is limited. When I visited Apolo, it took me over twenty hours to travel less than 500 miles on a public bus, including a stretch where passengers had to push the bus through the mud and walk a few kilometres carrying small children and luggage.

In Apolo, the creation of a new indigenous organisation called the Indigenous Council of the Leco People (Central Indígena del Pueblo Leco, CIPLA) triggered a conflict with the local peasant union – the Peasant Federation of the Franz Tamayo Province (Federación de Campesinos de la Provincia Franz Tamayo, FSUTC-FT), which in 2007 reached frightening peaks of violence. The conflict originated in the mid-1990s, when the FSUTC-FT – at that time the only social organisation in the region – was beset by division among its leaders. Following contact by peasant leaders with the growing Bolivian lowland indigenous movement, in 1997 a breakaway group decided to create a new organisation: the CIPLA. These leaders made rapid contact with local communities and began to popularise a discourse based on ethno-identitarian claims and on the revival of the culture, traditions and customs of the Leco people. The Leco were one of the dominant ethnic groups in the Apolo region during the sixteenth and seventeenth centuries, alongside the Aguachiles and Tacanas. Following colonisation by the Inca and then the Spanish, the Leco mixed with populations of different cultural and ethnic origins.[8] A few traces of Leco language and traditions still survive

---

[7] According to the Bolivian National Institute of Statistics (Instituto Nacional de Estadistica, INE, 2012), 77.7 per cent of the population of Apolo is poor or extremely poor.

[8] In the nineteenth and twentieth centuries, with economic growth and the decline of the Catholic missions, there was a wave of migration into the region, which facilitated the imposition of the Quechua language, the weakening of the Leco and the appearance of Spanish as the new *lingua franca*. Migrants came to Apolo attracted by possibilities of employment in the quinine and rubber industries. These changes in the local economy favoured the rise of the *hacienda* and of a local non-indigenous elite. The subordination of the local population to the *hacienda* system continued until the latter half of the twentieth century, when the National Revolution started the process of land redistribution and promoted the creation of the peasant unions (Assies 2002; Sotomayor 2009).

among contemporary Apolo inhabitants. However, nowadays, no evident cultural, physiognomic or class markers clearly distinguish peasant and indigenous affiliates in the region.[9]

Soon after its creation, the CIPLA was included in the network of eastern indigenous movements, joining the Council of Indigenous Peoples of La Paz (Central de Pueblos Indígenas de La Paz, CPILAP) at the departmental level, and the CIDOB at the national level. According to its statute, produced in 1999 with the support of the NGO Care-Bolivia (Dudley 2009), the organisation follows an 'identity-based development model' articulated around four points: (1) organisational strengthening; (2) territorial consolidation through the recuperation of traditional lands; (3) territorial planning based on sustainable management of natural resources; and (4) promotion of sustainable productive alternatives and the exercise of indigenous autonomy as a form of self-government and self-determination (CPILAP 2009).

The CIPLA has taken numerous steps to move towards achieving these goals. In 1999, an official demand for the titling of the TCO-Leco was submitted for a total of 654,000 hectares. At the same time, the organisation was recognised by the VAIPO through a Certification of Ethnic Identity and Actual Settlement. The VAIPO declared that 'the claimant people maintain their own identity and cultural practice as indigenous native people', and that this corresponds to the 'Leco Indigenous People/ Quechua Native People'. This highly ambiguous denomination brought about problems in the relationship with peasants.[10]

Between 1995 and 2005, seventeen out of eighty-six communities in the Apolo municipality joined the CIPLA (Sotomayor 2009). In practical terms, however, 'the form and procedures of local governance within the new indigenous communities did not vary considerably from the local peasant union forms that preceded them' (Dudley 2009: 309). In general, the fact that a community decided to join the indigenous organisation was linked to the role played by local leaders and to the awareness of an indigenous past

---

[9] Seventy-nine per cent of the Apoleños speak Quechua, 18 per cent Spanish, 1 per cent Aymara and 0.27 per cent other native languages. According to self-identification criteria, 72 per cent identify themselves as Quechua, 15 per cent do not identify with any indigenous peoples, 10 per cent identify as native or other indigenous peoples, and 3 per cent identify as Aymara (INE & UNDP 2006).

[10] One of the former officers of the vice-ministry in charge of the process of certification clarified that: 'We recommended calling the TCO "Leco-Quechua", to acknowledge the presence of Quechuas in the area. However, the INRA did not consider our recommendation and started the cadastral study as TCO-Leco' (interview, La Paz, August 2010).

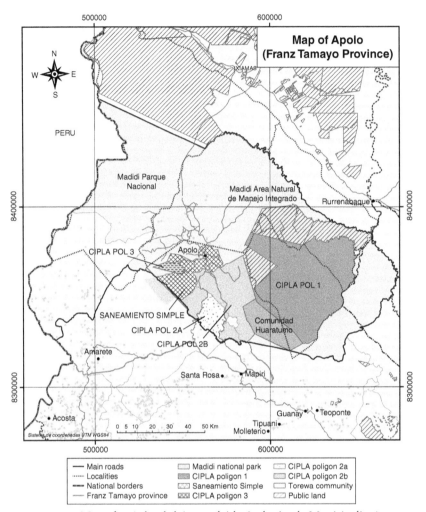

FIGURE 5.1. Map of main land claims and titles in the Apolo Municipality (source: Fundación Tierra)

among the local population. This was correlated with the community's remoteness, as well as to pre-existing tensions and power dynamics at the local level (interviews with CIPLA members, Apolo, July 2010).

In 2002, the demand for the TCO-Leco was included within the funding plan of Danida, and, in 2003, the cadastral study began. The area was divided into three zones (Figure 5.1). The study of Zone 1, almost entirely enclosed within the Madidi National Park, one of the most important biodiversity hotspots in Bolivia, proceeded very quickly (four months). In November 2006, the INRA issued the first title for the TCO-Leco in this zone, which, in turn, triggered the most violent phase of the inter-communal conflict. In May and June 2007, the conflict escalated to a critical phase: peasants began to mobilise, first by spearheading marches, blockades and hunger strikes, and by occupying public buildings. They also invaded the core protected area of the Madidi Park, with the occu-pants threatening to start felling trees if the government did not listen to their claims. These claims were, in brief: the construction of a road between Apolo and Ixiamas (cutting across the park), the beginning of hydrocarbon exploration[11] and the cancellation of the Zone 1 title (*La Razón* 2007).

After three attempts at negotiation, the government and peasant leaders reached a minimal agreement and tensions relaxed. The peasants presented a motion to the National Agrarian Tribunal (Tribunal Nacional Agrario, TAN) asking for the revocation of the TCO-Leco. Meanwhile, the INRA put all the land claims on hold, fearing that entrance into contested terri-tories would provoke a new wave of mobilisation and violence. This worry resurfaced after the rejection of the peasant demands by the TAN in 2010.

Within this context of rapid changes and high social tensions, it will be illustrative to take a closer look at how different people describe the facts, as well as how they portray new and old identities. Indeed, not only do social actors themselves possess divergent collective memories of the main historical phases of the conflict, they also cultivate narratives of 'self' and 'otherness' that serve to perpetuate tensions. There is evidence of identity playing an instrumental role in helping both peasant and indigenous narratives gain advantage in the political struggle and in response to international, national and local opportunities and constraints.

Affiliates of the CIPLA describe the conflict as a struggle for their rights and the recovery of their cultural identity, routines, customs and native origins. They do not deny their past within the peasant federation and they refer to the separation as a process of emancipation, motivated by the need to find the historical roots of Apolo. This break gave birth to an 'organisation with identity' – the CIPLA.

From that day on, we started to rescue all our traditions and customs; we are true indigenous with identity. Therefore, we had also to suffer a bit with the brothers of the Federation . . . they maltreated us, kidnapped and flagellated us. . . . Those are the roots of the claim for our culture. (Workshop with CIPLA leaders, Apolo, July 2010)

We keep on strengthening the fight for our rights and for the reproduction of our cultural identity . . . . When we discovered that the Leco existed here, that they organised a resistance, their way of living and all those

---

[11] On 13 May 2007, the government issued a decree that authorised the exploitation and exploration of energy resources in Apolo (*El Diario* 2007).

things, ... this was the root of Apolo. This is the identity, and we have gained possession of this identity. (Interview with CIPLA leader, La Paz, August 2010)

For the members of the CIPLA, the most important difference between a Leco and a peasant lies in their vision of the world: the indigenous person is community-oriented and has close ties with nature, while the peasant is individualist and 'emerges' from the colonial past. Nevertheless, the criteria for affiliation with the CIPLA are relatively blurred and simply imply a will to self-identify as indigenous. Concrete elements that would prove the contemporary existence of the Leco are the language (although, according to the indigenous leaders, it is currently spoken only by a few elders in remote communities) and its traces in toponymy, as well as typical local dances attributed to the Leco tradition.

Conflicting elements clearly emerge when the Leco's statements are juxtaposed with peasant narratives. The union uses the same rhetorical tools as those of the indigenous groups to highlight the alleged inconsistency of the indigenous identity. In particular, the fact that the Leco language is no longer spoken is presented as an argument to invalidate the legitimacy of the claim for recognition. Moreover, peasants deny the existence of typical Leco surnames and consider the Leco dance a local cultural feature shared by all the communities as a memory of the old inhabitants of the region.

There is only one Quechua people, native Quechua. In reality, these Leco people are only supposed Leco since they do not exist. Even in their own surnames, they don't have anything native. All their surnames are Spanish, while in the Federation we still have native [Quechua] surnames. (Workshop with peasant leaders, Apolo, July 2010)

According to the peasants, the Leco people are neither 'recognised' nor 'legitimate'. Their claim to Leco identity is an issue of 'belief' that has no ties with what really matters, that is, their roots and ancestry. Peasants refer to an alternative narrative of origin, which strengthens the present situation ('we are syndicalist'), by sinking their roots into an ancestral past ('we have always been syndicalist'):

Forever, *from our ancestors*, we have been syndicalist. We belong to the departmental Federation. But now the fellows [Lecos] believe they are another organisation. They believe that they are well linked to the government. They want to diminish us through concealments, misleading us. (Workshop with peasant grassroots, Apolo, July 2010)

Members of the peasant union have a strong sense of nativeness and connection to ancestral ties. This increases their resentment towards the CIPLA: 'They treat us as colonisers, as the Spanish that arrived here. We are not *colonos*[12] ... We are native. Our grandfathers were born in these lands' (workshop with peasant grassroots, Apolo, July 2010).

For peasants, the process of identity recognition is grounded in verifiable data such as place of birth, language and blood ties, rather than in the kind of self-identification process valued by the CIPLA. However, within the peasant union, discordant visions around identity issues coexist. By the second half of 2010 (at the time of my fieldwork), during a Federation meeting (*ampliado*) that I was observing, some peasant leaders proposed changing the name of the organisation to 'Native Indigenous Quechua' (*Indígenas Originarios Quechua*).[13] The argument was that this would improve the position of the organisation vis-à-vis the government and international agencies, enhancing their chances of gaining access to economic resources. Moreover, in some areas where there are conflicting land claims, identity-based demographic parameters could be used as a tactical tool to put 'CIPLA members in a minority' (FSUTC-FT meeting, Apolo, July 2010). This episode illustrates the consistent turn towards culture and ethnicity in collective self-identification as a strategy to fight 'multicultural' land battles. These dynamics are not unique to Apolo but emerge in equally remote and poor communities across the Andean region, in the framework of new conflicts for social reproduction linked to multicultural land reforms.

'PEASANTS WITH IDENTITY' AND 'COLONIAL INDIGENOUS' IN COLOMBIA

In Colombia, the distinction between indigenous and peasant groups has historically been less fluid than in other Andean countries such as Bolivia or Peru. Perhaps due to the influence of Marxist ideology on peasant movements, a discourse grounded in class inequalities and social justice has most commonly been used to underpin social struggles. Yet, in recent years, significant narrative shifts have brought identity to the forefront of rural politics for the first time. As in the case of Bolivia, new inter-communal land struggles have had the effect of strengthening both physical and identity boundaries, in contexts where those boundaries had maintained a high

---

[12] Literally 'settler'. For a discussion of the complex semantics and stigmatisation around this word, see Chapter 6.

[13] This option had already been explored by other Bolivian peasant organisations. For example, in the Chiuquisaca Department the departmental peasant federation is called Unified Federation of Chuquisaca Native Peoples Workers (Federación Unica de Trabajadores de los Pueblos Originarios de Chuquisaca). A similar discussion, which took place in the late 1990s in the Santuario de Quillacas municipality, is reported in McNeish (2002).

degree of fluidity and overlap for decades. Mirroring the Bolivian timeline, this kind of inter-communal land conflict in Colombia has emerged relatively recently and alongside the implementation of multicultural land reform.

Along the Colombian Andean slopes, most communities – indigenous and non-indigenous – have suffered the consequences of land scarcity and have put in place strategies to secure greater territorial control. Over the past two decades, a number of factors have played a role in converting long-standing territorial tensions into inter-communal conflicts of the kind I call social reproduction conflicts. Following the neoliberal reforms in the 1990s, which introduced new forms of collective land tenure, the presence of different groups in the same area led to a significant overlap of claims: *resguardos* for the indigenous, community councils for Afro-descendants and ZRCs for peasants. In these contexts, blurred territorial boundaries, which reflect customary and historical traditions of land sharing and group coexistence, complicate the evaluation of demands and the identification of negotiated solutions. Tensions have also been aggravated by state inefficiencies and slowness in dealing with an increasing number of claims for land tenure clarification.

Beyond long-standing issues with land tenure in the region, inter-communal land conflicts cannot be fully understood without considering the impact of the legal and institutional changes introduced in the 1991 constitution. This set of differentiated rights, designed to guarantee the cultural recognition and social protection of ethnic minorities, introduced very concrete opportunities for indigenous communities to consolidate and expand their territorial control. This process has accelerated since 2010, when a presidential decree granted a clear mandate to the Colombian Institute for Rural Development (Instituto Colombiano para el Desarrollo Rural, INCODER) to 'restructure *resguardos* of colonial origin following the clarification of the legal validity of the respective titles'. Using colonial titles to claim land has thus become one of the most common strategies adopted by indigenous groups to expand their territories, while in those cases where old titles did not exist or were lost, the *cabildos* often opt to use the revenue generated by state transfers to buy land plots in the vicinity of a *resguardo*, a de facto consolidation of the indigenous presence.

The recognition framework has opened new opportunities for indigenous peoples, but it has also been perceived as a threat by non-indigenous communities. Indeed, new indigenous claims have targeted neighbouring areas, which often consist of small peasant properties or state-owned land informally occupied by peasant and Afro-descendent communities, rather than big landowners' and agribusiness properties. This puzzle is rooted in geographies of social segregation and in a long history of what Harvey

(2007) calls 'accumulation by dispossession', resulting in the concentration of the most valuable and accessible land in the hands of a few, and the progressive push of indigenous groups towards the inhospitable mountain slopes. In the 1940s and 1950s, massive displacement caused by the civil war pushed waves of poor peasants into these same regions. Here, indigenous people and peasant dwellers entertained a generally peaceful coexistence until very recently, when indigenous communities started to pursue a strategy of territorial expansion. Moreover, while indigenous groups have had resources and legal protection on their side, over this same period, peasant communities did not see substantial changes in the recognition of their rights. As I have already mentioned, the creation of ZRCs has been stagnant since the 1990s and no other mechanisms have been available for peasants to combat similar economic and political challenges (e.g. land scarcity, demographic pressure, political violence, environmental degradation).

This imbalance in the institutional and legal options available to indigenous and peasant groups has suddenly made salient not only physical but also identity boundaries, fuelling new competition and conflict. A researcher who conducted a diagnostic of land conflicts in the Cauca Department for the Intercultural Studies Institute of the Universidad Javeriana de Cali put it as follows:

The whole process of implementing a multicultural state, beginning with the 1991 constitution and a differential system of rights, ... has generated inequalities within communities who were previously neighbours. In addition, this fuelled a struggle for recognition of territorial boundaries .... When it was not as important to create *resguardos* ..., the definition of who is peasant and who is indigenous was not as crucial. But recognition implies access to [monetary] transfers, health and autonomous education. It therefore becomes important to demarcate boundaries. But delineating these boundaries where there are intercultural territories is very difficult. This is why there is conflict. (Interview, Cali, November 2015)

As I illustrated in the case of Apolo, land struggles linked to multicultural reforms are often associated with a reshaping and strengthening of identity boundaries. Similarly, in the case of Colombia, land claims have been accompanied by the revitalisation of distinctive traditions in the form of language, symbols and mythology. Following the example of the indigenous movement, some peasant groups have recently engaged in the crafting of a new peasant identity, which goes beyond economic and class dimensions and focuses instead on its cultural uniqueness. This uniqueness is rooted in a universe of value, a special relationship with the territory, long-standing traditions and the historical role peasants played in the nation-building process (e.g. they were those that in practice opened and occupied the country's wilderness frontiers: Pontificia Universidad Javeriana de Cali, PUJC 2013). Changes in the collective identity of peasant movements coincided with a shift in the focus of their political battles towards the inclusion of explicit claims for the recognition of the peasantry as a distinct cultural entity, entitled to a differentiated set of rights. In so doing, peasant organisations have tried to bridge the judicial disadvantage that the 1991 constitution put them in vis-à-vis ethnic and racial groups.

The shift of the peasantry towards cultural identity is clearly rooted in their perceived marginalisation within the legal framework (as I illustrated in regard to the debate on FPIC in Chapter 4). Primarily, however, peasant grievances have developed at the local level, where different treatments are applied to groups that have shared the same geographical spaces and relatively similar livelihoods for decades. Indeed, according to the peasant movement, the multicultural state model envisioned in the 1991 constitution encouraged the formation of ethnically defined communities (either indigenous or Afro-descendants), while rendering the *mestizo* or peasant sectors invisible. A recent example of this is the fact that the 2014 National Agricultural Census did not include the 'peasant' category alongside the 'indigenous' and 'Afro-descendent' categories. Peasants ended up under either 'rural *mestizo* population' or 'unclassified population' (Verdad Abierta 2014). In response, peasant organisations from the Cauca Department filed a protection proceeding (*acción de tutela*) for the recognition of a 'peasant cultural identity'. The claim was, however, rejected by a departmental tribunal with the following justification: 'The peasant population does not have an ethnic tradition like indigenous or Afro-Colombian people. It is more about a socioeconomic reality that has to do with modes of production and not with racial origin' (*El Tiempo* 2014). Yet the tribunal's decision did not dissuade peasant organisations from pursuing a cultural turn. If it did not help with access to ethnic rights, this narrative shift may at least have contributed to reframing the peasant cause outside of classist and economic categories, and to dismantling the widespread association between peasant movements and Marxist guerrillas. The peasant struggle for recognition is synthesised here in the words of a local peasant leader:

The fight for recognition of a peasant identity has been hard. ... Peasants are considered the social base of the guerrilla. Until the government constitutionally recognises [the peasantry], coexistence will be very difficult because the rights of indigenous peoples are greater in scope than ours. This means that there must be recognition of the right to territory, as well as of the peasant as a cultural subject.

From the heart, one doesn't want them [indigenous peoples] to lose rights, but rather that they recognise that redistribution should be a chance for all those who have not had their opportunity yet. (Interview, Inzá, November 2015)

Peasant leaders certainly resent the difficulty of forging political alliances with indigenous organisations at the local level. At the same time, they recognise the need to look for alternative solutions to bridge gaps, instead of fractioning the rural movement. One example of this is the idea of constituting 'inter-ethnic territories', whose management and institutional arrangements would have to be the result of an agreement between different groups within a given social community.[14] Difficulties in creating such territories arise, however, from fears among indigenous sectors that they will lose the rights they have gained through long-standing social and political struggles:

[The peasants] want a new constitution. But how will we [the indigenous] end up with that? In the 1991 constitution we made some gains that really helped us. But if we have a new constitution, who knows how we are going to end up. (Interview, Inzá, November 2015)

More importantly, however, holes in the institutional and juridical frameworks impede the constitution of 'intercultural territories'. Although in many parts of Colombia complex social communities where different groups coexist and overlap are the norm rather than the exception, the available options in terms of collective land titles imply homogeneous social configurations (or at least the primacy of one group over others). Minorities within a given collective territorial unit either accept the authority of the majority and its forms of governance, or else leave. This rigidity and misrepresentation of social communities aggravates inter-group tensions, because it drastically reduces the potential for alternatives based around compromise. The lack of awareness and understanding of local dynamics on the part of state institutions simultaneously undermines the management and resolution of inter-communal conflict. The sub-units in charge of dealing with indigenous and peasant issues within the INCODER, for example, work as sealed-off units that pursue different and at times contradictory mandates.[15]

---

[14] See also the Catatumbo example and related referendum mentioned in Chapter 4.

[15] As one of my informants at the INCODER explained to me: 'The INCODER is divided into sub-administrations. There is a sub-management unit of ethnic issues that manages all policies related to indigenous and Afro-descendants, while there is also a sub-management unit of rural lands that handles all peasant issues. When I arrived at the INCODER, these two sub-administrations did not talk to each other. Then, each one was

The Cauca Department, in south-west Colombia, represents a particularly interesting case in which to study inter-communal land conflicts. It is one of the poorest regions of Colombia[16] and is also one of the most ethnically and culturally diverse.[17] As I mentioned in Chapter 3, the Cauca has been the cradle of the Colombian indigenous movement since the 1970s. The region also hosts some of the strongest, best-organised and most vocal peasant movements in the country, including the Unitary National Federation of Agricultural Trade Unions (Federación Nacional Sindical Unitaria Agropecuaria), the Popular Unity Process of the Colombian South-west (Proceso de Unidad Popular del Suroccidente Colombiano) and different Associations for the Constitution of Peasant Reserve Areas (Asociaciones Pro-constitución Zonas de Reserva Campesina). Both indigenous and peasant movements have been key local political actors and competing land claims have multiplied over the last decade (Figure 5.2). In the municipality of Inzá, in eastern Cauca, peasant and indigenous communities are engaged in two ongoing land disputes that represent paradigmatic examples of the new kinds of conflict that the region is experiencing.

Conflicts over Ancestral Territories and Local Governance in Inzá

Inzá is one of the main towns of a region known as Tierradentro, literally 'the inside land', in the eastern part of the Cauca Department. A geographic barrier formed by high swampy Andean plains separates Tierradentro from Tierrafuera ('the outside land'). Both Tierradentro and Tierrafuera have historically been occupied by the Nasa people, one of the biggest indigenous groups in this part of Colombia (Rappaport 2005); the regions are considered the strongholds of the Nasa culture and political activism. The difficulty of accessing the area kept Inzá in relative isolation until the mid-twentieth century, when peasant families fleeing the civil

---

following its own interests, some trying to do their duty to the indigenous and the Afros, and the others trying to do their duty to the peasants. So while one was constituting *resguardos* in one area, the other was titling private land for the peasants in the same area' (interview with former INCODER officer, Bogotá, November 2015).

[16] The incidence of poverty in the Cauca is 62 per cent, which is more than double the national average. The household per capita income is 46 per cent of the national average, and 25 per cent of the average in the capital city Bogotá (UNDP 2014).

[17] Fifty-nine per cent of the Caucan population is rural. Those declaring that they belong to an ethnic group make up 43 per cent, including Afro-descendants and indigenous peoples (UNDP 2014).

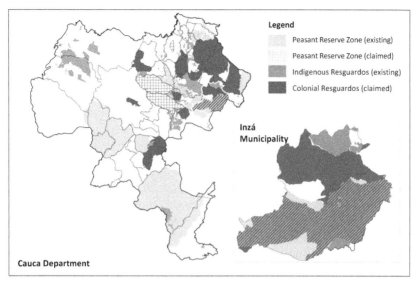

FIGURE 5.2. Map of peasant and indigenous collective land titles and claims in the Cauca Department (source: author's elaboration using data from the Intercultural Studies Institute at the Pontificia Universidad Javeriana de Cali, Colombia)

war were displaced there (Orlove & Custred 1980). The construction of a road between Inzá and the Cauca's capital Popayan (91 km) during the 1970s significantly improved the accessibility of the region and encouraged further migration inflow. Enhanced connectivity, however, was not a deterrent for guerrilla organisations: the FARC, for example, continued to regularly transit across this area, recruiting indigenous and peasant youths and limiting the freedom of assembly and movement of local communities (Rappaport 2005).

In contrast to other parts of eastern Cauca where the great majority of the population is Nasa (as in the case of Toribío that I discuss in the next chapter), Inzá has a complex human geography, in which indigenous communities make up only about half of the local population (UNDP 2014). These communities have historically shared their territory with *mestizo* peasants and Afro-Colombian farmers (Rappaport 2005). A relatively peaceful inter-ethnic and intercultural coexistence has been disrupted in recent years by demands for substantial territorial extension of Nasa land. Five out of six indigenous *resguardos* recently put forward demands for extension, while two more colonial *resguardos* are in the process of clarification. Indigenous claims have triggered tensions with other local inhabitants, and particularly peasant communities that occupy or hold claims over the same land. The situation has been aggravated by the new ambitions of the local peasant association – the Peasant Association of the Inzá Municipality (Asociación Campesina del Municipio de Inzá, ACIT) to create ZRCs in this region (Figure 5.2).

As a result, land disputes are widespread across the Inzá territory. A particularly tense front opened following the request for clarification, in 2008, of the two colonial *resguardos* of Turminá and San Antonio de Pedregal (about 20,000 hectares in total). The request provoked opposition from peasant inhabitants, who claimed that they had legally acquired property titles over that same land after the regional government declared the area vacant a few years back (PUJC 2013). The primary difficulty authorities faced in mediating the dispute was that, given the existence of overlapping ancestral and private property titles, both collective and individual rights ought to be considered legitimate. An agreement could only be reached if the parties were willing to negotiate and to agree not to fully exercise their rights.

Further tensions arose when the same territory was included in a ZRC (with an area of approximately 40,000 hectares), constituted de facto by the ACIT as part of its strategy to protect smallholder property against indigenous territorial expansion (interview with peasant leader, Inzá, November 2015). The constitution of a ZRC was not favourably received by the Nasa *cabildos*, who feared losing control over their territory and see ZRCs as jeopardising their expansionist efforts (interview with indigenous leader, Inzá, November 2015). For the peasants, however, the ZRC not only represents a way of securing land tenure but is also a matter of power, governance and recognition. Indeed, the ZRC would provide an alternative system of local governance to counterbalance the authority of the *cabildos*.

Peasants have become increasingly reluctant to accept indigenous authority, which comes as a precondition for being able to reside within the *resguardo*. As the former governor of the Yaquivá *resguardo* explains – himself a *mestizo* who has been part of the Nasa community for decades – non-indigenous residents must obey and follow indigenous institutions and the indigenous way of living in order to be accepted within a *resguardo*:

We are not going to violently evict those who think like a peasant .... They will continue to be part of the territory and of local politics because they also have reasonable rights. But they'll have to respect that this is already a *resguardo* and they'll have to be a part of the political life within it. (Interview, La Milagrosa, November 2015)

This, however, is easier said than done. Many peasants have begun to develop growing resentment towards indigenous authorities and consider the expansion of the *resguardos* a threat because it reduces access to resources and undermines their own culture and identity.

> The conflict is not only about [land] tenure but also about the territory's governability. Who governs the territory sets the conditions, and if they govern from an indigenous standpoint, we could lose our culture, our identity, our forms of production and our vision for the territory. (Interview with peasant leader, Guanacas, November 2015)

The tendency of land disputes to escalate and become violent is linked to the fact that land control is rarely the only issue at stake. These conflicts often occur when groups attempt to establish their authority over a given space. Thus, they are in fact about local governance or, as one peasant leader put it, about 'whom is exercising power over whom' (interview with peasant leader, Guanacas, November 2015). In this context, competition for power does not happen exclusively through traditional political channels (e.g. municipal elections), but also through the consolidation of customary or associational authority structures – namely the *cabildos* for indigenous groups, the community councils for Afro-descendants and the ZRC committees for peasants.

The expansionist strategy of indigenous communities has often been accompanied by efforts to strengthen the *cabildos*' authority, through adopting strong-arm tactics vis-à-vis peasant households living within or on the edges of a *resguardo*. One of the harshest conflicts between indigenous and peasant groups in the Cauca started in 2010 in San Andrés Pisimbalá, a *resguardo* within the Inzá municipality. The conflict reached national attention when, in 2013, the town's seventeenth-century church went up in flames as a result of an arson attack. Responsibility was never assigned, but the episode marked the peak of a conflict with multiple ramifications, from land to service provision to local governance.

The epicentre of the territorial dispute is the pueblo of San Andrés Pisimbalá, the main urban settlement within the homonymous *resguardo*, inhabited by a mix of indigenous and peasant populations. Following the rise of divergences around the local schools (which I discuss in detail in Chapter 7 as an example of an access conflict), the local peasant community began to challenge the authority of the *cabildo* and refused to be counted as residents of the *resguardo* any more. Peasants claim that they hold property titles (*escritura pública*) over the land that was granted to them, or to their ancestors, when they moved into the area – mainly as a result of violent displacements in the 1940s and 1950s. Indigenous leaders do not dispute the fact that peasants settled in the area with the consent of the *cabildo*, but they nevertheless consider those property titles invalid since they were not signed by indigenous authorities at the time. Hence, peasants do not have any formal entitlement over land they have been occupying for decades. Moreover, indigenous leaders are puzzled by the fact that peasants are suddenly opposing the *cabildo* authority, especially given that living on the *resguardo* brings a number of benefits to its residents, including peasants.

> Those that are part of the *cabildo* organisation have many benefits, many rights, many opportunities .... We have been recognised at the national level with the constitution .... We are ready to welcome everyone even if they are not indigenous, if they are willing to embrace our organisation. Here, we have always coexisted, indigenous or not, and that is what we want .... The majority of peasants are part of our [organisation]. Only a few of them are suddenly becoming blind. They have no vision for the future. (Interview with San Andrés indigenous governor, San Andrés, November 2015)

In an effort to settle the dispute, the *cabildo* offered to buy out peasant properties. However, the refusal of some families to sell generated resentment among indigenous residents, who began to occupy peasant estates (*fincas*) and cultivated fields (interview with San Andrés *resguardo* members, San Andrés, November 2015). In certain cases, houses and crops on those properties were set on fire. According to a peasant leader, between 2010 and 2015, twenty-seven claims against the *cabildo* were filed for land invasion, personal injury, damage to third party property, threats, kidnapping and murder (interview, San Andrés, November 2015). Peasants consider these actions part of a strategy to intimidate them and force them to leave, and ultimately 'to start recovering [indigenous] territory' (interview with peasant leader, San Andrés, November 2015). If territorial recovery is understood by indigenous peoples as a legitimate right based on their history and cultural attachment to the land, similar feelings and arguments are put forward by peasant dwellers as well.

> As those indigenous peoples who have lived on the territory for more than 400 years, we as *mestizos* or peasants have also lived here for more than 100 years. Our ancestors came here many years ago .... We also have ancestry, we have roots where we live. And morally, it affects one to be outside of one's territory. (Interview with San Andrés peasant leader, San Andrés, November 2015)

Peasants' attachment to their territory and their reluctance to leave, as well as their search for an alternative form of governance to the *cabildo*, motivated the declaration of a de facto ZRC around the town of San Andrés. In the union's view, the creation of a ZRC implies that peasants are also 'recognised and can continue to live here' under their own authority (interview with San Andrés peasant leader, San Andrés, November 2015). A committee will be in charge of producing a Peasant Development Plan that could receive funds from the state, design mechanisms to prevent exploitation and accumulation by private companies, and secure land tenure (interview with peasant leader, San Andrés, November 2015). This solution, however, is perceived as the second best for some members of the peasant organisation, who would prefer a more inclusive form of territorial and governance arrangement. This is the opinion of a woman of indigenous origins who, after the escalation of violence in San Andrés, decided to join the peasant organisation in protest against the 'acts of aggression' perpetrated by the *cabildo*:

> The state put us in this mess, in this fight for territory, when they said that indigenous territories should be distinctly indigenous, that is, there shouldn't be another organisation. ... So, when the state says that indigenous people have to cleanse their territory, it means that other people who have property titles [*escrituras públicas*] either donate it, sell it or leave. There is no way for us to live together because what they want, in reality, is for the territory to be purely indigenous. (Interview, San Andrés, November 2015)

Even if some local inhabitants would be in favour of a compromise solution, as I mentioned, the constitution of intercultural territories is not viable under the current legal framework. Communities, in other words, are left with very limited alternatives for peaceful, negotiated solutions. Meanwhile, the conflict between indigenous people and peasants has aggravated already high levels of endemic violence, and the two groups blame one other for that. On one hand, indigenous leaders consider that the peasants encouraged an increased army presence in the area as a deterrent to guerrilla activities, which placed local communities in the crossfire. On the other, peasants deem indigenous people responsible for the increased number of attacks by the guerrillas, who were constantly passing through indigenous territories but were acting particularly belligerently against peasant communities. In 2013, the FARC killed three peasant children, including the 14-year-old daughter of one of the local leaders of the ACIT, when they returned to their communities after leaving or abandoning the guerrilla ranks (interview with ACIT leader and mother of one of the victims, San Andrés, November 2015). The peace agreements signed between the Colombian government and the FARC in 2016 brought significant improvements for Inzá communities.

When I visited the region, a handful of tourists were wondering around to explore the local museum and some old Nasa graveyards up in the hills surrounding San Andrés. However, the departure of the guerrilla groups has not contributed to solutions for other issues that communities are facing, including land scarcity and secure control over their territories.

SPATIAL AND DISCURSIVE BATTLEGROUNDS

Land restitution for indigenous peoples is generally associated with common assumptions about the existence of long-standing cultural identities tied to an ancestral territory ruled by customary forms of governance in respect of the natural environment. These assumptions are often over-simplistic and overlook the complexity of social communities. In practice, as I have illustrated using examples from Bolivia and Colombia, drawing the lines of ethnic boundaries and ancestral territories is an extremely challenging and potentially tense process. As Fay and James (2009: xi) wrote:

> While restitution is an idea with an almost intuitive moral appeal, carrying it out inevitably enforces lofty principles of justice and restoration to confront the messy practicability of determining ownership, defining legitimate claimants, establishing evidence for claims and overcoming potential opposition . . ..

The history of multicultural land reforms is one of shifting relationships between indigenous peoples and the state, and indigenous peoples and other rural groups. Indeed, recognition reforms can embed policies and norms that can be at the same time empowering and exclusionary. If land restitution can generate a new sense of identity and community as well as promises of greater autonomy and well-being for indigenous groups, it can also fuel resistance from other social groups, who may feel excluded or unfairly treated (French 2009).

Feelings of exclusion and injustice on the part of non-indigenous groups are often justified by the fact that, over the last twenty years, non-indigenous claims have not received nearly as much attention as indigenous ones. In the Andean region, the titling of indigenous land has progressed rapidly and steadily since the 1990s, with Bolivia, Peru and Colombia becoming the countries with the greatest amount of titled indigenous land in South America (Rights and Resources Initiative 2015a). In contrast, only minor progress was made in the mapping and allocation of peasant land. In the case of Colombia, the creation of ZRCs was long postponed and remains highly contested. Even in Bolivia, where peasant unions have occupied a key position within the state apparatus in recent years, priority has been given to indigenous land titling. In Peru, where efforts were similarly put into titling native land, the weakness of the legal framework has made highland communities particularly vulnerable vis-à-vis the state-encouraged expansion of mining activities. Across these three countries, the situation has been exacerbated by the fact that indigenous land clarification was in many cases funded by international cooperation agencies (Assies 2006),[18] which often ended up reproducing long-standing racialised geographies (Andolina et al. 2009), while the budget to secure peasant land tenure was substantially lower or did not benefit from international aid at all.

As a result, the achievements of indigenous peoples have been more or less openly criticised by peasant sectors. One of the common complaints is that, under the indigenous rights framework, an 'unfair' amount of land is allocated to relatively small groups ('too much for too few', as Stock (2005: 85) put it). Throughout the region, it is not uncommon to hear peasant leaders referring to indigenous land as the 'new *latifundio*'. Even when peasants are sympathetic towards indigenous rights, they still incubate a sense of exclusion and injustice. From their perspective, indigenous peoples are extremely and unjustifiably protective of the advances made in the recognition of ethnic rights and are reluctant to show solidarity with other groups' demands because they fear this will jeopardise their own achievements. In this context, it is not surprising that the implementation of a differentiated set of rights rooted in ethnic recognition has reinforced identity boundaries and prevented inter-rural alliance in recent years.

The strengthening of social boundaries and identity disarticulation are the result of a new emphasis on culture and ethnicity that strives to justify claims for rights and resources. Across Bolivia, Colombia and Peru, these discursive shifts are not the prerogative of indigenous groups but are increasingly mirrored by peasant organisations. The latter have started to incorporate references to a sense of belonging, or 'ancestral' attachment to the land, in their discourse in order to justify their demand for recognition. This turn towards identity can be understood as a tactic in response to a normative framework that favours identity-based claims for resource allocation. The discursive space becomes indeed a privileged 'battlefield'. Here, new identities are formed and stories and mythologies

---

[18] A telling example is the ten-year-long programme by the Danish cooperation Danida, 'Support to the rights of indigenous peoples', discussed earlier in the chapter.

are reinvented. A new semantic repertoire contributes to the generation of a collective representation of the adversary, while at the same time dialectically influencing the representation of the 'self'. This 'self' is mainly constructed in opposition to what the 'enemy' is, or is assumed to be. In the words of Noel Castree (2004: 152), 'This is more than just a semantic issue of signifiers and signifieds. It is also an issue of how identities are claimed or made, of how "insiders" and "outsiders" are created through the identification process, and of how real place-projects are pursued in the name of these identities'. Besides questions of authenticity and legitimacy, what is interesting is the trajectory that leads to the emergence of new identities, and the reasons why drawing from an ancestral past is a recurrent feature of contemporary social struggles in the Andes.

The turn towards identity goes beyond the aesthetics of discourse. It grants a new dimension to land struggles: parties' positions have increasingly shifted from resource-based claims to ethno-identitarian issues, traditionally more resistant to bargained agreements (Taras & Ganguly 2008). In this process, other grievances beyond land access have resurfaced in regard to power and local governance. It is in looking beyond the more obvious aspects of land struggles, especially around the definition of physical boundaries, that the effects of recognition reform become evident. Whether through the constitution of new indigenous territories or the expansion of existing ones, the implementation of multicultural land reforms fails to account for the existence of 'complex territorialities', in which different groups coexist and form equally complex social communities.

On one hand, an astigmatic regard for local contexts is not suited to capturing the historical processes that have shaped contemporary social landscapes. It fails, for instance, to reveal why certain groups prefer not to identify as indigenous even if this makes the fight for land more difficult (such as in the case of Apolo), or to explain why indigenous leaders embark on radical eviction campaigns of peasant neighbours (as occurred in Inzá). On the other hand, the myopic range of options available for addressing territorial claims consolidates geographies of segregation and hinders any attempt to find alternative solutions. This is the case with land restitution claims based on colonial titles. Such restitution politics is explicitly designed to redress injustices and a lack of recognition by seeking to reinstate the conditions of the past. Doing so, however, is grounded on a weak precondition: the arbitrary chance of a community getting their land recognised by colonial authorities and of being able to provide evidence through the preservation of a colonial title. At the same time, this segregationist approach to land restitution has, in practice, impeded the creation of intercultural territories based on the coexistence of different land ownership regimes (collective and private) and of multiple systems of local governance. The failure by the recognition framework to account for historical complexity and social contingency is responsible for other kinds of social tensions rooted in demographic change and human mobility, which I examine in the next chapter.

6

Unsettled Demographies

Changes in local demographics have introduced new challenges for the coexistence of different social groups in the post-recognition phase. These changes are rooted in both exogenous and endogenous factors. On one hand, sustained migration has created new settlements, expanded the agrarian frontier, and pushed indigenous groups to assume a more hostile and protectionist attitude towards non-indigenous settlers. On the other, indigenous groups' increasing population rates have encouraged an expansionist strategy that involves targeting new territories already occupied by other groups. This chapter considers both exogenously and endogenously driven changes in rural demographics as factors that contribute to the new relevance of social heterogeneity and of distributive measures embedded in recognition reforms. As I illustrated in the previous chapter, land is often at the root of recognition disputes in the context of resource scarcity. In this chapter, I analyse how changes in social heterogeneity can fuel land conflicts as well as conflicts for social provisions (e.g. access to water and electricity), linked to the implementation of recognition reforms. As in the previous chapter, norms around land tenure work as 'means of redistribution' embedded in a recognition framework that dramatically influences communities' access to key resources and is often an object of contention. I discuss these tensions in relation to shifts and shocks in social communities' demographic composition which result in increased social heterogeneity. Because these conflicts are all related to changes in local demographics, I call this type of recognition conflict demographic conflict. I rely on empirical cases from the inter-Andean regions of Peru to illustrate the challenging coexistence of rural migrants and indigenous communities; and on the case of the Cauca Department in

Colombia to analyse how population growth, combined with a situation of widespread and acute violence generated by the civil war, has aggravated resource competition. Based on these empirical cases, I argue that the recognition framework is poorly equipped to account for the more fluid aspects of social communities embedded in migration dynamics and other demographic changes.

EXOGENOUS PRESSURE: RURAL MIGRATION AND NEW SETTLEMENTS

In Latin America, migration studies have mainly been concerned with international flow towards Western countries and, on the domestic level, with the exodus from the countryside and processes of mass urbanisation. Yet, since the 1980s, migration to secondary cities and rural frontiers has been increasing even when compared to urban migration (Mougeot 1985; Altamirano et al. 1997; Carr 2009). In countries such as Brazil, Ecuador, Honduras and Peru, rural–rural or urban–rural migrants represent a third of total migrants (Bilsborrow 2002). These flows have often been encouraged by state-sponsored resettlement programmes, as part of nation-building strategies of territorial occupation and control of peripheral land. Investment in infrastructure and development initiatives in remote areas have worked as indirect pulls towards the frontier (Findley 1984). In the Colombian Amazon, for example, institutional subsidies and public investment spawned a land market distortion whereby existing farmland was overpriced, while frontier land remained under-priced, leading to population movement towards these regions (Heath & Binswanger 1996). In Peru, in the late 1980s, the government put in place incentive programmes for the creation of new settlements with the aim of consolidating its control over remote areas and increasing food production. In this framework, communities or settlements had to register as Agrarian Associations in order to be eligible to receive plots of land and loans to purchase agricultural tools (Newing 2009). Meanwhile, Bolivian highlanders have increasingly migrated to the valleys and lowlands (Rudel 2009), after a new Agrarian Law (1996) established that unproductive land had to be recovered by the state and redistributed through colonisation programmes (Vargas & Osinaga 2009).

Across the region, multicultural agrarian reforms implemented in the 1990s have greatly influenced internal migration dynamics. As I mentioned in Chapter 5, over the last twenty years many indigenous groups have taken advantage of the receptiveness of the state vis-à-vis their land claims and have successfully secured a certain degree of control over their territories. The extension of these territories,[1] however, has not always proved consistent with population needs. While Amazonian groups have generally obtained very generous extensions of land, higher demographic density and the contiguity and sometimes overlap of indigenous and non-indigenous communities in the highlands and valleys have resulted in the titling of smaller plots, which are often unsuited to providing decent standards of living. As a result, indigenous highlanders have increasingly joined the ranks of rural migrants.

Along the fertile inter-Andean valleys, dramatic changes triggered by the arrival of rural migrants, as well as informality and a lack of planning following the initial phase of territorial occupation, have contributed to the rise in social tensions between old inhabitants and newcomers. These tensions often persist throughout the process of redefining new territorial boundaries. Migratory pressure has indeed been one of the main reasons behind the need to formalise (through cadastral studies and issuing of property titles) areas that have traditionally been characterised by very loose and fluid territorial boundaries. As I illustrated in Chapter 5, reterritorialisation processes are in certain cases coupled with identity redefinition, with the consolidation of new collective identities and the dilution of others, and with increased identity rigidity and social closure (Coate & Thiel, 2010).

Migration-related conflicts are present across the Andean region. They are linked to the movement of populations from highland to lowland areas, especially along the subtropical fertile strips at the edge of the rainforest. These conflicts, however, are not exclusive to the Andes. In Nicaragua, for example, tensions between Miskito peoples and *colonos* (as rural migrants are commonly called across Latin America) over the control of land have been mounting in recent years, leading to numerous victims, displacements and continuous violent attacks (Mollett 2011; Robles 2016). Similar conflicts are ongoing in Costa Rica, where the murders of Bribri indigenous leaders in early 2020 have been linked to land disputes with peasant settlers (Lakhani 2020). Even though migration is known to be a source of social disruption (Alexiades 2009; Dancygier 2010; Cochrane 2015) and is commonly associated with the

---

[1] This is established by a combination of objective and subjective criteria, including more or less sophisticated projections of needs to maintain decent conditions of subsistence, as well as reference to colonial titles and proofs of ancestral occupancy.

rise of inter-group tensions, social conflict linked to rural–rural migration is still poorly understood in the Latin American context.

With the aim of offering an insight into migration-related conflicts and their relevance for recognition politics, I present here cases from Peru, drawing both on data collected during my fieldwork in the Selva Central region (Satipo and Oxapampa provinces) in March and April 2016, and on secondary sources and archival research concerning other emblematic cases in departments with similar migration patterns (Cajamarca and San Martín).

MIGRATION DYNAMICS AND LAND DISPUTES IN SELVA CENTRAL, PERU

The Selva Central is a subtropical region in the heart of Peru. It is home to around 230 native communities, mainly Yanesha and Ashaninka, all belonging to the Arahuac linguistic family. Their ancestors have occupied the region since 1800 BC (Lathrap 1970). During the colonial period, a few Franciscan missions were established in the area. It was only in the late nineteenth century, though, that a broader occupation of the region began, in conjunction with the establishment of *latifundia* for agriculture and livestock production. Economic development started to attract a labour force from other regions, particularly from Andean peasant communities. International migrants from Europe, especially from the Austro-Hungarian Empire, were also redirected towards these fertile valleys through government-sponsored programmes. Major infrastructural projects in the 1940s and 1970s brought new migration to the region and contributed to rapid population growth (from 23,000 inhabitants in 1940 to approximately 213,000 in 1981) (OAS 1987). Since the early 2000s, Selva Central has become even more attractive to internal migrants, especially from the Andean departments of Huancavelica, Junín and Apurímac, following the de-escalation of the conflict with the guerrilla movement Sendero Luminoso. According to the most recent household census, the provinces of Oxapampa and Satipo have both seen positive migration rates in recent years (Sánchez Aguilar 2015).

As in other similar areas situated on the fringes between highlands and lowlands, in Selva Central rural migrants have followed two main settlement strategies: creating informal settlements on unoccupied land, often alongside new-built roads; or purchasing their plots from regional governments and private owners before resettling. Migrants usually gather in one area called a *caserío* or *sector*. In certain cases, they organise in associations of producers (*asociaciones de productores*), especially in crop-intensive production areas (e.g. coffee, coca).

Following the creation of new settlements, conflicts are usually triggered by the overlapping of the areas occupied by the migrants with land either formally belonging to or claimed by indigenous groups. This is often the case in the context of informal land occupation. However, the acquisition of land titles prior to relocation does not guarantee less conflictive outcomes. In fact, many land conflicts are rooted in administrative mismanagement, whereby local and regional governments allocated land titles to areas formally belonging to indigenous communities, or awaiting formal recognition. Besides the cases of local corruption that certainly exist, these errors are grounded in institutional inefficiencies and a lack of centralised information. Indeed, in Peru there is no computerised register of communal and land tenure at the regional or national level.[2] Even when titles are issued, property boundaries are not mapped and georeferenced (interviews with officers at the Peruvian Ombudsman's Office, Lima, April 2016). This has been fuelling a widespread problem of overlapping land titles between migrants and indigenous territories due to the poor geographical information and incomplete maps handled by the public administration (Greene 2009). Title overlap and a lack of clarity on property boundaries make it very difficult to find solutions to the emerging conflicts before entering a judicial process. Informality and mismanagement are aggravated by delays in state intervention, and it is obvious that the more the settlers are left to occupy a given territory, the greater their resistance will be towards relocation or other compromise solutions.

Settlements in the San Matías San Carlos Protected Area: Environmental Protection or Service Provision?

It is often the case that new settlements not only overlap with community land, but also with areas that have some special environmental protection status – either as a protected area or a national park. This complicates the tenure scenario further and is no guarantee of a quicker or more efficient

---

[2] Complaints are even more justified by the fact that a centralised and computerised register of around 50,000 mining concessions does exist (managed by the Mining and Metallurgic Geologic Institute, Instituto Geológico Minero y Metalúrgico), while no such equivalent exists for individual properties nor even for the few thousand indigenous and peasant communities.

state response. The protected area San Matías San Carlos offers a telling example of this complexity. San Matías San Carlos was created in 1987 with an allocation of 145,818 hectares of tropical moist forest ranging between 300 and 2,250 metres of altitude. Since its creation, it has received waves of migrants from highland regions as well as from nearby towns. Pushing factors for these movements were displacements caused by the civil conflict during the late 1980s and 1990s, as well as the search for additional land, especially land apt for coffee production (interview with Ashaninka advisor at the Centre for the Development of Amazonian Indigenous People, La Merced, April 2016). The existence of a protected area did not deter the creation of new settlements. In fact, the almost complete absence of state institutions and monitoring mechanisms encouraged, for over twenty years, land occupations in a framework of total impunity and lack of regulation. This resulted in an incredibly complex land tenure landscape and has generated occasional friction with the native communities already living in the area, who claim ancestral rights over the protected forest.

In the late 2000s, indigenous inhabitants created a committee of self-defence to resist new occupations, called the Army of the Ashaninka Nationality of Pichis (Ejercito de la Nacionalidad Ashaninka del Pichis; Gaspar 2009).[3] Although no one was killed in the conflict between indigenous communities and migrants, house burning, physical confrontations and verbal threats have been common. In recent years, the already tense situation has been exacerbated by allegations of land trafficking within the protected area. According to local sources, illegal activities involve both settlers and native leaders. In 2011, the National Service of State Natural Protected Areas (Servicio Nacional de Áreas Naturales Protegidas por el Estado) issued a warning to dissuade people from engaging in land purchases within the protected area (Inforegión 2011). One of the indigenous land claims in Valle Orito has been suspended, awaiting investigations about land trafficking in the area (interview with Ashaninka advisor, La Merced, April 2016). To be sure, land trafficking is only one of the illegal activities that affects the protected area, which is also threatened by the construction of roads for lumber extraction and by the expansion of illicit crops (coca and poppy) (Gaspar 2009).

---

[3] Probably inspired by the experience of the Ejercito Ashaninka formed in the 1990s to resist Sendero Luminoso incursions (information retrieved from database of indigenous peoples, Ministry of Culture, http://bdpi.cultura.gob.pe/node/15, accessed 10 November 2017).

In 2008, after years of illegal occupation and mounting tensions, a protected area headquarters was eventually established. This was a first step towards ensuring a greater institutional presence within the region, although it would take another seven years for the publication of the first management plan. The protected area's administration was given a very broad mandate, which went beyond environmental protection. It included, for example, the preservation of agricultural soil, towns and infrastructure against the effects of water erosion. This has probably facilitated the adoption of a very pragmatic attitude towards the issue of illegal settlements. In the words of the Director of the San Matías San Carlos Protected Area:

> There are people that have been living there for more than twenty years, mainly producing coffee. It is a reality and we have to see how we manage it . . .. One goal is to improve the productivity of those plots that are already there in order to avoid the expansion of the agrarian frontier. (Interview, Pichinkeni, April 2016)

Between 2014 and 2015, the first effort to count the settlers estimated their number at around 3,500 (interview with Director of the San Matías San Carlos Protected Area, Pichinkeni, April 2016). The oldest settlements, which in certain cases date back more than two decades, are organised in associations of plot holders (*asociaciones de parcelarios*), who have been lobbying local government for access to service provisions such as electricity, sanitation, health and education. While the park administration has adopted a rather moderate position and is keen to compromise, these claims have generated strong resistance from indigenous communities, who interpret them as a sign of more permanent arrangements. As a result, settlers' claims have triggered new tensions even in cases that had not generated conflict in the first place, or that had already been peacefully resolved.

The resurgence of tensions around claims for social provisions is common in many migration-recipient areas. The conflict between the Awajún (also known as the Aguaruna) community of Los Naranjos and the Sawinsa sector in the district of San José de Lourdes, Cajamarca Department, represents another such case. Here, too, there was an agreement in place between the community and the migrants. However, the sector's demands for access to basic services have led to a change of heart on the part of the community leaders, who are now keen for the migrants to leave (interviews with Ombudsman officers, Lima, April 2016).[4]

---

[4] Similar conflicts between migrants and Awajún communities over land rental arrangements and service provision are described in Greene (2009, Chapter 5). These practices also carry the risk, as noted by Greene, of fuelling new intra-community inequalities, with the formation of an indigenous economic elite of landowners.

The development of the situation in Los Naranjos is closely monitored by the Ombudsman's Office, especially because in the early 2000s this same community witnessed the worst episode of violence against migrant settlers in recent Peruvian history. Indeed, this case merits closer attention for its exceptional levels of violence, as well as for the insight it provides on widespread attitudes towards this kind of dispute.

Flor de la Frontera: From Usurpation to Massacre

In the late 1990s, the Awajún community of Los Naranjos had approximately 1,100 members, divided between 150 households. The community was recognised and granted a land title in 1977, which was expanded in 1993 to include an additional 60,000 hectares. In 1996, a group of migrants occupied some plots in the community forestry area and their possession was formalised a year later through a resolution of the Sub-regional Agrarian Unit of the Ministry of Agriculture. One hundred and sixteen (116) plots were allocated for a total of 793 hectares. In 1998, following a complaint by the indigenous community, the provincial public attorney filed criminal charges for usurpation against the President of the Agricultural Association La Flor de la Frontera. At that point it was clear that the migrants' plots fell within the native territory, as the Ministry of Agriculture itself acknowledged, which nullified the land titles previously issued. Between 2000 and 2002, four judicial injunctions were issued instructing the settlers to leave. However, the four eviction attempts failed either because of institutional inefficiencies or the settlers' resistance. On one occasion, the settlers were supported by armed members of peasant *rondas* from the region,[5] and declared that they were 'ready ... to lose their lives because they did not have anywhere else to go' (Defensoria del Pueblo 2002: 34). Meanwhile, two mediation attempts were led by the Ombudsman's Office, which partnered with the Ministry of Agriculture to relocate the migrant families to a new area. However, relocation proposals were dismissed by the Association because, it was argued, the settlers were not ready to give up the labour and money they had invested in their plots over the years.

---

[5] The *rondas* are autonomous peasant patrols active in northern Peru. They were originally formed as a protection force against theft, especially cattle rustling, and they evolved into community paramilitary units in charge of the enforcement of order and justice during the Sendero Luminoso insurgency war.

In the early morning of 17 January 2002, members of the indigenous communities unexpectedly entered the Flor de la Frontera sector to evict the inhabitants. The intervention left sixteen people dead (including three women and seven children), seventeen wounded (including five women and five children), one missing person and one kidnapped girl, who was later returned to her family (Guerrero Figueroa et al. 2002). The investigation of the event was poorly managed by local authorities from the beginning, starting with a failure to conduct post-mortem examinations on the bodies (Defensoria del Pueblo 2002). The judicial trial was also questionable: the provincial attorney filed charges against six members of the native community, but responsibilities for the murders were never fully established despite the clear acknowledgement by a parliamentary commission that 'it was not a confrontation between settlers and natives. What took place is an attack with firearms and sharp cutting weapons of the natives against the invading settlers' (Guerrero Figueroa et al. 2002).

Considering the unprecedented levels of violence that characterised this episode, it is surprising to observe that the case did not generate a strong reaction within the media or academia, or among human rights organisations. A few articles and editorials in national newspapers were published soon after the fact and some international media outlets picked up the news. However, after the initial fuss, the story vanished. The case is briefly mentioned in a couple of academic works (Steinert 2003; Garcés Trelles & Echevarría Mejía 2009) and the only attempt at analysis is in Greene's book *Customizing Indigeneity* (2009), where the case is cited as an example of violent 'customization' of indigenous rights. Reports were issued by the Peruvian Ombudsman's Office and the Parliamentary Commission investigating the case, but no mention of Flor de la Frontera was made in publications and press releases of international human rights organisations, such as Amnesty International and Human Rights Watch.

Interestingly, almost all these sources share common narratives in their accounts and analysis of the episode. The conflict is often described as the result of a 'socio-cultural problem' (Guerrero Figueroa et al. 2002); the violent outbreak is understood as the symptom of a clear external threat represented by the settlers, coupled with legitimate long-standing frustrations from the aborted efforts to follow the legal path on the part of the Awajún community. Discussing land conflict in the Alto Mayo region of Peru, the authors of an academic article published by the Colombian journal *Jangwa Pana* wrote:

A cultural conflict of perceptions between the settlers and the native members is also manifest ... Once the territory that corresponds to the community is identified, territorial autonomy is firmly established against the settlers, particularly because the settler not only occupies the land but represents a death threat for the native. (Garcés Trelles & Echevarría Mejía, 2009: 58–59)

In the aftermath of the Flor de la Frontera massacre, editorials of one of the major Peruvian newspapers, *La República*, included statements such as: 'the Aguaruna-Huambisa exhausted the legal means and were forced to respond forcefully' (*La República* 2002) and 'the absence of hope in the law (of the state and of the Aguaruna) fuelled the spirit of force that first penetrated the invaders and their promoters and, then, infected the Aguaruna' (Ballón Aguirre 2002).

The blame for the outbreak of violence was often attributed to institutional inefficiencies and corruption and, ultimately, to the state. Both indigenous people and migrants were positioned as victims. The anthropologist Imelda Vega Centeno was quoted by the news agency InterPress Service commenting on the case: 'The greater responsibility does not correspond to the Aguaruna elders who ordered and perpetrated the attack, nor to the peasant leaders, but to the double and hypocritical legal normativity of our country' (Lama 2002). Again, a *La República* editorialist (2002) wrote: 'What is being demonstrated is the inefficiency and incompetence of a state ... incapable of satisfying the basic needs of the people [and] that ends up putting the poor up against the poor'.

These narratives surrounding the Flor de la Frontera case share common features that are representative of public opinion towards land conflicts linked to rural migration. There is a sense of inevitability and predictability, which relates both to state inefficiencies and to a sort of unavoidable conflictive seed embedded in intercultural relationships. On one hand, the members of the Association of Producers are always referred to as *colonos* or 'invaders' (*invasores*), never as migrants and very rarely as highland peasants.[6] This stereotypical and arguably prejudicial language contributes to reducing any possible sense of empathy and encourages moral judgment, which implicitly attributes the responsibility for the violence, at least in part, to this group. On the other hand, indigenous communities are portrayed as victims rather than perpetrators. The prolonged injustice they have suffered with the occupation of their lands, when not explicitly justifying, at least permits to understand

---

[6] On their side, the migrants clearly reject these labels: 'We are not invaders. The judge told us that these lands were free' (cited in Torrejón 2002).

their violent reaction. In other words, the murder of the migrants appears almost as an act of legitimate violence, in this view, or at least a legitimate defence. In other cases, the classic paternalistic approach to indigenous peoples led to Awajún actions being described as the result of '"uncivilized" indigenous ignorance', undermining the agency and decision-making ability of this group (Greene 2009: 153).

Many commentators on this case have tried to address what they consider to be the root of the problem. In so doing, however, they often neglect to provide a comprehensive account of the facts. Elements which the press tends to linger upon, such as the ferocity of a crime, the stories of the victims and graphic details about the murders, are completely absent here. For instance, the fact that the majority of the victims were women and children is never mentioned, with the exception of the Parliamentary Report (which includes a list of the names and ages of all the victims). This report also makes reference to another hypothesis in justification of a violent reaction, which is not addressed by any other source: not long before the massacre, the indigenous community had signed agreements with two mining companies, and the prospect of increased future benefits might have incentivised their efforts to push for the rapid eviction of the migrants (Guerrero Figueroa et al. 2002). This is relevant as it points to economic and distributive claims, which are often embedded – and neglected – aspects of inter-communal conflicts linked to recognition.

The document on the Flor de la Frontera case produced by the Ombudsman's Office also shows clear analytical biases. The most outstanding is that it exclusively focuses on the violation of the rights of the native community. In the conclusions, it is stated that:

The members of the peasant association Flor de la Frontera had no right to justify their presence in the lands of the native community Los Naranjos .... These people violated the property and possession rights of the native community Los Naranjos as well as the rights of use, administration and conservation of the natural resources existing on their lands. [... This conflict] highlights the lack of material protection that the native communities of the Peruvian Amazon suffer. (Defensoría del Pueblo 2002: 64)

There is no reference to the murder of sixteen migrants as a crime or even as a human rights violation. Migrant settlers are clearly portrayed as the ones that are violating rights and there is no mention of the fact that they were victims of administrative mismanagement. Finally, their resistance to relocation is not analysed through a rights-based framework, which would at least help to raise the issue of whether migrants should also be entitled to some form of compensation for the violation of their rights or, at least, for the economic loss that the relocation process would involve.

In fact, this conflict deserves more nuanced and complex interpretation. One such interpretation is offered by Greene (2009), who observes in his book how this conflict is an example of the difficulties both indigenous peoples and peasant settlers have in negotiating market dynamics through rejection, despite needing to somehow be part of them. In particular, he uses this case to illustrate a process that he calls 'aggressive customisation' of the rights of indigeneity, where custom results in a blend of traditional conflict resolution methods and the indigenous rights legislative framework (i.e. rights to land are 'customised' through armed action). This is an interesting alternative way of describing how the recognition framework is indeed shaping strategies of adaptation/articulation (or customisation, to use Greene's term), following ethnic groups' interpretation and enactment of indigenous rights. Greene also makes another important remark: although local actors have agency (and therefore responsibility) in shaping the outcomes of their interactions, the state is not a neutral actor here. Indeed, this case should have raised awareness about state complicity in fuelling conflict through the misleading and unlawful handling of land titling claims by both migrants and indigenous communities, which is something I have observed in other contexts and countries as well.

The Flor de la Frontera case constitutes an extreme example in terms of the level of violence and number of casualties in a migration-related conflict. Yet this brief analysis clearly exemplifies the simplistic way in which conflicts between migrants and indigenous peoples are understood by authorities and public opinion in Peru, and similarly in other Andean countries. Manichean frameworks are often also applied to make sense of disputes over land and resources triggered by endogenous, rather than exogenous, changes.

ENDOGENOUS PRESSURE: POPULATION GROWTH AND POLITICAL VIOLENCE

Demographic pressure can sharpen issues around social cohesion in different ways. If exogenous demographic growth through migration increases social heterogeneity, endogenous population growth can also contribute to making subtle social differences more relevant and contentious. Population growth, for example, can make a group stronger compared to other groups, while at the same time placing greater stress on local social structures and resources.

After a long period of population decline, many indigenous groups have experienced sustained growth in recent decades linked to high fertility and low mortality rates (McSweeney & Arps 2005). Demographic growth is a complex phenomenon that goes beyond head counting and involves important economic factors. As Mitchell (1991: 19) notes, 'population pressure is not an ecological threshold, but an ecological-economic continuum. It refers to the entire relationship between population and resource production, not simply the number of people per hectare'. Environmental changes such as soil erosion and a more extreme climate can dramatically affect local agricultural production, which constitutes the major source of income for most peasant and indigenous communities in the Andes. Political violence and civil conflict also have an impact on resource access. The presence of armed groups can limit access to land and significantly reduce communities' control over their territories. Moreover, communities are usually keen to receive land titles as compensation for conflict-related losses, in order to deal with resource scarcity and livelihood issues. Across the Andean region, population growth in the context of economic and political fragilities has pushed communities to look for new strategies of social reproduction, such as territorial expansion. In Colombia alone 'there are more than 800 requests for constitution, cadastral study and extension of indigenous *resguardos* that have not yet been resolved' (Colombian Constitutional Court, Sentence C-371/14, 2015), particularly concentrated in the Cauca Department.

Cases of territorial expansion through invasion of neighbouring lands can also be found beyond the Andean region. The Michoacán state in Mexico presents an incredibly similar scenario to the one of Cauca. In an effort to resolve hundreds of land disputes following the implementation of a policy for the individualisation of peasant and communal land (*ejido*), the government gave priority to communities self-identifying as native peoples (*pueblos originarios*). Tepehuan people started to invade *ejido* lands, forcing the *mestizo* residents to leave. Ironically, the official evaluation speaks of the 'emigration' of the peasants who, to be sure, also consider themselves 'natives' of that territory. Their 'crime', as Vásquez León (2016: 42) writes, 'was to be thought of as *mestizos* in an area imagined to be exclusively inhabited by a single ethnic group'.

In the following section, examples from the Cauca region help illustrate how endogenous demographic changes driven by environmental and political crises have increased perceived identity differentiation and heterogeneity in social communities; at the same time, multicultural land reforms with high redistributive impact have provided a framework in which ethnic groups have pursued expansionist strategies, generating new demographic conflicts.

RESISTANCE AND OCCUPATION IN THE CAUCA, COLOMBIA

Since the 1950s, the Cauca Department has been one of the epicentres of the civil war between the Colombian government and a plethora of guerrilla movements. An indigenous guerrilla group called Armed Indigenous Movement Quintín Lame (Movimiento Indígena Armado Quintín Lame) had its main base in northern and eastern Cauca between 1985 and 1990, while all other major guerrilla armies, including the FARC and the National Liberation Army (Ejército de Liberación Nacional), considered Cauca a strategic region because of key communication routes. The significant presence of insurgent actors has converted the area into a crucial location for counterinsurgency operations, with a massive army deployment and almost constant confrontations and human rights abuses.

Not only have the northern and eastern regions of the Cauca paid the highest price as a result of the civil war, they are also those that have been most affected by a recent wave of inter-communal land struggles, as I discussed in Chapter 5 (PUJC 2013; UNDP 2014). Some of these conflicts can be linked to endogenous demographic changes, and in particular the growth of indigenous communities in areas where land access is limited: to the east, by the presence of guerrilla actors and the establishment of protected natural reserves, and to the west, by agribusinesses.

A report on inter-ethnic and inter-rural relationships in the Cauca identifies thirty-nine *resguardos* with a conflict situation, including twenty-four active and nineteen latent (PUJC 2013). Demographic pressure seems to be a key factor in explaining disputes between indigenous, peasant and Afro-Colombian groups. Many of these conflicts emerge in relation to claims to expand existing indigenous territories (*resguardos*) or to constitute new ones. In the following section, I analyse how these conflicts have manifested in the municipalities of Toribío, where I travelled and conducted research in November 2015 – when the period of detente opened by the peace talks had improved levels of security and made it possible to access the region.

Caught in the Frontline: Compensation and Land Disputes in Toribío

'We'll keep fighting until the sun stops shining' ('Seguiremos luchando hasta que se apague el sol'). This verse from one of the hymns of the Caucan indigenous movement is written on the stairs of the central square of Taqueyó, a village in the municipality of Toribío, north-east Cauca. The statement recalls the long-standing story of resistance by this Nasa community, caught for decades in the confrontation between guerrilla movements and the Colombian army. The central square of the nearby town of Toribío reveals less poetic evidence of recent attacks: only the skeleton of the military headquarters that occupied the south-west corner remains standing, after the FARC launched a bus loaded with explosives into it on a crowded Saturday morning in July 2011. It resulted in the death of four people, with a further 103 injured and 460 damaged houses (Semana 2011). This is only the most recent in a long series of violent episodes and massacres perpetrated by armed actors in this municipality (PUJC 2013).

Marking the last populated frontier at the edges of the western mountain ridge and the Huila massif, Toribío has been an important corridor for irregular troops. The FARC had traditionally boasted a sizable contingent of supporters within indigenous communities and relied on the recruitment of indigenous youth. However, the influence of the FARC and the Communist Party has been challenged, since the 1970s, by the CRIC. The indigenous organisation pursued a political agenda focused on ethnic self-determination and autonomy, in contrast with the mainstream leftist discourse of other social groups, such as peasants and workers (Rappaport 2005). Toribío hosted the foundational meeting of the Caucan indigenous movement and has been at the forefront of the indigenous struggle ever since. Intra-communal tensions between FARC supporters and the CRIC leadership persist, although the indigenous movement has now been in control of local politics for more than a decade. The rising power of indigenous authorities with a strong vision of self-determination has complicated the relationship with the Colombian army, which increased its military presence (by more than 8,300 troops) with the aim of re-establishing control over strategic areas (as part of the National Policy of Territorial Consolidation and Reconstruction) (UNDP 2014).

Particularly since 2010, Nasa communities have been the target of political violence. Between January 2012 and May 2013, CRIC denounced sixty-five murders of community members by the FARC, among them four spiritual leaders accused of being informants for other armed groups (CRIC 2013). The upsurge in violence brought the situation in northern Cauca under the radar of the peace negotiation committees in La Habana and, since 2015, the ceasefire and then a peace agreement have reduced the presence of armed actors and drastically improved the security conditions of these communities.

The civil war that has so deeply conditioned the life of the Nasa communities of northern Cauca for decades has also had an impact on inter-group relationships. Toribío is one of a number of municipalities experiencing ongoing conflict over land with neighbouring Afro-descendent groups. At the root of this dispute is the acquisition of the San Rafael estate by the Ministry of Agriculture, who subsequently handed it over to the Toribío *resguardo* as compensation for the massacre of twenty-one indigenous people, killed in 1991 by the Colombian police and armed civilians in retaliation against the occupation of the El Nilo estate. The state admitted its responsibilities and agreed to buy 15,663,000 hectares of land for the Nasa people. In 2007, the San Rafael estate was included in the compensation plan, without consideration that these lands had been occupied by Afro-descendant communities, who hold ancestral claims over them. The relocation of Nasa families to the area led to violent clashes with Afro-descendants, which resulted in two fatalities and many injured people. Following this outbreak of violence, different national and local authorities established mediation commissions. According to one of the Afro-descendent community council leaders, an agreement was eventually reached, although there is still a need to be vigilant to prevent other rights violations:

We have reached agreements. One of them is that if you are going to buy land, the Inter-ethnic Commission is called in to review the case and verify that communities do not already live in that area. [Also] there have been difficulties with the issue of education. Now we have difficulties with the issue of *resguardos*. So we told the government: 'let's review the matter well before buying land'. (Cited in PUJC 2013: 403)

Commenting on the land conflicts with neighbouring Afro-Colombian and peasant communities, the indigenous governor of Toribío minimised the inter-ethnic dimension of territorial claims and focused on political and ideological barriers and on external influences at the root of tensions:

[The San Rafael estate] was not Afro-Colombian land; it was land of the *hacienda*. It was the [white] politicians who began to push [Afro-Colombians] to reclaim those lands and create a conflict. So, that's not an inter-ethnic conflict, it's a provocation. They are using the pain, the need, the right surely of Afro-Colombians, to generate a conflict. The same has happened with the peasants [referring to another conflict with peasant dwellers]. Here the indigenous people are not violating a peasant right. ... What has happened is that the right was politicised. ... Some ideologues of the FARC, some politicians who are against the peasant sector are saying that this is peasant land when it is *resguardo* land. So, it is the indigenous movement that has been assaulted by merely ideological intentions to generate conflict. (Interview, Toribío, November 2015)

Indigenous leaders perceive their process of political organisation as more advanced and autonomous than the Afro-Colombian and peasant processes, which still suffer the influence of traditional powers and leftist ideologies obstructing their claims for emancipation and self-determination (interview with Toribío governor, Toribío, November 2015). This position might at least partially explain the scepticism and distrust of the peasants towards indigenous organisations, because they feel delegitimised and unable to claim rights based on cultural identity and ancestral ties to the territory:

The difficulty with the indigenous comrades is that they think that the only legitimate fight is theirs ... that this is in the law and that they have a special power, while the peasant struggle is not so legitimate because they are *llegados* [aliens ...]. They [indigenous] are claiming everywhere that they are ancestral, that they were the first and, as such, they have more rights than the rest of us. One doesn't say that they are not right, but with that discourse they simply don't want to recognise [other peoples' rights]. (Interview with an advisor to the PUPSOC, Popayan, November 2015)

Peasant frustrations led to a claim for the formation of two ZRCs in the neighbouring municipalities of Caloto and Corinto. As in the case of Inzá described in Chapter 5, the ZRCs are perceived by indigenous leaders as threats to the *resguardos* and particularly to their new claims of expansion in the lower valleys. Here, efforts to recover ancestral territory occupied by 'peasant *colonos*' have been ongoing since the 1970s (interview with the president of the Nasa Project Association, Toribío, November 2015).

   Besides the problems linked to the civil conflict, uncooperative indigenous attitudes are motivated by a perceived urgency to find new land to cope with the sustained demographic growth of indigenous communities. As the governor of Tacueyó told me, 'The first problem we have is that we have grown a lot in population and this is generating a very complicated problem of land tenure ... because, as we say, "the landless indian is condemned to disappear"' (interview, Tacueyó, November 2015). The indigenous leadership has attempted to encourage people to migrate by purchasing land in other departments (e.g. the southern Putumayo Department), but as the governor admitted:

It hasn't been easy because, according to our worldview, 'the indian always wants to be where his navel is'. So, we made several attempts to move several families to Putumayo last year, we bought land there, but that didn't work. One came back, the other came back and so on. (Interview, Tacueyó, November 2015)

According to local leaders, an expansion towards the western ridge could be made possible by the retreat of the guerrilla forces. However, this will jeopardise the conservation of higher elevation ecosystems (*paramos*) in the area, which are now protected as natural reserves.

The demographic problems that concern indigenous authorities in Toribío are far from unique to this *resguardo*. Very similar issues of land scarcity related to population growth are reported in the *resguardo* of San Andrés de Pisimbalá. These issues are exacerbating conflicts with the neighbouring peasants, described in Chapter 5. As the indigenous governor of San Andrés reported: 'The population is growing, but the territory is the same. So we are tight. The council makes projects so that the state can extend us. That's why we talk about extension of *resguardos*' (interview, San Andrés, November 2015). Another indigenous authority mentioned a study conducted to estimate projections of land needs:

Here between fifty and sixty children are born each year. Now we have more than a thousand children. In about fifteen years we'll be overpopulated. ... Here there is a shortage of land. A study was done and we need about 1,800 hectares. Maybe if we were to do another census, it would go up. At the moment the *resguardo* has 4,330 hectares, of which forty-five per cent is suitable for work. The rest are sacred sites, rocks, reserves ... So, here, we are gonna need more land. (Interview, San Andrés, November 2015)

DEMOGRAPHIES OF IDENTITY AND THE LIMITS OF STATIC RECOGNITION

Growing demographic pressure driven by both exogenous and endogenous factors has had a major impact on local geopolitics in many Andean regions, triggering new tensions that I have called demographic conflicts. Over the last two decades, the recognition framework has offered tactical tools (particularly through 'means of redistribution' embedded in recognition norms) with which indigenous communities can confront new demographic challenges related either to the arrival of new migrants or to population growth. The strategy of highlighting a group's ancestral ties to a territory as a requirement for cultural survival has been incredibly effective in gaining land claims. This strategy, however, has also led to the strengthening of social boundaries and opened new conflict fronts in the context of generally peaceful inter-group coexistence. These conflicts are linked to a very specific and static understanding of ethnic identities, which excludes indigenous migrants, as well as to a simplistic and crystallised view of socio-historical processes exemplified by the 'ancestrality' concept. These conceptual constraints make it very difficult for the recognition framework to account for the fluid and changing nature of human interaction and heterogenous social communities.

Despite growing historical and contemporary evidence documenting the patterns of mobility and migration of indigenous peoples, an assumption of spatial stasis is still widespread and, in recent years, has strongly influenced national and international frameworks of ethnic rights and recognition. As Alexiades (2009: 1) notes, 'there seems to be a widespread residual tendency to view indigenous societies, and their ethnoecologies, as historically emplaced: that is, as the product of a long history of engagement with particular locales'. This 'indigenous rootedness' is conceptualised as:

[a] long-standing connection to a rural, ancestrally defined, and communal land base. For a claim to indigeneity to become recognisable by institutions of governance (even if it is not fully recognised), it typically must be articulated in terms of a bounded territory of 'origin' associated with the group in question. (Greene 2007: 340)

In fact, however, the displacement, mobility and migration of indigenous populations is common across different historical phases. As a result of post-conquest demographic and political disruptions, relatively few indigenous groups today occupy the same territory they did a century ago, or in certain cases even a few decades ago (de Oliveira 1994). While the early expansion of the agri-extractive frontier triggered a process of spatial dispersion and a return to nomadism on the part of Amazonian groups – a phenomenon called 'agricultural regression' by Balée (1994) – new economic opportunities and changes in the commodity and crop markets have pushed people from the scarcely productive highlands towards urban centres, the coast and lowlands. This means that many among the so-called *colonos* are in fact of indigenous origin (from Quechua and Aymara communities in the central Andes). Yet migration often has the effect of erasing their ethnic identities. This can be partially explained by a change in self-identification preferences and modes of collective organisation, whereby the resettlement process makes ethnic ties less relevant, while at the same time debilitating traditional systems of authority and governance. However, ethnic dilution is also linked to established assumptions about the way ethnicity is conceived within the recognition framework and, in particular, the understanding of indigeneity as tied to a group's relationship to the land and its ancestral occupancy.

In the case of rural migration, not only are people leaving behind what are considered their ancestral lands, but the relocation within or close to a territory belonging to another ethnic group means that these migrants are confronted with competition over ethnic authenticity. In these contexts, even more than in urban settlements, it becomes incredibly difficult to reconstitute an identity and sense of community based on ethnicity. This is particularly challenging for highland migrants for whom the delineation of a discrete 'Aymara' or 'Quechua' territory, or ethnic identity for that matter, can be challenging even in their regions of origin (Albó et al. 1995). In most cases, migrants abandon ethnicity as the primary source of individual and collective self-identification in favour of a new sense of belonging as *colonos*. This new identity becomes, for many, a source of meaning that can form the basis for effective political mobilisation. This has been the case for coca-growing peasants in Bolivia who have organised in powerful 'colonisation associations' (recently rebranded as 'intercultural') at the local and national level. It was among the settlers of the Chapare region that the political career of the former Bolivian President Evo Morales started.

In general, however, the *colono* universe is densely suffused with negative stereotypes. The very word *colono* is charged with a derogatory connotation associated with the alleged greedy and self-centred attitudes of these groups and their unsustainable way of managing the environment.[7] In certain cases, these views are grounded in long-standing prejudices against highland inhabitants, exemplified in this quote from an interview with an officer of a Peruvian civil society organisation working in the Selva Central:

The people here are from Huancayo, Tarma, Huancavelica, Andahuaylas [highland departments], and they are people whose ancestors had been in litigation their whole lives. They are the ones who faced the Incas. If they are not fighting, they don't keep calm. They have that in their blood. So, those people who are increasingly entering, entering, for me, are a great threat to [indigenous] communities. (Interview, Oxapampa, April 2016)

---

[7] Other examples of such stereotypical and derogatory discourse are discussed in Chapter 7.

This kind of ethnic-based prejudice is not uncommon in other countries across the region. In Bolivia, the rivalry between indigenous peoples
and Andean *colonos* has added to the old tensions between highlands and
lowlands, and is yet another example of rural identity disarticulation. As
López Pila (2014) documented with an ethnography among the Tacana
communities in the Beni Department, the election of Evo Morales in
2005 contributed to generating new-found irritation towards the *colonos*
among the lowland communities,[8] who view migrant settlers as more
aggressive and better off. The quote below from a Tacana woman is a
good example of the kind of discourse used by indigenous peoples to
make sense of the difference between the two groups and describe the
threat posed by migrants:

> The *colonos* always try to get more, to make a profit . . . . [In contrast] we (Tacana)
> want to live peacefully and comfortably. We sell a chicken here or a tree-trunk
> there, but only in order to live in peace. But how can we do this, if the *collas*
> [highlanders] advance on us like termites taking our land and cutting down our
> trees to sell? (Cited in López Pila, 2014: 430)

This portrait becomes even more vivid when it is juxtaposed against
equally stereotypical narratives of indigenous peoples as the legitimate
inhabitants of the 'colonised lands'. Indigenous people are described as
community-oriented, innately devoted to protecting nature and committed to sustainability. Reality, however, is far more complex and diverse.
Indigenous peoples are neither 'good savages', nor is the colonisation
frontier an 'empty land', as governments have often claimed. Common
rhetoric surrounding migrants is in sharp contrast to evidence suggesting
that these social groups are often 'the poorest of the poor – the most
marginalised, least educated, largest households' (Carr 2009: 370),
among already impoverished and marginalised highland communities.
Given the vulnerable initial conditions of many among them, migration
strategies may in fact be closer to securing household survival rather than
accumulation of wealth and rent-seeking (Carr 2009). To be sure, this
is not to say that there are no differences between migrant settlers
and indigenous peoples in their modes of production and land management. It is, however, important to point out the effect of the distortions

---

[8] In contrast with Peru, in Bolivia the term *colonos* is exclusively reserved for indigenous
highlanders who migrate to the lowlands, and never used to indicate white/*mestizo*
migrants (López Pila 2014).

introduced by widespread stereotypes on interpreting social processes and collective identities, which in turn exacerbate inter-group differences.[9]

These migration disputes are common across Latin America. My main interest here is not to offer evidence for which group is better entitled to a given territory, but rather to illustrate how these controversies can often be linked to the shortcomings of recognition reforms. I argue that the recognition framework is not well equipped to deal with the fluidity of social interaction. These policies fail to acknowledge the historical depth and changes that territories have experienced throughout the centuries, as well as the current issues that communities are facing. It is certainly true that indigenous communities have been subject to a history of dispossession and marginalisation, for which they deserve some form of compensation. But it is often also the case that changes have been rooted in other less dramatic and disruptive events, or that contingent circumstances had been peacefully settled with the agreement and sometimes even in the interest of indigenous groups. Long-standing historical processes, whether rooted in violent or peaceful change, are condensed in contemporary social landscapes. In this context, recognition reforms should at least acknowledge this complexity, engage with broader questions about what social and cultural justice means for all the groups that inhabit a given territory (or what I call social communities), and discuss what are, in these specific contexts (and not in abstract, ahistorical scenarios), the moral grounds for reparatory action (particularly land distribution/restitution) as well as for denial of recognition (as in the case of migrants' illegal settlements). Moreover, more attention should be paid to understanding what lies behind indigenous claims. Endogenous demographic changes, for instance, have not been on the radar of researchers and governmental agencies. Problems faced by indigenous communities would require a more holistic approach, including, for example, economic initiatives to improve land productivity, which would contribute

---

[9] It is not only recent migration but, in certain cases, also historical migration that contributes to contemporary demographic conflict. A well-known example is the case of the indigenous Lacandone in southern Mexico and the long series of land conflicts with Choles and Tzeltales indigenous communities (Viqueira 1995; Trench 2005). Ethno-historical evidence was central to this dispute. Indeed, the origin of the contemporary Lacandones outside of Chiapas and their proved presence in the region for 'only' 300 years have been used (in contrast to the Choles and Tzeltales's presence, estimated at over 1,000 years) to discredit their status and land titles and to question their 'authenticity' as Maya descendants (de Vos 2002).

to a reduction in social and economic anxieties and prevent conflict linked to indigenous expansionistic strategies.

Finally, tensions surrounding migratory processes and demographic change are at least in part the result of a series of assumptions, embedded in international norms and then translated into domestic policy frameworks, which ground the right to ethnic recognition on territorial ancestrality, or 'a group's original relationship to the land' (Engle 2010: 163). As the cases in this chapter illustrate, establishing this 'original relationship' is an extremely complicated endeavour, and the determination of winners and losers is the result of factors that have little to do with historical and ethnographic evidence. It is rather linked to narrative competition, alliance-building and state biopolitics. As Greene (2007: 334) puts it, states seem to 'engage in a strategic recognition of certain Afro-Indigenous subjects in part as a strategy to not recognise certain others'. Moreover, even recognised groups 'are expected to remain, from the state's point of view, largely rural and immobile; those who represent themselves as more urban and mobile usually do not enjoy the benefits of collective recognition' (2007: 349).

Even a more culturalist argument that stresses the existence of customs and traditions, rather than physical primacy, is often unhelpful in providing for the resolution of demographic conflicts in practice. The logical step is to begin wondering whether a narrow understanding of recognition based on ancestry is in practice a good criterion for rights allocation, and whether indigenous peoples should be the only collectivities entitled to land and other rights (e.g. service provision) on the basis of their cultural ties with a given territory. This would imply renegotiating the grounds upon which international norms on indigenous recognition are built, and openly addressing the issue of whether collective rights can be made compatible with a more dynamic understanding of social communities. Rather than constructing artificial arguments to justify ancestry and tradition and viewing migration and changing ethno-cultural boundaries as deviations from the norm, it might be worth putting more effort into understanding how these dynamics are influencing ethnic self-identification, inter-ethnic relationships and, ultimately, access to rights. In the next chapter, I discuss other examples of how social boundaries rooted in new ethnic claims play out in the context of disputes triggered by recognition-inspired education reforms.

7

Struggles for Inclusion *and* Exclusion

Since the 1970s, the rise of identity politics has had a crucial impact on debates about the relationship between education and diversity. A new focus was placed on cultural and linguistic differences, as both sources of discrimination in the school environment and indispensable components of multicultural curricula (Vavrus 2015). In normative terms, this perspective contributed to popularising two major policy initiatives: intercultural (bilingual) education (IBE) and race-focused affirmative action (AA) measures. I term these initiatives, which, in different ways, have sought to account for ethno-cultural diversity in education, the 'identity policies in education'. More than three decades after these initiatives were launched, IBE and AA remain popular policies for ethno-cultural management in education across the world. I include these policies under the 'means of recognition' category, as their main effect rests on the crystallisation of ethnic categories in education norms and implementation, while their impact on redistribution is indirect and less substantial compared to other explicitly distributive recognition policies (e.g. agrarian reforms).

This chapter[1] includes examples of a type of recognition conflict that I have called access conflict. These conflicts lie at the intersection between means of recognition (affirmative action and policies with a weak redistributive vocation) and high heterogeneity in social communities in which they are implemented. Relying on case studies from Colombia and Peru, I question here some of the key arguments put forward by the advocates

---

[1] This chapter is based on Fontana (2019).

of identity policies in education regarding their potential to redress historical discrimination by levelling horizontal inequalities (inequalities between groups) and by granting equal value to different cultures and languages in the schooling system. This potential, I will show, is considerably weakened if one of the main assumptions of this framework is lost: that is, groups live in relatively homogeneous or segregated communities. Although it is certainly true that highly unequal and diverse societies are often characterised by limited social mobility and constrained inter-ethnic relationships, a closer look at local realities can in fact reveal, as I have already shown in several cases throughout this book, that communities are often more heterogeneous and interconnected than we might expect. In heterogenous social communities, changes to educational arrangements can therefore trigger horizontal inter-group competition and new claims for inclusion and exclusion that can become entrenched in protracted conflicts.

EDUCATION AND DIVERSITY IN THE ANDES

Intercultural (bilingual) education (IBE) refers to pedagogical models aimed at improving education for ethnic groups and tackling discrimination within society through teaching different cultures and languages on an equal footing (Cortina 2014: 3). Learning different languages also encourages increased receptiveness towards different cultures, and greater respect for ethnic and cultural diversity (López 2014). In practice, what intercultural education means and how it is implemented vary significantly depending on the country and time period in question. I adopt here a broad definition of IBE, which includes measures ranging from minimalist interventions such as the incorporation of intercultural concepts in nationwide curricula, to substantial reforms that grant autonomous administration of education and schooling to ethnic groups.

Affirmative action (AA) is a broad term that includes different measures used to 'give members of traditionally disadvantaged groups a better shot at social advantage' (Hasan and Nussbaum 2012: 12). Within the education sector, affirmative action has been implemented mainly through positive discrimination mechanisms that give an extra boost to members of disadvantaged groups (e.g. ethnic minorities, women) in competitive contexts. These measures typically concern increasing access to higher education through quota systems and differentiated entry requirements. AA measures usually exclusively target racial minorities, although in certain cases class-based and caste groups are also included (e.g. in India). Their implementation is generally motivated by 'compensatory justice' arguments (the need to remedy past discriminations), although they have also been used as conflict management tools aimed at reducing political instability and violence (Brown et al. 1990).

Latin America provides a very rich context in which to explore the impact of identity policies in education on the social fabric. Andean countries in particular have pioneered the implementation of a variety of identity-based education policies over the past thirty years. Education is a key component of their contemporary process of recognition of ethno-cultural diversity. Laws and regulations were passed recognising the right of indigenous peoples to education in their own languages (López 2009), and IBE was embraced by indigenous movements as part of their self-determination agendas (Gustafson 2014). Changes in multicultural language rights have also emerged in contexts of relatively weak indigenous mobilisation, as a 'side effect' of other institutional transformations such as decentralisation and new electoral systems, which resulted in the election of indigenous language speakers who then pushed for the official recognition of indigenous languages (Rousseau & Dargent 2019). As a result of social mobilisation and institutional reforms, different policy measures have been implemented to address the education gap and to acknowledge cultural specificities in education across the region.

In Bolivia, IBE started as a bottom-up endeavour (López 2014). In the late 1980s, indigenous and other grassroots organisations formulated IBE proposals that led to the implementation by the Ministry of Education of a nationwide IBE project, involving 114 rural schools and teaching in three indigenous languages (Aymara, Quechua and Guaraní) throughout primary school (Sánchez García 2007). These early experiences set the groundwork for the creation of an IBE National Directorate within the comprehensive educational reform of 1994 (Albó & Anaya 2003; López 2005). This reform made interculturality and popular participation the new pillars of the national education system (Sánchez García 2007). In order to guarantee qualified personnel, half of all Bolivian teacher-training colleges adopted an IBE curriculum with the direct involvement of indigenous leaders (Delany-Barmann 2009).

Since the early 2000s, however, IBE in Bolivia has lost momentum. The approach was questioned both because of its ties with the neoliberal policies of the 1990s (IBE was formally endorsed by the World Bank and the Inter-American Development Bank; Gustafson 2014) as well as its inability to become a nationwide model, being in practice relegated only to certain rural areas. The strongest opposition came from teachers' unions, who felt excluded from the negotiations on reform strategies and implementation from the outset (López 2014). The discussion on IBE was revitalised in the framework of the Constitutional Assembly from 2006. A new educational discourse, rooted in postcolonial theory and decolonisation ideology, emerged among indigenous activists and intellectuals and informed a new legal framework (Jiménez Quispe 2014). The Law 'Avelino Siñani – Elizardo Pérez',[2] approved in 2010, states in Article 3 that education is:

decolonising, liberating, revolutionary, anti-imperialist, depatriarchalising and transforming economic and social structures; oriented to the cultural reaffirmation of the indigenous nations and peoples, the intercultural and Afro-Bolivian communities in the construction of the Plurinational State.

The new framework also attempted to remedy some of the shortcomings of the 1994 reform. The new Intracultural Intercultural and Plurilingual Education (Educación Intracultural Intercultural and Plurilingüe) is conceived not as indigenous education but as education for all citizens (Ströbele-Gregor et al. 2010). In terms of implementation, at the local level, IBE seems to be slowly re-gathering momentum, but independently from broader reform. At the national level, indeed, most efforts have been directed towards the transformation of the university system at the expense of basic education. Indigenous universities have multiplied across the country and programmes targeted at training indigenous professionals have flourished in various academic fields (López 2014).

In Colombia, the first official initiative that attempted to address ethnic diversity in the education sector dates back to 1985, when the Ministry of Education approved the first Ethno-education Programme (Programa de Etno-educación). The main goals were to strengthen indigenous teacher training, improve pedagogic materials and incentivise research on indigenous culture (Enciso Patiño 2004). Since these early years, the policy-making process has been informed by the active participation of Colombian indigenous movements, which have been able to advance proposals based on concrete experiments in autonomous indigenous education. From the late 1970s, indigenous organisations in the Cauca Department have resisted both state and religious schooling and developed their own IBE projects (focused on pedagogical training and indigenous knowledge revitalisation), as well as a more radical proposal

---

[2] The law was named in memory of the founders of the Ayllu Warisata School Project (1931–1940), a pioneering example of agrarian indigenous education in Latin America.

for the implementation of an autonomous education system. Education programmes were conceived by the indigenous leadership as key components of their socio-political strategies: teachers were supposed to work as political mediators in their communities and autonomous schools were first established in communities with strong organisational capacities (Rappaport 2005). In the Cauca, schools run by the CRIC have been so widespread (over 600 according to the CRIC[3]) that, after 1985 and the approval of a national framework for intercultural education, they entered into competition with state-sponsored schools (Rappaport 2005).

The exceptional strength of indigenous movements contributed to the approval of a number of legal changes following the 1991 constitutional reform. In 1994, the General Law on Education included a chapter on ethnic education, and in 1996 the Ministry of Education published new guidelines that, for the first time, were directed also at Afro-descendent people (Rojas 2011). In the early 1990s, the Ministry of Education and the Colombian Institute of Educational Credit and Technical Studies Abroad (Instituto Colombiano de Crédito Educativo y Estudios Técnicos en el Exterior), with the support of international aid, created a fund to finance ethno-education, including a programme of credit directed at indigenous students enrolled in higher education (DNP et al. 2009). The wave of legal reforms throughout the 1990s, however, was followed by a very slow process of policy regulation and implementation.

In 2007, a National Working Commission for Indigenous Peoples Education (Comisión Nacional de Trabajo y Concertación para la Educación de los Pueblos Indígenas) was created, which included twenty-one regional leaders and aimed to craft a proposal for an autonomous indigenous education system (*sistema educativo indígena propio*, or *educación propia*). The work of the Commission led to the approval of a National Decree (2500) in 2010 to regulate the administration of local schooling by 'certified territorial entities', including traditional indigenous authorities and indigenous organisations. The Decree establishes that official schools could become subject to the autonomous regime when they are located in territories where the majority of the population is indigenous, and when they have been developing community projects and a full proposal for the implementation of autonomous indigenous education. The Decree also offers indigenous organisations the possibility of recruiting teaching personnel directly, based on criteria such as their

---

[3] Interview with CRIC's Education Secretary, Popayan, November 2015.

'sense of belonging and consciousness of cultural identity' (Art. 5) as well as their proficiency in the indigenous language. These provisions, as we shall see, raised a number of questions around the compatibility of indigenous and standard education, including critical details such as how to deal with the presence of non-indigenous students and teachers within or near to indigenous territories.

Peru has one of the longest histories of identity-based education policies in Latin America. Early indigenous bilingual education experiments date back to the first half of the twentieth century (López 1998; Schmelkes & Núñez 2009). Since the 1980s, in line with the rest of the region, the Peruvian government has intensified efforts to account for ethnic diversity in education policy. One of the first measures was the creation of a Directorate of IBE (that still exists under the name of the General Directorate of Bilingual and Rural Intercultural Education, Dirección General de Educación Intercultural Bilingüe y Rural), and the incorporation of a national IBE policy within the 1992 World Bank-sponsored education reform. This policy was renewed in 2002 (with the approval of IBE Law 27818). The 1993 constitution also introduced cultural and linguistic rights. In practice, however, little was achieved throughout the 2000s, particularly during Fujimori and García's right-wing governments (Aikman 2012; Rousseau & Dargent 2019). Recently, after a process of consultation with seven national indigenous organisations, a new impetus resulted from the approval of a sectorial policy on IBE by the Ministry of Education through Supreme Decree 006-2016 and of a National IBE Plan 2016/2021. The Plan sets some ambitious targets: 67 per cent indigenous students should complete secondary education; 85 per cent of pre-schools and primary schools should implement IBE pedagogy; and 100 per cent of IBE schools should possess adequate materials. The effort is to move towards a less targeted and more widespread implementation of IBE. It is a very ambitious goal considering that, according to the school census, in 2008 only 38 per cent of indigenous children attended intercultural bilingual schools; that IBE schooling had been offered almost exclusively in rural areas, completely excluding the rising population of indigenous urban residents; and that 46 per cent of teachers working in IBE schools did not have adequate training and few spoke the local indigenous language (PRONABEC 2014).

In order to address the lack of indigenous teachers, in 2014 a new scholarship programme was put in place that provides financial support to indigenous students pursuing university training to become IBE teachers. The scholarship, called the IBE Scholarship (Beca EIB), forms part of a wider National Scholarships and Educational Credit Programme (Programa Nacional de Becas y Crédito Educativo), and specifically of a programme called Beca 18, which targets the most vulnerable sectors of the population.[4] The Ministry of Education created another scholarship within the Beca 18 programme targeted at indigenous students from Amazonian communities (Scholarship for Amazonian Native Communities, Beca de Comunidades Nativas Amazónicas). These students require lower grades than their non-indigenous peers, based on the assumption that their schooling experience has generally been worse and on the subsequent impact of this on standardised test scores (Hernandez-Zavala et al. 2006). In 2015, 1,223 students received support through this programme (PRONABEC 2015). Affirmative action in higher education has only very recently been implemented in Peru and still represents a minimal percentage of the total number of scholarships issued by the government: by 2016, the Scholarship for Amazonian Native Communities only represented 3 per cent and the IBE Scholarship 2 per cent (1,030 in total) of all Beca 18 scholarships (Chaikuni 2016). Moreover, the former has a narrow focus on indigenous peoples from the Amazon, excluding the more numerous highland groups (Quechua and Aymara). This is a relevant difference that, as we shall see, is at the heart of local inter-group tensions.

STRUGGLE FOR *EXCLUSION* IN INZÁ, COLOMBIA

The town of San Andrés Pisimbalá, in the Inzá Municipality of western Cauca, is a paradigmatic example of how the implementation of *educación propia* can escalate into protracted violent conflict. It is also an interesting case by which to illustrate the complexity of recognition conflicts and the shifts and overlapping of underpinning mechanisms. This is indeed a conflict for social reproduction that has evolved into an access conflict. As I described in Chapter 5, San Andrés is one of the areas of the Inzá municipality affected by violent territorial disputes between indigenous and peasant communities. Over the past decade, the San Andrés *cabildo* has undertaken an expansionistic strategy by advancing new claims on peasant land based on ancestral holdings, directly occupying some of the peasant *fincas* scattered across the indigenous territory,

---

[4] Seventy-three per cent of recipients were in conditions of extreme poverty, while the remaining 27 per cent were below the poverty threshold (Chaikuni 2016).

which has resulted in outbreaks of violence. The focus of the contention then shifted to service provision issues, and particularly the control of the local school and the implementation of *educación propia*.

At the origin of this access conflict is a Decree (0591) issued by Cauca's Education Secretariat on December 2009, listing 666 schools across the Department as complying with the *educación propia* requirements. In line with national law, these schools could pass under the control of indigenous authorities. The Decree, however, triggered hostile reactions from communities, including San Andrés, where part of the population was in disagreement with the implementation of ethno-education in local schools. In an effort to de-escalate tensions, a second Decree (0102) was issued in 2010, which excluded thirty-two of the schools listed in the previous order. In San Andrés, however, the provision had the opposite effect, resulting in a new wave of aggression in the context of an already tense situation around territorial claims. Indigenous leaders initiated legal action against local and departmental authorities (CRIC 2010) and, just a few days after the approval of the new decree, indigenous protestors took over the local high school buildings, locking out more than 300 students. In the following months, the two opposing groups (those in favour of and those against *educación propia*) set up segregated informal schooling services. After two failed negotiation attempts (PUJC 2013), the *cabildo* opted to unilaterally proceed with the implementation of the *educación propia* project. With the support of the CRIC, teachers were hired and the buildings were re-occupied by indigenous students (interview with *cabildo* members, San Andrés, November 2015). The rest of the students, in the meantime, had been receiving their education in private or rented houses from some of the former teachers of the local school (interview with a member of the peasant organisation, San Andrés, November 2015).

The occupation of the school also exacerbated tensions between community factions, and led to the escalation of a conflict that took the form of a complex, multi-layered confrontation over control of local power and territory. Some residents, both indigenous and non-indigenous, reported that they were told they would lose the public benefits they received (through the *cabildo*), if they decided to withdraw their children from the indigenous school. According to local sources, around 160 were in fact excluded from the Family in Action (Familia en Acción) programme, which offers financial aid to families with children in school. This is an example of how, in the framework of recognition policies, indigenous organisations have become central brokers to accessing land

and other basic services, and how this brokerage function performed by ethnic leaders can be a key asset in recognition conflict.[5]

Some peasant families decided to leave the area as a result of the conflict. Among them were the parents of Alonso Secundino Pancho Tencué, a 21-year-old student killed in May 2011 on his way home from school. Those responsible for the crime were never identified. The guerrillas of the FARC, very active in the area until the peace talks started in 2012, claimed responsibility but, according to local residents, the murder was also linked to the school conflict (interview with members of the peasant organisation, San Andrés, November 2015).

Blackmail and threats continued to exacerbate tensions among local residents, particularly peasants, who felt the indigenous authority was preventing them from expressing their opinions. An indigenous woman who decided to leave the *cabildo* and join the peasant organisation, in protest against the way indigenous authorities managed the education dispute, told me: 'education is supposed to be a right and to be free ... but here they said "you have to go to the indigenous school", with teachers without degrees and with a very poor quality of education. So they force you to put your children there' (interview, San Andrés, November 2015). The quality of education under the new system was indeed one of the main concerns for some parents. Peasant families felt that an education mostly in Nasa Yuwe (the language of the ethnic majority) with a strong emphasis on Nasa culture, traditions and leadership skills was not appropriate for their children.

Peasants feel increasingly unsafe and unwelcome in a place they consider their home. Yet they do not oppose the idea of an indigenous school. Rather, they propose having two local schools, one adopting the *educación propia* model under the authority of the *cabildo* and the other managed by state institutions and offering a standard curriculum. Departmental authorities were open to this option and potentially to funding the construction of a second school. What might seem like a reasonable way out of the conflict from an external perspective, however, is challenged by an entrenched history of colonisation and discrimination. The two-school solution was, in fact, completely dismissed by the *cabildo*,

---

[5] Albeit without direct links to recognition reform, Pablo Lapegna's work (2016) on peasant organisations in Argentina provides useful insight into how the windows of political opportunity opened by the indigenous rights framework in many Latin American countries, and particularly the latter's redistributive implications, might have favoured the constitution of new clientelist networks and brokerage functions for ethnic organisations.

which considers it yet another expression of racism against indigenous peoples. With two different schools, 'the discrimination of us here and them there will continue' (interview with a former member of the CRIC secretariat, San Andrés, November 2015). As the indigenous governor put it, 'in such a small community we are not supposed to have such differences, because with that it just means there is racism, there is discrimination, they do not want us to be part of it [the school system]' (interview, San Andrés, November 2015).

Yet, only a few kilometres west of San Andrés, a two-school solution was pursued as a way to resolve a similar conflict between the indigenous *resguardo* of La Gaitana and the peasant community of Guanacas. As in San Andrés, the local school was first included in the Decree 0591 and then excluded from the list soon after. The school was neither on indigenous land, nor was it serving a majority of indigenous students. Yet the legal actions of the *cabildo* managed to bring the case before the Colombian Constitutional Court, which ruled in favour of the indigenous party, arguing that the right of prior consultation for indigenous peoples (established in international human rights law and incorporated in the Colombian constitution) had been violated when the school was excluded from the *educación propia* list (Sentence T-116/11). Peasants, on their part, also claimed their right to be consulted. As a result of the bipartisan consultation process, a new indigenous school was built on the *resguardo* land while the old school was downsized to serve the remaining students.

Before the two-school solution became inevitable, however, negotiation efforts were carried out to implement an experimental intercultural education model (neither indigenous nor standard), which would accommodate the needs of a complex demographic landscape consisting of a roughly half peasant and half ethnic population (including Nasa, Guambiano and Afro-Colombian people). Issues surrounding resource management and the hiring of teaching personnel prevented the parties from reaching an agreement. Peasants were keen to keep these elements under the control of the state, while the indigenous party was in favour of shifting towards an autonomous *cabildo*-led administration. Indeed, they considered that:

the project of appropriation of the school as a political and cultural strategy necessarily means that the [indigenous] authorities should control the management and orientation of this educational process, because the state, during all these years, has never guaranteed inclusion or interculturality in education. (Interview with the education secretary of the La Milagrosa indigenous association, La Milagrosa, November 2015)

This growing autonomy however raised concerns about the lack of formal protection for school personnel, including the right to unionise. Many of the peasant leaders are indeed teachers themselves. Originally from the area, they had access to higher education through scholarship programmes (some of them have degrees from elite Colombian universities) but decided to return to the region and contribute to its development. They now perceive that the radical take on education of the *cabildo* prevents them from engaging in an effort towards a better, more inclusive education arrangement that they had been pursuing for years:

We can transform this region, this country, through education, because knowledge is another form of power; but that knowledge has to be in everyone's hands. That's why we're still here; that is why many of us had opportunities in the city or to continue studying but we preferred to return and stay here because we want to change [the situation] with our example for our children and contribute to what we believe. (Interview with high school teacher and peasant leader, Guanacas, November 2015)

STRUGGLE FOR *INCLUSION* IN PANGOA, PERU

San Martín de Pangoa is a typical Amazonian town. A handful of mostly dirt roads form a chessboard on which brick buildings and partially unfinished houses surround the main square, overlooked by a modern version of a colonial church. The town is the capital of the Pangoa district, in the Junín region of central Peru. Its territory forms part of the Valleys of the Apurímac, Ene and Mantaro rivers (Valles de los Ríos Apurímac, Ene y Mantaro, VRAEM) – the only area in Peru still formally in state of emergency due to the presence of active guerrilla groups as well as drug trafficking. The district has a population of around 61,000, of which 6,525 are indigenous from two major Amazon ethnic groups (called 'native' as opposed to highland ethnic groups): Ashaninka and Nomatsiguenga (Cosavalente Vidarte 2017). The rest of the population is formed by peasant settlers, mostly of Quechua origin, who arrived over the last fifty years from coastal or highland regions, either through government-led 'colonisation' programmes or through spontaneous migration in search of land (Newing 2013). Natives and migrants live in small villages in close proximity to each other and, in some cases, in mixed settlements. This coexistence has generally been peaceful, although tensions, mostly around land tenure, are not uncommon. Lately, education has also become a contentious issue in Pangoa.

In 2014, the creation of a scholarship for Amazonian ethnic communities (within the Beca 18 programme) was applauded as an opportunity to improve access to higher education for students in the region. Some Quechua students were keen to apply, but soon realised that their application process was not as smooth as that of their Ashaninka and Nomatsiguenga colleagues. Alongside their application, students had to submit proof of belonging to an indigenous people and of residence in a native Amazon community (from those included in the Ministry of Culture's Register of Native Communities), signed by three communal authorities and endorsed by the regional or national indigenous organisation. Since Quechua migrants are not organised in ethnic associations and their communities are not among those recognised by the Ministry of Culture, it was practically impossible for Quechua students to comply with the scholarship's requirements.

Quechua parents were puzzled by this outcome and considered the exclusion of their children an act of discrimination on at least two grounds. Firstly, they argued, migrant children often attend the same local schools as native children (some of which are IBE schools). They also share similar conditions of poverty, marginalisation and insecurity. They therefore experience the same social gaps in their education and living conditions. Secondly, migrant families interpreted the Ministry's decision as an act of denial and misrecognition of their Quechua identity and culture (interview with a leader of the Quechua association, Satipo, April 2016).

Quechua families began to mobilise and won the support of the mayor of the Pangoa District, who issued a decree granting them recognition as an ethnic group. Yet the action failed to gain traction at the national level. The Ministry of Education remained strongly in opposition to the inclusion of Quechua students from the Amazon. The official view is that these students do not meet the ethnic criteria and should therefore compete for the income-based scholarship programme available to all Peruvian students. Moreover, their attempt to access the native peoples' scholarship is perceived as a way of 'tricking the system' unrelated to recognition and rights. In the words of a manager in the national IBE programme:

This [Beca 18 for native communities] is a national affirmative action initiative for some indigenous peoples, not for all indigenous peoples. And beyond that, one thing is a native community and another thing is a peasant community. In the Selva Central there are no Quechua peasant communities; there are only Quechua *colonos*. (Interview, Lima, April 2016)

In other words, only those Quechua communities from the highlands recognised by the Ministry of Culture have the right to an ethnic status.

Yet they are still not able to apply for this particular scholarship, which is only for Amazonian communities. Quechua people from the Amazon, for their part, cannot apply because their ethnic identity is not recognised.

This is not just a matter of bureaucratic labelling. It is yet another example of how group differences (between native and peasant, peasant and *colono*) can mark strong social boundaries of inclusion and exclusion, recognition and discrimination, articulation and disarticulation. These boundaries permeate the discourse, not only of bureaucrats, but of indigenous leaders themselves:

> The Amazonian indigenous peoples have reacted [to the Quechua mobilisation], because that does not apply: they are not peasant communities, they are groups of individuals that do not represent a people, as in the case of a native community. The native communities have territory, they have their identity, their own language, a whole culture and they have been here for years. They have history here in the jungle. That is not what the *colonos* have, because they have migrated, they have come from over there, their history is elsewhere. (Interview with indigenous leaders and local representative of the Ministry of Education, Satipo, April 2015)

> We [Ashaninka] have been living here for a long time, so we are a native people. The Quechua-speaking people have migrated to the jungle from the highlands and also from the coast. We call them *colonos*, because they have settled here. ... The Beca 18 is directed to the indigenous peoples that exist here in the Amazon rainforest.[6] (Interview with leader of the native organisation Ashaninka Council of the Rio Tambo, Central Ashaninka de Rio Tambo, CART, Satipo, April 2015, emphasis added)

This is precisely the discourse that generates resentment among Quechua residents. As I mentioned in Chapter 6, the very labels commonly used to describe the Quechua are derogatory: the term *colono* (not uncommonly coupled with 'invader') is associated with characteristics of greed, selfishness and environmental destruction. And for Quechua leaders, the expression 'Quechua-speaking people' also has discriminatory connotations:

> I am not a Quechua-speaking person. I am a Quechua person. I didn't learn Quechua afterwards, I was born Quechua from my ancestors and I am still

---

[6] Indigenous leaders were not satisfied with the scholarship programme. They highlighted how many native beneficiaries returned before finishing their programmes. They pointed the finger at the local schooling system, arguing that it is not adequate to prepare native students to compete with students from urban areas: 'the government says "I put you in the best university", but that child of the VRAEM cannot compete with a child of the upper class of Lima, it is impossible and all those young people come back frustrated' (Interview with CART leader, Satipo, April 2016).

Quechua. This is why we started to mobilise, because they were giving us names that do not correspond to our culture, to our vision. (Interview with Quechua leader, Satipo, April 2015)

An organisation of Quechua families was created in 2013. This organisation fights racism against migrant communities and supports the revitalisation of the Quechua language and culture, ultimately striving for the inclusion and recognition of 'Quechua native people with shades of the jungle' (interview with Quechua leader, Satipo, April 2015). The education issue is where Quechua migrants' struggles begin. Aside from the possibility of Quechua children from Amazonian communities accessing affirmative action programmes for native peoples, their demands include the implementation of an IBE in Quechua to reverse the vertiginous drop in the rates of Quechua-speaking children from migrant families. Attempts have also been made to reach out to universities and to set up bilateral agreements such as those that already exist with other indigenous groups.

The Quechua organisation is struggling to find support and funding. Cooperation agencies and NGOs, which have been major sponsors of indigenous movements in Latin America, have shown no interest in the Quechua migrants' cause. One of the main reasons behind their reluctance may be the widely documented impact that internal migration has on the pristine Amazon rainforest (Bierregaard 2001). If Quechua migrants are often considered the ones to blame, from their perspective there have been instances in which their rights have been violated too. In Pangoa, for example, settlers complain about their exclusion from a consultation process on a hydrocarbon exploration initiative that affected their land, but on which only native communities were consulted (interview with Quechua leader, Satipo, April 2015). Although the idea of a Quechua ancestral territory in the Amazon still sounds like an oxymoron, the Pangoa organisation is in many ways pioneering the struggle for inclusion and recognition of migrant communities in the Peruvian Amazon. It has done so by embracing the transnational discourse of the indigenous rights movement, emphasising discriminatory practices and referring to international human rights law for legal leverage. As a leader of the organisation told me, while proudly displaying the traditional Quechua straps wrapped around her braids:

If you don't make yourself visible, you are automatically *colono*, a synonym of Hispanic. ... Here in the jungle, it would seem that Quechuas have no legality, they should not exist in [regard to] rights or duties. The whole administrative and political system considers us Hispanic, from the city, and therefore we don't have any rights. But the ILO says that all native people have rights, under the political constitution. Why is it that this part of the jungle can't have any? (Interview, Satipo, April 2015)

INCLUSION AND EXCLUSION: THE TWO SIDES OF ACCESS CONFLICTS

Education policies are not rational, technocratic solutions to problems in wider society. They are inherently political because they are underpinned by ideas of identity, community, justice and rights. The politics of education are important 'means of recognition' as they define who (or which groups) can and should be recognised as bearers of rights and claims, ultimately reflecting 'the very shape and configuration of the society and the power relationships it entails' (Bacevic 2014: 18). Education policy-making not only responds to the claims of specific groups, but actively contributes to the re-creation, strengthening or dismantling of those very groups. In this chapter, I have illustrated how education policies both implicitly and explicitly affect social processes by reshaping inter-group relationships, collective identities and power dynamics. The two case studies are quite different in terms of levels of violence and social disruption, as well as in the type of policy measures at the heart of the controversy. Yet San Andrés and Pangoa exemplify the kinds of tensions and claims that identity-based education policy can trigger at the micro level, particularly in the framework of social communities already characterised by high levels of ethnic heterogeneity as a result of both long-standing colonisation and more recent migration processes.

As for other recognition reforms discussed in previous chapters, identity policies in education problematically target ethnic groups in an abstract fashion and as if they exist in isolation from specific social communities. Multicultural education approaches often assume the existence of 'bounded communities solidified through geographic and racialised borders' (McCarthy 1998: 159). In normative terms, these limitations are reflected in the tendency to treat racial and ethnic definitions as immutable and existing a priori, and to disregard historical variation in the practices of inclusion and exclusion and the redefinition of ethnic categories. It can of course be said that it would be hard to account for such complexity in national policymaking and that a certain level of generalisation is unavoidable. Yet issues of culture and identity are considerably less stable than what is proposed in the identity politics within the education framework. In practice, this overly simplistic view of ethnic and cultural differences prevents assessment of the consequences and impact of these policies in terms of the broader social community. Indeed, most groups that are targeted by these policies do not live in isolation, but rather share their environment with other groups, who are also likely to react to the implementation of identity policies. The two cases offer examples of how reactions to policy changes are not unidirectional, as it is often assumed. While they can lead to the rise of new grievances for inclusion, as in the case of Pangoa, they can also trigger demands for exclusion, as in Inzá. The dichotomous relationship between inclusion and exclusion should not be misleading. In this case, inclusion and exclusion are two aspects of the same problem, and particularly of the inability of recognition reforms to incorporate social heterogeneity and account for spill-over effects between groups.

Claims for exclusion are rooted in a narrow understanding of IBE as a distinct schooling model for ethnic communities, rather than a broader endeavour to strengthen intercultural exchange across society. As scholars have noted (García 2005; Aikman 2012), the emphasis on the bilingual rather than intercultural aspect of IBE is problematic because it can be perceived as perpetuating the process of differentiation and silencing of ethnic communities. But it also has nothing whatsoever to say to groups who might have needs or feel they have claims, but who cannot be defined in ethnic terms. It is not surprising therefore that *educación propia* is unlikely to be the solution for mixed communities struggling for truly intercultural education – and that the implementation of IBE in these contexts will hardly be successful if it ends up creating new mechanisms of exclusion.

Claims for inclusion clearly illustrate how assumptions of ethnic culture and identity as bounded, coherent and static fail to make sense of the multiplicity of identities that people embrace and the rapid changes in self-identification processes. The Quechua people in Peru are a clear example of how ethnicity can quickly go from being a derogatory category to an empowering tool. Until very recently, among peasant communities, being 'indigenous' was synonymous with backwardness, economic poverty and a lack of political power (García 2005; Aikman 2012). Now, it is increasingly common for Quechua people to embrace ethnic labels in claims for rights and recognition. The Pangoa case is indeed one of the first documented examples of how the ethnicisation of Peruvian peasants is slowly spreading from mining communities in the highlands (as in the case of Las Bambas, mentioned in Chapters 2 and 4) to the Amazon lowlands. This case also illustrates how narrow understandings of identity in education policies are unable to account for contingent social processes, such as migration dynamics and, again, the existence of complex, non-homogeneous schooling communities. Indeed, the very separation between school and community should be overcome and spaces for engagement and active social participation in school and education should be encouraged (Catalán Colque 2007; Zavala et al. 2007).

Issues of inclusion and exclusion are not only grounded in the way identity policies in the education framework conceptualise how social communities work, but also in the way these policies offer their own vision of a just society. At the macro-level, social differentiation criteria are generally justified by the need to tackle horizontal inequalities. Indeed, such policies are based on the idea that we should prioritise reducing inter-group inequalities over vertical inequalities across all identity groups (Brown et al. 1990). The micro perspective adopted here, focused on how these policies work in multicultural environments, contributes to high-lighting new normative dilemmas. In particular, it forces us to ask how inclusive identity-based education policies are in practice; or, more pre-cisely, whether the degree of exclusion they entail can be justified in moral terms and in terms of outcomes. On one hand, an 'empowering through strong boundaries' model can strengthen traditionally marginalised ethnic sectors, but can also widen social and intercultural gaps and weaken social cohesion. On the other hand, an 'equalising through melting boundaries' model closes social and cultural gaps, but also reduces the political power and internal cohesion of ethnic communities. To imple-ment these different models, AA and IBE can take very different forms. If the first model is better served by a demanding definition of ethnicity (e.g. language-based) as entry criterion for AA measures, the second model necessitates a variable framework that considers economic and spatial factors. For IBE, the two main options are a bilingual curriculum model targeted towards specific ethnic groups or the 'intercultural education for all' model. Different models better serve different national and local contexts. In a general sense, the experiences of San Andrés and Pangoa highlight the need for a thorough discussion about the meaning of social justice in multicultural education policymaking and recognition reforms more broadly (Gewirtz 1998). I take up the task of organising the evi-dence discussed throughout the empirical chapters, and reflect on their contributions to debates on equality and diversity, and recognition policy-making, in the final chapter.

8

Rethinking Recognition: What Are the Implications for Identity Governance?

This book argues for the need to closely examine recognition theories and politics in light of social facts. After digging into the very detailed empirics of recognition conflicts, it is now time to go back to the analytical and theoretical frameworks spelled out at the beginning of the book, and to consider the implications of my findings for broader debates on ethnic diversity and social justice. This concluding chapter makes three main contributions. The first is to summarise the main findings about recognition conflicts and how these can contribute to building bridges across the rigid continental divide that characterises recognition and ethnic conflict scholarship. I then discuss how the empirical evidence should encourage new thinking around the way in which recognition is theorised as a justice principle. Finally, I offer some recommendations on how to incorporate the book's findings into a policy agenda, or how to tackle these empirical and normative puzzles through concrete action and policy measures. In sum, I argue that the 'costs' and seeds of conflict linked to recognition politics should be addressed not by eliminating or curtailing recognition but, on the contrary, by 'levelling up' the recognition field so that more social groups can have access to it, and by implementing mitigation strategies that would reduce the 'side effects' of recognition on conflict and inequality.

TOWARDS A COMPARATIVE POLITICS OF RECOGNITION

Why are social groups that have peacefully cohabited for decades suddenly engaging in hostile and violent behaviours? What relationship do these conflicts have with changes in collective self-identification, claim-making and rent-seeking dynamics? And how, in turn, are those changes driven by broader institutional, legal and policy reforms? Through extensive empirical data, I have shown that the key feature recognition conflicts have in common, besides being horizontal conflicts involving two or more social groups, is that they are related to the implementation of recognition reforms. Specific legal or policy measures vary significantly, ranging from land titling to education policies, affirmative action, and participatory governance. Whether at the national, regional or local level, these measures are all part of the project of incorporating ethnic groups into the framework of multicultural or plurinational models of citizenship and statehood. In contexts of high multidimensional fragility, linked in particular to social heterogeneity and the endemic lack of resources experienced by social communities, the legal protection and rights offered by the recognition framework are perceived by certain groups as an opportunity to gain access to power and resources. And rightly so. In remote rural areas, the state generally has a very weak presence and rural communities have for decades been looking for opportunities to either be included in the state-building process, or to be granted some degree of autonomy. For indigenous peoples, recognition serves both purposes: it formalises self-government and territorial control, while creating new spaces for the integration of ethnic groups within a new multicultural or plurinational state. It also offers access to very concrete resources, including land, and, in certain cases, direct monetary transfers from central government, which can significantly improve situations of widespread poverty and marginalisation.

In these contexts, ethnicity has acquired new social and political salience following the implementation of recognition reforms. Through a more or less radical process of 'reinvention of tradition' (Hobsbawm & Ranger 1983), ethnic identities have been strengthened (as in the Nasa communities of the Cauca), revitalised (as for the Quechua migrants of Peru) or created anew (as for the Leco people of Apolo). This does not imply that they are less authentic or real than other identities, or that they are alien to pre-existing cultural markers and systems of beliefs. There is no doubt that identity-based claims reflect the real aspirations, desires and frustrations of groups that have been living at the margins of Latin American societies and have experienced persistent discrimination and abuse. In other words, I do not intend here to undermine in any way the problems that communities have been facing and their choices in terms of self-identification and collective mobilisation strategies. What I have tried to highlight is that claiming allegiance to an ancestral past and an ethnic identity is contingent upon a given socio-political context, which has not always been the case even in relatively recent times (as I discussed in Chapter 3).

The process of ethnic boundary-remaking shaped by the 'means of recognition' is often accompanied by tensions. Indeed, while for certain groups claiming allegiance to an ethnic culture has been relatively smooth, other groups have been unable or unwilling to be recognised as ethnic subjects. They have therefore been excluded from accessing the new rights and resources that recognition reforms have made available for ethnic groups. This differential treatment is fuelling resentment and a feeling of injustice, particularly in those locations where ethnic and non-ethnic groups have been coexisting in generally peaceful social communities for decades. In other cases, it is the increase in social heterogeneity triggered by migration and population growth that is at the root of new tensions. Finally, as I have shown throughout the book, the endemic lack of resources is also a key factor to consider for understanding the occurrence of new conflicts. Indeed, recognition reforms are generally particularly tense in remote rural areas characterised by widespread poverty and precarious livelihoods. In these communities, the 'means of redistribution' embedded in recognition reforms offers certain groups the opportunity to gain access to strategic resources (particularly land), while leaving other local groups in a worse-off position.

The seeds of conflict embedded in recognition reforms that I have analysed throughout the book are the unintended social costs of recognition. These costs emerge only when we look 'in the shadow' of recognition reforms, at the margins of Andean societies where broader vertical struggles for rights and resources spill over into horizontal inter-communal conflict and competition. These horizontal conflicts offer empirical grounds for a powerful critique of one of the key arguments of proponents of recognition concerning the potential of indigenous rights to resolve social tensions linked to inequality and marginalisation. In Latin America recognition has certainly provided effective and popular solutions for the inclusion of ethnic minorities within national societies. Yet, as I document in this book, it can at the same time increase inter-group competition and worsen social cohesion in ethnically heterogeneous and economically fragile communities. These findings show that Latin America shares more similarities with other contexts than scholars have generally considered. Similar tensions around the implementation of indigenous rights and their potential to reinforce a class system that marginalises the poorest even further have been documented by Alpa

Shah in the case of India (2010), while in southern Africa, the redistribution of land to San indigenous peoples excluded the landless San farmers who did not conform to the indigenous stereotype (Sylvain 2014). Latin American countries are characterised, on average, by a lower degree of ethnic diversity, better economic performance and more effective state institutions compared to many Asian and African countries. The evidence presented here should therefore encourage a closer look at the conditions under which a recognition agenda might be pursued in other regions, particularly when it comes to the implementation of regimes tasked with the local governance of ethnicity.

There is at least one other key finding of this book that will be of particular interest to scholars working on ethnic politics beyond Latin America. This relates to the complexity and variation in the reshaping of ethnic boundaries. As I described in the introduction, there is a general consensus on the difficulty of negotiating ethnic categories in Asia and Africa. In the case of Asia, the question of who is indigenous has been referred to as the 'Asian controversy' (Kingsbury 1998). On one hand, groups across the region have started to mobilise as indigenous peoples and to participate in international meetings and be part of transnational networks. On the other, Asian states have argued that the concept of indigenous peoples is a product of European colonialism and is therefore not applicable to most parts of Asia. In Africa, a continent that experienced widespread European colonisation, one of the core arguments behind the reluctance of scholars and policymakers to embrace the indigenous rights framework has been precisely around the difficulty of discerning who is indigenous. African states have successfully fought for their independence and they do not consider themselves to be responsible for decolonising their tribal populations (Kymlicka 2007). In contrast, Latin America is generally perceived as a context in which the distinction between indigenous minorities and white/*mestizo* majorities is relatively straightforward. The cases of recognition conflicts presented in this book, however, are examples of how contentious ethnic categorisation can be even within the Latin American context. Again, Latin America may have more similarities with other regions and countries across the Global South than has generally been assumed.

Since the 1980s, ethnic studies in Latin America, Asia and Africa have taken completely different paths and, thirty years later, attempts to bridge the gap between extraordinarily siloed and non-overlapping debates remain quite limited. Yet there are clear advantages in comparative cross-continental approaches. As I argued in this book's introduction,

considering context-dependent variables when studying the implementation of recognition reforms is paramount to understanding variation in
policy effectiveness as well as unintended consequences. To this end,
cross-continental perspectives could add important insights that have
yet to be fully explored.

SOCIAL JUSTICE AND THE POLITICS OF RECOGNITION

Recognition conflicts certainly need innovative analytical tools in order to
fully understand the characteristics of the norms as well as the features of
social communities that underpin them. They also encourage new thinking around how recognition is theorised as a justice principle. Critical
scholars of recognition have extensively discussed the limitations of theories of recognition (Remotti 2001; McNay 2008; Dick 2011; Pilapil
2015). Most of them, however, ground their critiques exclusively
in political philosophy arguments. My contribution adds to these critical
perspectives by discussing theoretical arguments in the light of
empirical evidence. As Miller (1999: 56) acknowledges, 'greater weight
to empirical evidence about justice' should be a key component of
theoretical justification.

   One common criticism of recognition is that it too often succumbs to
essentialism. Identities are taken as given and as part of an individual or
group essence that tends to remain constant across cultural and historical
boundaries. This perspective is particularly attractive when trying to
explain collective action grounded in concepts of ancestrality, authenticity
and culture – as in the case of indigenous claims. In this framework,
identities are also understood as expressions of common and long-
standing experiences of oppression. Yet this perspective is clearly in
tension with constructivist understandings of how collective identities
work. It is also incompatible with any conceptualisation of identities as
endogenous to economic, political and social processes. One of the most
powerful ways recognition reforms generate performative effects on collective identities is by setting the rules for the very access to recognition
based on positive discrimination criteria. There are three main arguments
commonly used to justify special group rights. These arguments rely on
both moral and empirical observations, and, although they all have some
degree of validity, they also contain some relevant flaws. These flaws are
important to understanding why the implementation of recognition can
ultimately be a very tense and conflict-prone endeavour.

The first argument is a historical one and makes the case for the need to redress past experiences of domination and segregation due to some ascriptive characteristics as the main roots of current inequalities (Richardson 2012). As Brown et al. (1990) note, this criterion makes sense when every member of one group is better off than every member of another group. It can, however, become problematic in cases of intra-group heterogeneity or when the outcomes of recognition bring the discriminated group not to a position of equality but of advantage compared to other groups. It can be argued that this is the case for certain indigenous communities that benefitted over a significant period of time from access to land, public services and state resources, while other non-indigenous communities were left behind. These situations have fuelled perceptions of relative injustice for peasants across the Andean region, particularly in Peru and Colombia, where peasants' claims for recognition have remained almost completely unattended to, especially if compared to indigenous rights, which have been included in these countries' constitutions and legal frameworks.

The second argument is a cultural one. It is grounded in the acknowledgement that indigenous peoples have a unique relationship with the territory they occupy and that that specific territory is constitutive of their identity. Article 3 of ILO Convention 169 mandates governments to 'respect the special importance for the cultures and spiritual values of the peoples concerned of their relationship with the lands or territories . . . and in particular the collective aspects of this relationship'. It is certainly true that indigenous communities have a long history of living in symbiosis with their natural environment and that they attribute to it religious and spiritual value. This argument has two major flaws, however. On one side, it ignores the fact that indigenous communities do move, and while identity is portable, territory is not. Linking recognition with a given territory, therefore, prevents indigenous migrants from gaining access to recognition. More broadly, it raises questions around the definition of citizenship: 'how can one attain full political citizenship at the national level if one's special rights are constrained by residence in a particular place' (Shneiderman & Tillin 2015: 35)? On the other side, this argument focuses on the exclusiveness of this relationship, failing to acknowledge that other social groups may share a similar sense of belonging to a place, as indigenous peoples do. In other words, cultural attachment to physical space is not unique to indigenous communities, but it is common, although in different shapes and forms, among rural communities in general. Moreover, given the importance of land control for any communities making a living from subsistence farming, would a certain type of cultural attachment to a territory be the best proxy to establish whether and in what form communities deserve secure access to land?

The third argument is economic and is based on the observation that indigenous people are the poorest within Latin American societies. According to the World Bank, 'indigenous peoples worldwide continue to be among the poorest of the poor and continue to suffer from higher poverty, lower education, and a greater incidence of disease and discrimination than other groups' (World Bank 2010). According to the Food and Agriculture Organization (FAO), 'although they account for less than 5 per cent of the global population, they comprise about 15 per cent of all the poor people in the world'.[1] At the end of the 'indigenous decade' (1994–2004), in Bolivia, Ecuador and Guatemala, three-quarters of the indigenous population were classified as poor (Hall & Patrinos 2005). This situation has traditionally been linked to the impact of colonisation and unequal economic development which, as the director of the pro-indigenous NGO Survival International wrote, 'turned most of the survivors into dispossessed paupers' (Corry 2011). A strong correlation certainly exists between poverty and ethnic belonging. Yet these two variables are not always synonymous (Seligmann 1995). In 2017, almost half of the rural population in Latin America was poor and about one-third indigent (FAO 2018). If we consider that indigenous peoples represent around 8 per cent of the region's population and that nearly half of them now live in urban areas, most of the rural poor are in fact not indigenous, or not recognised as such. In sum, not all indigenous are poor and not all poor are indigenous (World Bank 2018). Moreover, macro-data are sometimes poor indicators of micro-social realities. Local contests, as I have shown, are usually quite heterogeneous and, at this scale, the economic divide between ethnic and non-ethnic groups tends to become less sharp. It is indeed a common trait in all the cases analysed in this book that a significant percentage of the local population live in conditions significantly below the poverty threshold, independently of whether they identify as indigenous or peasants. If socio-economic features within specific social contexts are not considered, recognition is likely to lose its equalising potential. This is particularly the case when measures with a significant redistributive component are applied as necessary steps towards full ethnic recognition.

---

[1] Information retrieved from FAO website, http://www.fao.org/indigenous-peoples/en/.

Analysis of recognition conflicts inevitably steps into the long-standing discussion on recognition and redistribution as the two poles of social justice and collective mobilisation. The redistributive component is particularly relevant in contexts characterised by high levels of poverty and precarious livelihoods, as those where inter-communal conflicts are most likely to occur. Yet redistribution has generally been neglected by recognition scholarship. Bringing redistribution 'back into the picture' also has, I argue, a theoretical merit: it contributes to challenging the mainstream epistemological shift from class to identity, and from redistribution to recognition. It is indeed legitimate to wonder whether the criticisms of ethnically blind twentieth-century interpretations that I described in Chapter 3 have not, in fact, transitioned towards equally unbalanced class-blind analytical frameworks. Social scientists have tended, in recent years, to overlook existing social class structures and the role still played by class in shaping society, from global political economies to local social hierarchies (Gibson-Graham 1997). In fact, class analysis may very well benefit studies of indigenous movements and ethnic populations, whose complexity has been growing in recent decades. In particular, they are instrumental in understanding these movements' new political roles and patterns of social mobility linked to their incorporation into market economies and urban environments (also referred to as 'cholification' in the Andean context; Greene 2007). The key example here is probably the one of Bolivian Aymara traders who, taking advantage of the growing inflow of contraband goods and increasing access to Asian markets, are now in control of a major part of the Bolivian retail economy, while running thriving transnational businesses. These new entrepreneurs have been undergoing a 'cultural renaissance', maintaining strong bonds with the indigenous world while still failing to fully integrate within the national bourgeoisie (Tassi 2010; 2017). The classic Marxist discussion about status differences among the peasantry (Wolf 1969; Alavi 1973) and their implications for peasants' progressive vs conservative attitudes could perhaps be of inspiration in developing a class analysis of contemporary indigenous groups that fully considers their socio-economic heterogeneity.

We should be careful, however, to avoid 'throwing the baby out with the bathwater'. Replacing redistribution with recognition is not desirable either. The merits of recognition as an analytical and policy tool are not negligible. Recognition has allowed a key dimension of social claims that has to do with the importance of culture, identity and sense of belonging to be captured and debated. Yet, in its most widespread interpretation, recognition has a rather narrow focus on specific social groups, often conceptualised in terms of ethnically differentiated minorities (Kymlicka 2001; Postero & Zamosc 2004; Stavenhagen 2007; Canessa 2012). These social groups are also considered for their collective action potential (as social movements) in claiming differentiated rights, inclusion and citizenship (Le Bot 2009). This framework, in other words, implies a highly normative interpretation of recognition.

As the cases presented in this book illustrate, however, more than a claim proper only to ethnic minorities, recognition seems rather a necessary attribute for each and every collective actor. As Hannah Arendt (1958) pointed out, identity is not so much a substance as a requirement: that of knowing (and being able to define) who we are dealing with. To recognise is, therefore, first and foremost the operation through which an observer identifies something or someone as durable and different from whatever surrounds it. Recognition operates by selecting those identities that enable the establishment of a cognitive order in a differentiated social landscape. Hence, it would be more appropriate to talk about the recognition needs of each and every individual and collective actor, where recognition is a general form of identity distinction that includes a plurality of elements (not just ethnicity) and that is compatible with strategic decision making. Indeed, recognition could be a *need* that is not necessarily beneficial for the whole population, but, in certain cases, responds to the agenda of a small group, for example, an elite or a few leaders. In this sense, recognition claims cannot be understood only through the lens of rights. The dimensions of power and interests must be considered as well.

This broader perspective on recognition allows us to reconceptualise recognition as an analytical rather than a normative concept, and focus on its descriptive rather than prescriptive potential. Following Rossi's (2017: 18) conceptualisation of recognition in his book on the *piquetero* movement in Argentina, recognition can be understood as the 'initial quest linked to the popular sectors' disruptive emergence in protest', which is generally followed by socio-economic conflict and the quest for political incorporation. This broader analytical understanding of recognition also has the merit of shedding light on struggles that have shifted into the background, as in the case of labour movements but also peasant and Afro-descendant movements – mainly because of the narrow focus taken by mainstream debates on recognition.

There is another aspect that common arguments supporting recognition reforms fail to consider: setting the rules for recognition is a highly contentious process imbued with politics, whose outcomes are determined not only by moral arguments but by contingent relationships of power and prevailing interests involving different groups. This aspect is best illustrated in this book by the debates on FPIC. This new tool for participatory governance generated intense discussions around who should be the subject of this right, and notably whether peasant communities should be entitled to consultation or not. What is at stake here, rather than a moral paradigm, is a procedural approach to defining who holds rights and deserves recognition. In the case of FPIC, as we have seen, Andean countries diverge in how they define the subject of consultation, with Bolivia including peasant communities, Colombia excluding them and Peru adopting a case-by-case approach. In practice, these differences imply that millions of people are either included or excluded from the right to be consulted. And even after an agreement is reached in principle, the porous boundaries of ethnic identities mean that rules can be challenged on a case-by-case basis. For example, Quechua settlers in the Peruvian Amazon are now engaging in a process of revitalisation of ethnic markers in order to support their claim for inclusion in affirmative action measures. If the entitlement to an ethnic identity is questionable, the concept of cultural distinctiveness is even more open to debate. Indeed, as peasant associations in Inzá argue, the unique culture and identity of peasant communities should also give them access to special rights (including some degree of territorial autonomy as well as prior consultation).

The process of tracing ethnic boundaries is not only contentious, but always implies a certain degree of arbitrariness. It is indeed about establishing a cut-off point along a number of continuous variables, such as groups' collective sense of belonging, cultural differentiation and even language proficiency. Those groups that, for historical reasons, are better able to comply with the established criteria will be more likely to be granted recognition, compared with those groups that cannot easily subscribe to those criteria, or refuse to do so. There is, in other words, a problem of distribution of opportunities that may, in certain cases, not even reflect a common understanding of indigeneity. Visiting highland communities in Peru may be perceived by an outsider as a close approximation to what stereotypical imaginaries of Andean indigenous peoples look like. Many would be surprised to know that most of those communities do not consider themselves, nor are they recognised, as indigenous. Equally, first-time visitors are often disappointed to travel to remote Amazon communities and find that indigenous peoples commonly wear Western clothes, carry around the latest generation smartphones, and move up and down the river in fast motorboats. It would perhaps be easier to establish cross-cutting criteria if all indigenous peoples looked like the 'avatars' portrayed in Hollywood movies. Such homogeneity is far from the reality of ethnic communities in Latin America. The relative arbitrariness of recognition criteria, therefore, ultimately undermines the value of identity fitness as a moral metric. Are those groups that can better adapt to state-crafted indigeneity more worthy of cultural and social recognition? And, if ethnicity is often endogenous to institutional change, can identity then be considered a sufficiently robust criterion for the allocation of differentiated rights and resources?

TOWARDS A MUTUAL CONSTRUCTION OF INCLUSION

Fairness is not only a moral but an empirical puzzle. It is now clear that recognition conflicts open up new moral dilemmas around the implementation of recognition reforms and their underpinning model of social justice. These dilemmas often complicate the quest for practical solutions. Given the prolonged and sometimes violent nature of recognition conflicts, parties are generally stuck in confrontational and competitive patterns of behaviour, supported by narratives of estrangement and resentment. Even when parties are both willing to engage in dialogue and negotiation, the path towards resolution remains scattered with many uneasy questions. I summarise here some of the questions that I have already more or less explicitly raised throughout this book. They concern both larger issues and specific cases, and they are all underpinned by moral and empirical puzzles. Given the complexity of the Andean ethnic landscape, what criteria would be most appropriate for tracing recognition boundaries? Is a loose self-identification criterion more appropriate than stricter markers, such as language proficiency, or vice versa? Should FPIC be a right only for indigenous/native peoples or should it be expanded to other rural communities? Should Quechua migrants in Pangoa be granted an ethnic status and therefore be entitled to the same scholarship as their native neighbours? Should peasant students in Inzá have the right to opt out of the *educación propia* system, or should indigenous peoples have the right to enforce their educational model within the territory they control? Is two-school modelling a fair or a discriminatory solution? Who are the victims of the Flor de la Frontera conflict: the indigenous peoples who suffered illegal occupation of their land or the peasant settlers who were granted illegal land titles? Are the expansionistic strategies put in place by Cauca's *resguardos* a legitimate means of consolidating their territory and autonomy? Should indigenous peoples in Apolo be given priority over peasants in the process of land titling? Is the Colombian peasants' appeal to a unique identity and cultural recognition as a way of claiming differentiated rights legitimate?

These questions have no simple answers. More importantly, it is clear that the recognition framework does not offer a clear map or moral horizon to navigate these dilemmas. New thinking is needed around the effects of recognition and the chain of actions and reactions triggered by recognition reforms. This is particularly important when it comes to the local governance of recognition. The outcomes of policymaking are often uncertain; yet, after more than twenty years of implementation of recognition reforms, it is time to look closely at both their broader and localised impact. Recognition conflicts offer a window on a number of problematic issues around recognition. Most of these issues, however, can be prevented or moderated. In fact, simple awareness of these dilemmas may inspire a more cautious design and implementation of recognition reforms. Furthermore, other strategies could be considered to mitigate the seeds of conflict inherent in recognition.

One of the problems with recognition politics is that they are self-referential in their assessment and they generally predict a win–win scenario. Yet, as we have seen, recognition can trigger zero-sum games. This is particularly the case when recognition relies on redistribution of scarce and valuable resources – such as land – or when it is implemented in highly heterogeneous and deprived social communities. A telling example of a zero-sum game is the strategy of expansion of *resguardo* territories in the Cauca region through the acquisition or occupation of surrounding peasant and Afro-descendant lands. When zero-sum dynamics are at play, the post-recognition scenario is likely to be populated by winners and losers. Some measures can, however, be taken to prevent or moderate potential conflict. The most obvious is to refrain from evaluating the outcomes of recognition policies only with respect to those groups that directly benefit from recognition, and to introduce instead evaluation methods that include the broader social communities. Otherwise, successful outcomes for one group may result in negative effects for other groups, or the deterioration of the overall situation.

Before getting to the evaluation, which by definition happens after policy implementation, other strategies could be adopted to prevent conflictive outcomes. An example is to account for the need to offer compensatory measures to groups that may be negatively affected by the implementation of recognition reforms. Rather than monetary compensation, these measures should aim at expanding and consolidating communities' rights and should answer distributive claims. For example, while granting land titles to indigenous peoples, offering peasant communities the resources and technical expertise to be able to secure land tenure could prevent feelings of resentment and horizontal conflicts. In the case of Apolo, for example, peasants' perceived injustice is fuelled not only by the fact that the Leco's land claim was fast-tracked and ultimately successful, but by the realisation that the costs of the technical procedures to issue the title were taken care of through international cooperation funding, while no funds were made available for peasants to title their land. The conflict could probably have been moderated by offering poor peasants the means to secure control of their communal territories.

Conflict mitigation through compensatory measures is, however, not always possible and does not generally offer any long-term solutions for a sustainable intercultural coexistence in ethnically diverse territories. Heterogeneous social communities require more inclusive arrangements, rather than the exclusive model offered by recognition reforms. This is clear from looking at how, in some of the cases analysed in this book, the parties seemed to be converging around compromise solutions acceptable to all groups. One example is the case of the land conflicts in Inzá, where innovative models of 'intercultural territorialities' were at some point on the negotiation table. Yet a rigid understanding of territorial configurations and the lack of institutional instruments to support solutions involving compromise prevented this proposal from being seriously taken into consideration. Another example is the informal agreements that are in some cases signed between indigenous communities and migrant settlers in order to regulate their relationship and access to resources. These arrangements are often imperfect and do not offer a priori any guarantees about either sustainable environmental management or respect for accountability and broad participation in decision making. This is, however, partially because they happen outside any legal or institutional framework. It is not a matter of signing off any successful local negotiations or arrangements, but it is nevertheless important to learn from these experiences. It should now be clear that the existing models of recognition do not resolve issues of social justice in many complex scenarios. Efforts should therefore be put into developing alternative models that address the needs for intercultural governance and peaceful coexistence.

But taking seriously the proposals coming from the territories is unlikely to be enough. Broader claims for recognition and redistribution will also need to be addressed to prevent recognition conflicts from arising. Following the conceptualisation of recognition as a universal need, the state should opt for an inclusive approach to recognition that acknowledges the cultural value of both ethnic and non-ethnic identities. A claim for recognition is now explicit in the discourse of Colombia's peasants, while in Peru peasant organisations are in the process of pursuing ethnicisation campaigns of their grassroots in the hope of gaining visibility and a voice in the political arena. Ethnicisation has proved to be an effective strategy to gain recognition. Yet a broader understanding of recognition would allow social groups to choose among a range of collective identities, rather than force people into categories that they do not truly embrace or feel represented by. Andean countries have done a lot in recent years to tackle racism. In Bolivia, for example, a historic law was passed in 2010 with the aim of establishing 'mechanisms and procedures for the prevention and sanction of racism and any forms of discrimination' (Law 045). Focusing on ethnic diversity was indeed an important step towards the redressing of long-standing discrimination rooted in the colonial past. But building a more inclusive society requires addressing different forms of stigmatisation, even those that have no direct colonial origin. Across the Andes, peasants and particularly internal migrants are highly stigmatised groups. As indigenous peoples, they are also over-represented among marginalised and poor communities. A broader recognition framework could offer powerful tools to redress many forms of social and racial stigmatisation in these societies, beyond the indigenous question.

A broader approach to recognition should be accompanied by policies with a wider redistributive potential. There remains a long way to go to significantly reverse the conditions of poverty and marginalisation in indigenous communities. However, recognition reforms have achieved some notable improvements in addressing distributive claims by offering land security, access to financial resources and service provisions. However, the redistributive effects of these policies benefit only a small percentage of the rural poor, while strategies to improve the condition of rural communities more broadly have been lacking. The main reason for this may be political. As we have seen, indigenous recognition has been unanimously embraced across the political spectrum. This can be explained by the relatively limited material and immaterial costs that these reforms entail for political elites. A paradigmatic example is agrarian reform. Since the 1990s, a substantial amount of land has been titled in favour of indigenous peoples. In Colombia, a third of the national

territory is now in the hands of indigenous communities. How can we
make sense of the fact that arguably the most conservative among the
Andean countries agreed to cede property rights over such a huge expanse
of land? I argue that this (as with most agrarian reforms across Latin
America since the 1990s) can be understood as a strategy adopted by
elites to minimise the costs of redistribution, while maximising the volume
of redistributed land. Territories claimed by indigenous peoples are usually remote, often overlap with national parks and public land, and do not
have strategic value in terms of agricultural exploitation. They do, however, have significant commercial value when other commodities are
considered, such as hydrocarbons and other natural resources. This is
why countries have carefully crafted what kind of control communities
retain over their territories, generally excluding subsoil resources. At the
same time, Andean countries are still waiting for substantial agrarian
reforms to be carried out. Colombia, where two-thirds of agricultural
land is concentrated in just 0.4 per cent of farmland holdings, is the worst
case in the entire Latin American region (Guereña 2017). In Bolivia,
where land titling has been carried out at a faster pace over the last
decade compared to other Andean countries, problems remain around
the unequal agrarian structure and modes of production (Colque et al.
2016). In Peru meanwhile, between 1994 and 2012, there was an increase
of more than 40 per cent in the number of smallholder farms (less than
five hectares), but the total area occupied by them did not increase,
resulting in the shrinking of holding size from 1.7 to 1.3 hectares on
average (Guereña 2016). The real challenge in these countries is to
implement strategies of redistribution for the rural poor as a whole.
Indigenous recognition is only one piece of the puzzle and alone does
not address burning issues around social inequalities.

Yet tackling broader issues of inequality is a necessary condition to
ensure that the implementation of recognition is less conflictive.
A different, integrated model of governance of cultural differences and
social inequalities would need to replace the incentive mechanisms that
have fuelled, over the past thirty years, higher levels of social competition.
This model should incorporate mechanisms oriented towards the mutual
construction of inclusion, rather than exclusion. In other words, it is not
that recognition should be curtailed or eliminated, but rather it is a matter
of 'levelling up' the field of recognition so that more social groups can
access it, while strengthening horizontal cooperation, rather than fuelling
conflict. Designing a radically different approach to recognition means
looking closely at what happens 'in the shadow of recognition', beyond

the epics of indigenous struggles, where normal life takes its course. The roots of violence tend to be remarkably similar across cultures and geographies, and they are often nested in our 'inability to think ... from the standpoint of somebody else' (Arendt [1963] 2006: 49). Politics of recognition can be crucial to shape the imagination of difference and to prevent the darkest side of human communities from prevailing.

References

ABC (2015). Campesinos e indígenas siguen en conflicto por tierras en San Pedro. 23 March. www.abc.com.py/edicion-impresa/interior/campesinos-e-indigenas-siguen-en-conflicto-por-tierras-en-san-pedro-1348903.html.

Abelson, Julia, Forest Pierre-Gerlier, Eyles John et al. (2003). Deliberations about deliberative methods: Issues in the design and evaluation of public participation processes. *Social Science & Medicine*, 57(2), 239–51.

Adelman, Irma (1975). Growth, income distribution and equity-oriented development strategies. *World Development*, 3(2–3), 67–76.

AIDESEP (2015). Consultation and compliance review request. 27 August. http://idbdocs.iadb.org/wsdocs/getdocument.aspx?docnum=40097617.

Aikman, Sheila (2012). Interrogating discourses of intercultural education: From indigenous Amazon community to global policy forum. *Compare*, 42(2), 235–57.

Alavi, Hamza (1973). Peasant classes and primordial loyalties. *Journal of Peasant Studies*, 1(1), 23–62.

Albertus, Michael (2015). *Autocracy and Redistribution*. New York: Cambridge University Press.

Albó, Xavier (1991). El retorno del indio. *Revista Andina*, 9, 299–345.
  (2002). *Pueblos Indios en La Política*. La Paz: CIPCA.
  (2009). *Movimientos y Poder Indígena en Bolivia, Ecuador y Perú*. Vol. 71. La Paz: CIPCA.

Albó, Xavier & Amalia Anaya (2003). *Niños Alegres, Libres, Expresivos: La Audacia de la Educación Intercultural Bilingüe en Bolivia*. Vol. 58. La Paz: CIPCA.

Albó, Xavier & Franz X. Barrios Suvelza (2006). *Por una Bolivia Plurinacional e Intercultural con Autonomías*. La Paz: PNUD.

Albó, Xavier, Libermann Kitula, Godinez Armando & Pifarre Francisco (1995) [1989]. *Para Comprender las Culturas Originarias de Bolivia*. La Paz: CIPCA and UNICEF.

Albro, Robert (2006). The culture of democracy and Bolivia's indigenous movements. *Critique of Anthropology*, 26(4), 387–410.

Alexiades, Miguel N. (ed.) (2009). *Mobility and Migration in Indigenous Amazon: Contemporary Ethnoecological Perspectives*. Oxford: Berghahn.

Altamirano, Teófilo, Lane Ryo Hirabayashi & Xavier Albó (eds.) (1997). *Migrants, Regional Identities and Latin American Cities*. Washington, DC: American Anthropological Association.

Althusser, Louis (1971). Ideology and ideological state apparatuses. In Luis Althusser (ed.), *Lenin and Philosophy, and Other Essays*. London: New Left Books, 127–88.

Anderson, Benedict (1991). *Imagined Communities*. London and New York: Verso.

Andolina, Robert, Nina Laurie & Sarah A. Radcliffe (2009). *Indigenous Development in the Andes: Culture, Power and Transnationalism*. Durham, NC: Duke University Press.

Andolina, Robert, Sarah A. Radcliffe & Nina Laurie (2005). Development and culture: Transnational identity making in Bolivia. *Political Geography*, 24(6), 679–702.

Arendt, Hanna (1958). *The Human Condition*. Chicago, IL: University of Chicago Press.

  (2006). *Eichmann in Jerusalem: A Report on the Banality of Evil*. New York: Penguin Books.

Armstrong, Chris (2006). *Rethinking Equality: The Challenge of Equal Citizenship*. Manchester: Manchester University Press.

Asociación Unión de Comunidades Campesinas de Influencia Directa e Indirecta Afectadas por el Proyecto Minero Las Bambas UCCAMBA (2016). Perú: ¡Abajo la represión judicial contra las comunidades campesinas que luchan contra proyecto minero Las Bambas! Derecho Sin Fronteras, 26 April. https://derechosinfronteras.pe/peru-abajo-la-represion-judicial-contra-las-comunidades-campesinas-que-luchan-contra-proyecto-minero-las-bambas/.

Assies, Willem (2002). From rubber estate to simple commodity production: Agrarian struggles in the northern Bolivian Amazon. *Journal of Peasant Studies*, 29(3–4), 83–130.

  (2006). Land tenure legislation in a pluri-cultural and multi-ethnic society: The case of Bolivia. *Journal of Peasant Studies*, 33(4), 569–611.

Bacevic, Jana (2014). *From Class to Identity: The Politics of Education Reforms in Former Yugoslavia*. Budapest and New York: Central European University Press.

Balée, William L. (1994). *Footprints of the Forest: Ka'apor Ethnobotany – The Historical Ecology of Plant Utilization by an Amazonian People*. New York: Columbia University Press.

Ballón Aguirre, Francisco (2002). El Derecho Aguaruna y el Derecho del Estado. La República, 23 January. http://larepublica.pe/politica/339698-el-derecho-aguaruna-y-el-derecho-del-estado-por-francisco-ballon-aguirre.

Barth, Frederik (1969). *Ethnic Groups and Boundaries*. Boston, MA: Little, Brown.

Bascopé Sanjinés, Iván (2010). *Lecciones Aprendidas sobre Consulta Previa*. La Paz: CEJIS.

Bauer, Brian S. & Lucas C. Kellett (2010). Cultural transformations of the Chanka homeland (Andahuaylas, Peru) during the late intermediate period (AD 1000–1400). *Latin American Antiquity*, 21(1), 87–111.

Bauman, Zygmunt (2001). The great war of recognition. *Theory, Culture & Society*, 18(2–3), 137–50.

Bebbington, Anthony (2009). The new extraction: Rewriting the political ecology of the Andes? *NACLA Report on the Americas*, 42(5), 12–20.

Bebbington, Anthony & Denise Humphreys Bebbington (2011). An Andean avatar: Post-neoliberal and neo-liberal strategies for promoting extractive industries. *New Political Economy*, 16(1), 131–45.

Bebbington, Anthony & Jeffrey Bury (2013). *Subterranean Struggles: New Dynamics of Mining, Oil, and Gas in Latin America*. Vol. 8. Austin, TX: University of Texas Press.

Bengoa, José (2000). *La Emergencia Indígena en América Latina*. México and Santiago de Chile: Fondo de Cultura Económica.

Bermúdez Liévano, Andrés (2014). La Cumbre Agraria: el movimiento político del posconflicto. La Silla Vacía, 2 October. http://lasillavacia.com/historia/la-cumbre-agraria-el-movimiento-politico-del-posconflicto-48711.

Béteille, André (1998). The idea of indigenous people. *Current Anthropology*, 39 (2), 187–91.

Bierregaard, Richard O. (2001). *Lessons from Amazonia: The Ecology and Conservation of a Fragmented Forest*. New Haven, CT: Yale University Press.

Bilsborrow, Richard E. (2002). Migration, population change, and the rural environment. *Environmental Change and Security Project Report*, 8(1), 69–84.

Boccara, Guillaume (2014). Tous homo œconomicus, tous différents. Les origines idéologiques de l'ethno-capitalisme. *Actuel Marx*, 2, 40–61.

Boccara, Guillaume & Paola Bolados (2010). ¿Qué es el multiculturalismo? La nueva cuestión étnica en el Chile neoliberal. *Revista de Indias*, 70, 651–90.

Bottazzi, Patrick & Stephan Rist (2012). Changing land rights means changing society: The sociopolitical effects of agrarian reforms under the government of Evo Morales. *Journal of Agrarian Change*, 12(4), 528–51.

Boyer, Véronique (2016). The demand for recognition and access to citizenship: Ethnic labelling and territorial restructuring in Brazil. In David Lehmann (ed.), *The Crisis of Multiculturalism in Latin America*. New York: Palgrave Macmillan, 155–78.

Brass, Tom (2000). *Peasants, Populism and Postmodernism: The Return of the Agrarian Myth*. London: Frank Cass.

Brinks, D. M., Steve Levitsky & M. Victoria Murillo (2019). *Understanding Institutional Weakness: Power and Design in Latin American Institutions*. Cambridge, MA: Cambridge University Press.

Brown, Graham, Arnim Langer & Frances Stewart (1990). *Affirmative Action: Foundations, Contexts, and Debates*. Basingstoke: Palgrave Macmillan.

Brysk, Alison (2000). *From Tribal Village to Global Village: Indian Rights and International Relations in Latin America*. Stanford: Stanford University Press.

Buchanan, Ian (2010). *A Dictionary of Critical Theory*. Oxford: Oxford University Press.

Burt, Jo-Marie & Philip Mauceri (eds) (2004). *Politics in the Andes: Identity, Conflict, Reform*. Pittsburgh, PA: University of Pittsburgh Press.

Cameron, John (2010). *Struggles for Local Democracy in the Andes*. Boulder and London: First Forum Press.

Cameron, Maxwell A., Eric Hershberg & Kenneth E. Sharpe (2012). *New Institutions for Participatory Democracy in Latin America*. Basingstoke: Palgrave Macmillan.

Canessa, Andrew (2006). Todos somos indígenas: Towards a new language of national political identity. *Bulletin of Latin American Research*, 25(2), 241–63.

(2012). *Intimate Indigeneities: Race, Sex and History in the Small Spaces of Life*. Durham, NC and London: Duke University Press

(2018). Indigenous conflict in Bolivia explored through an African lens: Towards a comparative analysis of indigeneity. *Comparative Studies in Society and History*, 60(2), 308–37.

Cardoso, Fernando H. & Enzo Faletto (1979). *Dependency and Development in Latin America*. Berkeley, CA: University of California Press.

Carr, David (2009). Population and deforestation: Why rural migration matters. *Progress in Human Geography*, 33(3), 355–78.

Castree, Noel (2004). Differential geographies: Place, indigenous rights and "local" resources. *Political Geography*, 23, 133–67.

Catalán Colque, Ruth L. (2007). *Encuentros y Desencuentros: Luchando Por Una Educacion Propia y Participativa*. La Paz: UMSS, PROEIB Andes, Plural Editores.

Chaikuni, Instituto (2016). *Programa Beca 18 y Pueblos Indígenas. Diagnóstico Region Loreto – Peru*. http://d2g1dofgkbpvym.cloudfront.net/2016/10/21/15/14/02/414/2016.10.DIAGNOSTICO_BECA_18.VFINAL.pdf.

Chandra, Kanchan (ed.) (2012). *Constructivist Theories of Ethnic Politics*. Oxford: Oxford University Press.

Chong, Natividad Gutiérrez (2010). Indigenous political organizations and the nation-state: Bolivia, Ecuador, Mexico. *Alternatives*, 35(3), 259–68.

Choque, María Eugenia & Carlos Mamani (2003). Reconstrucción del Ayllu y derecho de los pueblos indígenas: el movimiento indio en los Andes de Bolivia. In Esteban Ticona (ed.), *Los Andes desde los Andes. Aymaranakana, Qhichwanakana, Yatxatawipa, Lup'iwipa*. La Paz: Yachaywasi.

Clifford, James (2001). Indigenous articulations. *The Contemporary Pacific*, 13 (2), 467–90.

Coate, Roger A. & Markus Thiel (eds) (2010). *Identity Politics in the Age of Globalization*. Boulder, CO: First Forum Press/Lynne Rienner.

Cochrane, Feargal (2015). *Migration and Security in the Global Age: Diaspora Communities and Conflict*. London and New York: Routledge.

Collier, Ruth Berins & David Collier (1991). *Shaping the Political Arena: Critical Junctures, the Labor Movement, and Regime Dynamics in Latin America.* Princeton, NJ: Princeton University Press.

Colombian Constitutional Court (2015). Sentencia C-371/14 Creación de Zonas de Reserva Campesina. Realización de consulta previa si en área existen territorios indígenas o si están habitados por pueblos indígenas o tribales, 12 May. http://prensarural.org/spip/spip.php?article16823.

Colque, Gonzalo, Efraín Tinta & Esteban Sanjinés (2016). *Segunda Reforma Agraria: Una historia que incomoda.* La Paz: Fundación Tierra.

Comaroff, John & Jean Comaroff (2009). *Ethnicity, Inc.* Chicago, IL: University of Chicago Press.

Comisión de la Verdad y Reconciliación (2003) *Informe Final.* Lima: CVR.

Comisión Interinstitucional de la Iglesia Católica and Asamblea Permanente de Derechos Humanos en Bolivia (2012). Resumen de Informe Visita a las Comunidades del TIPNIS. Archivo documental Isiboro Sécure https://tipnisboliviaorg.files.wordpress.com/2018/10/pri-com-apdh-00087-2012.pdf.

CONAIE (2007). *Proyecto Político de las Nacionalidades del Ecuador.* Quito: CONAIE.

Connor, Walker (1973). The politics of ethnonationalism. *Journal of International Affairs*, 27(1), 1–21.

Coombes, Brad, Jay T. Johnson & Richard Howitt (2012). Indigenous geographies I: Mere resource conflicts? The complexities in land and environmental claims. *Progress in Human Geography*, 36(6), 810–21.

Corry, Stephen (2011). Do indigenous peoples benefit from "development"? *The Guardian*, 25 November. https://www.theguardian.com/global-development/poverty-matters/2011/nov/25/indigenous-peoples-benefit-development-tribal.

Cortina, Regina (ed.) (2014). *The Education of Indigenous Citizens in Latin America.* Bristol: Multilingual Matters.

Cosavalente Vidarte, Jose (2017). Municipalidad Provincial de Satipo. Memoria Institucional Anual 2016. https://www.scribd.com/document/386419698/Memoria-Anual-2016.

Coxshall, Wendy (2010). "When they came to take our resources": Mining conflicts in Peru and their complexity. *Social Analysis*, 54(1), 35–51.

CPILAP (2009). *Plan Estratégico Institucional de la Central de Pueblos Indígenas de La Paz, 2008–2012.* La Paz: CPILAP.

Crabtree, John (2003). The impact of neo-liberal economics on Peruvian peasant agriculture in the 1990s. In Tom Brass (ed.), *Latin American Peasants.* London: Frank Cass Publishers.

CRIC (2013) Intereses políticos y económicos se sobrepone a la vida de los pueblos. https://www.cric-colombia.org/portal/intereses-politicos-y-economicos-se-sobrepone-a-la-vida-de-los-pueblos/

Dancygier, Rafaela M. (2010). *Immigration and Conflict in Europe.* Cambridge, MA: Cambridge University Press.

Dandler, Jorge (1969). *El Sindicalismo Campesino en Bolivia: Los Cambios Estructurales en Ucureña (1935–1952).* México, DF: Instituto Indigenista Interamericano.

(1984). Campesinado y reforma agraria en Cochabamba (1952–1953): Dinámica de un movimiento campesino en Bolivia. In Fernando Calderón & Jorge Dandler (eds), *Bolivia: La fuerza histórica del campesinado*. La Paz: UNRISD/CERES.

Danida & IWGIA (2010). *The Rights of Indigenous Peoples: The Cooperation Between Denmark and Bolivia (2005–2009)*. La Paz: Danida/IWGIA.

Davalos, Pablo (2005) *Pueblos Indígenas, Estado y Democracia*. Buenos Aires: CLACSO.

de Castro, Fábio, Barbara Hogenboom & Michiel Baud (eds). (2016). *Environmental Governance in Latin America*. Basingstoke and New York: Palgrave Macmillan.

Defensoría del Pueblo (2002). La defensoría del Pueblo y los derechos territoriales de las comunidades nativas. El conflicto territorial en la comunidad nativa Naranjos. *Informe Defensorial N° 68*. http://www2.congreso.gob.pe/sicr/cendoc bib/con4_uibd.nsf/0EE62EC509AA95CB05257CE0005A5099/$FILE/informe_Defensoral68.pdf.

(2016). *Reporte de Conflictos Sociales N. 152*. Lima: Defensoria del Publo. https://www.defensoria.gob.pe/wp-content/uploads/2018/07/Reporte-Mensual-de-Conflictos-Sociales-N-152-Octubre-2016.pdf.

de la Cadena, Marisol (2000). *Indigenous Mestizos: The Politics of Race and Culture in Cuzco, Peru, 1919–1991*. Durham, NC: Duke University Press.

(2005). Are "mestizos" hybrids? The conceptual politics of Andean identities. *Journal of Latin American Studies*, 37, 259–84.

(2008). *Formaciones de Indianidad: Articulaciones Raciales, Mestizaje y Nación en América Latina*. Lima: Envión.

(2010). Indigenous cosmopolitics in the Andes: Conceptual reflections beyond "politics". *Cultural Anthropology*, 25(2), 334–70.

Delany-Barmann, Gloria (2009). Bilingual intercultural teacher education: Nuevos maestros para Bolivia. *Bilingual Research Journal*, 32(3), 280–97.

de Oliveira, Adélia Engrácia (1994). The evidence for the nature of the process of indigenous deculturation and destabilization in the Brazilian Amazon in the last three hundred years: Preliminary data. In Anna Roosevelt (ed.), *Amazonian Indians from Prehistory to the Present: Anthropological Perspectives*. Tucson, AZ: University of Arizona Press, 93–119.

de Vos, Jan (2002). *Una Tierra para Sembrar Sueños: Historia Reciente de la Selva Lacandona*. Mexico: CIESAS.

Dick, Caroline (2011). *The Perils of Identity: Group Rights and the Politics of Intragroup Difference*. Vancouver: UBC Press.

Dietz, Kristina (2019). Direct democracy in mining conflicts in Latin America: Mobilising against the *La Colosa* project in Colombia. *Canadian Journal of Development Studies / Revue canadienne d'études du développement*, 40(2), 145–62.

DNP, MEN, ICETEX (2009). *Asistencia a Comunidades Indígenas A Traves Del Fondo de Creditos Condonables*, 2009–10. https://spi.dnp.gov.co/App_Themes/SeguimientoProyectos/FichaEBI/2011_002000045000.pdf.

Dudley, Meredith E. (2009). *The Historical Ecology of the Lecos of Apolo: Ethnogenesis and Landscape Transformation at the Intersection of the Andes and Amazon.* PhD thesis, Tulane University.

Eckstein, Susan E. & Timothy P. Wickham-Crowley (eds). (2003). *Struggles for Social Rights in Latin America.* New York: Routledge.

EJOLT (2015) 'Environmental Justice Atlas'. *EJOLT,* accessed 12 June 2015. http://ejatlas.org/.

El Diario (2007). Autorizada la explotación de hidrocarburos en Norte paceño. *El Diario.* Digital edition, 14 May.

El Espectador (2012). No se sabe cuántos campesinos hay. *El Espectador,* 16 October. https://www.elespectador.com/noticias/economia/no-se-sabe-cuantos-campesinos-hay-articulo-381588.

El Tiempo (2014). Niegan derechos de minoría étnica a campesinos. *El Tiempo,* 30 June. http://www.eltiempo.com/archivo/documento/CMS-14189755.

EMRIP (2011). Final study on indigenous peoples and the right to participate in decision-making. Report of the expert mechanism on the rights of indigenous peoples. www.ohchr.org/Documents/Issues/IPeoples/EMRIP/AEVfinalreportStudyIPRightParticipate.pdf.

Enciso Patiño, Patricia (2004). Estado del arte de la etnoeducación en Colombia con énfasis en política pública. *Ministerio De Educación Nacional,* Dirección de Poblaciones y Proyectos Intersectoriales Subdirección de Poblaciones

Engle, Karen (2010). *The Elusive Promise of Indigenous Development: Rights, Culture, Strategy.* Durham, NC: Duke University Press.

Esman, Milton J. (1994). *Ethnic Politics.* Ithaca: Cornell University Press.

Eversole, Robyn, John-Andrew McNeish & Alberto D. Cimadamore (eds). (2005). *Indigenous Peoples and Poverty: An International Perspective.* London: Zed Books.

Faguet, Jean Paul (2012). *Decentralization and Popular Democracy: Governance from Below in Bolivia.* Ann Arbor, MI: University of Michigan Press.

Faguet, Jean-Paul (2013). Can subnational autonomy strengthen democracy in Bolivia? *Publius: The Journal of Federalism,* 44(1), 51–81.

(2014). Decentralization and governance. *World Development,* 53, 2–13.

Fajardo, Darío (2000). *Las Zonas de Reserva Campesina: Primeras Experiencias.* Bogotá: Mimeo.

FAO (2018). A new alliance for the elimination of rural poverty in Latin America. *FAO,* 30 August. http://www.fao.org/americas/noticias/ver/en/c/1033344.

Fay, Derick & Deborah James (2009). Restoring what was ours: An introduction. In Derick Fay & Deborah James (eds.), *The Rights and Wrongs of Land Restitution: "Restoring What Was Ours".* Oxford: Routledge.

Feola, Giuseppe (2017). Adaptive institutions? Peasant institutions and natural models facing climatic and economic changes in the Colombian Andes. *Journal of Rural Studies,* 49, 117–27.

Findley, Sally E. (1984). *Colonialist Constraints, Strategies and Mobility: Recent Trends in Latin American Frontier Zones. World Employment Programme Research Working Paper* No. 145. Population Studies and Training Center, Brown University. https://www.econbiz.de/Record/colonist-constraints-strat

egies-and-mobility-recent-trends-in-latin-american-frontier-zones-findley/
10010966473.

Finnemore, Martha & Kathryn Sikkink (1998). International norm dynamics and
political change. *International Organization*, 52, 887–917.

Flemmer, Ricarda & Almut Schilling-Vacaflor (2016). Unfulfilled promises of the
consultation approach: The limits to effective indigenous participation in
Bolivia's and Peru's extractive industries. *Third World Quarterly*, 37(1),
172–88.

Fontana, Lorenza B. (2013a). On the perils and potentialities of revolution:
Conflict and collective action in contemporary Bolivia. *Latin American
Perspectives*, 40(3), 26–42.

(2013b). Evo Morales at the crossroads: Problematizing the relationship
between the state and indigenous movements in Bolivia. *Ibero-Americana*,
43(1/2) 19–45.

(2014a). Indigenous peasant "otherness": Rural identities and political processes in Bolivia. *Bulletin of Latin American Research*, 33(4), 436–51.

(2014b). Indigenous peoples vs. peasant unions: Land conflicts and rural movements in plurinational Bolivia. *Journal of Peasant Studies*, 41(3), 297–319,
https://www.tandfonline.com/doi/abs/10.1080/03066150.2014.906404.

(2014c). The "indigenous native peasant" trinity: Imagining a plurinational
community in Evo Morales's Bolivia. *Environment and Planning D –
Society and Space*, 32(3), 518–34.

(2019). Identity policies of education: Struggles for inclusion and exclusion in
Colombia and Peru. *Journal of Education Policy*, 34(3), 351–73.

Fontana, Lorenza B. & Jean Grugel (2016). The politics of indigenous participation through "Free Prior Informed Consent": Reflections from the Bolivian
case. *World Development*, 77, 249–61.

Fox Piven, Frances, and Richard A. Cloward. (1979). *Poor People's Movements:
Why They Succeed, How They Fail*. New York: Vintage Books.

Fraser, Nancy (1995). From redistribution to recognition? Dilemmas of justice in
a "post-socialist" age. *New Left Review*, 212, 68–93.

(2000). Rethinking recognition. *New Left Review*, 3, 107–20.

(2009). *Scales of Justice: Reimagining Political Space in a Globalizing World*.
Vol. 31. New York: Columbia University Press.

Freire, Germán N., Steven D. Schwartz Orellana, Melissa Zumaeta Aurazo et al.
(2015). *Indigenous Latin America in the Twenty-First Century: The First
Decade*. Working Paper, The World Bank Group. http://documents
.worldbank.org/curated/en/145891467991974540/Indigenous-Latin-
America-in-the-twenty-first-century-the-first-decade.

French, Jan Hoffman (2009). Ethnoracial land restitution: Finding Indians and
fugitive slave descendants in the Brazilian Northeast. In Derick Fay &
Deborah James (eds.) *The Rights and Wrongs of Land Restitution*. New
York/Oxon: Routledge-Cavendish, 143–60.

Galeano, Eduardo (1971). *Las Venas Abiertas de. América Latina*. México, DF:
Siglo XXI.

Galindo, J. Fernando (2010). Cultural diversity in Bolivia: from liberal intercul-
turalism to indigenous modernity. In Maddy Janssens, Myriam Bechtoldt,

Arie de Ruijter et al. (eds.), *The Sustainability of Cultural Diversity*. Cheltenham: Edward Elgar Publishing, 97–115.

Garcés Trelles, Kenneth E. & V. Javier Echevarría Mejía (2009). Entre propietarios y migrantes: los encuentros y desencuentros entre Colonos y Aguarunas en el alto mayo. *Revista Jangwa Pana*, 8(1), 50–73.

García, María Elena (2005). *Making Indigenous Citizens: Identities, Education, and Multicultural Development in Peru*. Stanford: Stanford University Press.

Gaspar, Arlen (2009). Territorio y bosques nuevas amenazas sociales. *Articulo. org*, 11 December. http://www.articulo.org/articulo/10294/territorio_y_bosques_nuevas_amenazas_sociales.html.

Gelles, Paul H. (2002). Andean culture, indigenous identity, and the state in Peru. In D. Maybury-Lewis (ed.), *The Politics of Ethnicity: Indigenous Peoples in Latin American States*. Cambridge, MA: Harvard University Press, David Rockefeller Center for Latin American Studies, 239–65.

Gewirtz, Sharon (1998). Conceptualizing social justice in education: Mapping the territory. *Journal of Education Policy*, 13(4), 469–84.

Gibson-Graham, Julie K. (1997). The end of capitalism (as we knew it): A feminist critique of political economy. *Capital & Class*, 21(2), 186–88.

Goodland, Robert (2004). Free, prior and informed consent and the World Bank Group. *Sustainable Development Law & Policy*, 66(4), 66–74.

Gordillo, José (2000). *Campesinos Revolucionarios en Bolivia. Identidad, Territorio y Sexualidad en el Valle Alto de Cochabamba, 1952–1964*. La Paz: Plural.

Greene, Shane (2005). Incas, Indios and Indigenism in Peru. *NACLA Report on the Americas*, 38(4), 34–41.

 (2006). Getting over the Andes: The Geo-Eco-Politics of Indigenous Movements in Peru's Twenty-First Century Inca Empire. *Journal of Latin American Studies*, 38(2), 327–354.

 (2007). Introduction: On race, roots/routes, and sovereignty in Latin America's Afro-indigenous multiculturalisms. *The Journal of Latin American and Caribbean Anthropology*, 12(2), 329–55.

 (2009). *Customizing Indigeneity: Paths to a Visionary Politics in Peru*. Stanford: Stanford University Press.

Grugel, Jean & Enrique Peruzzotti (2012). The domestic politics of international human rights law: Implementing the Convention on the Rights of the Child in Ecuador, Chile and Argentina. *Human Rights Quarterly*, 34(1), 178–98.

Gudynas, Eduardo (2012). Estado compensador y nuevos extractivismos: Las ambivalencias del progresismo latinoamericano. *Nueva Sociedad*, 237, 128–46.

Guereña, Arantxa (2016). *Unearthed: Land, power, and inequality in Latin America*. Oxfam International. https://www.oxfam.org/sites/www.oxfam.org/files/file_attachments/bp-land-power-inequality-latin-america-301116-en.pdf.

 (2017). *A snapshot of inequality: What the latest agricultural census reveals about land distribution in Colombia*. Oxfam International. https://d1tn3vj7xz9fdh.cloudfront.net/s3fs-public/file_attachments/colombia_-_snapshot_of_inequality.pdf.

Guerrero Figueroa, Luis, Rosa Florián Cedrón, Jorge Luis Mera Ramírez et al. (2002). *Informe del grupo de trabajo encargado de la investigación de los hechos ocurridos en la provincia de San Ignacio, departamento de Cajamarca, producto del enfrentamiento entre colonos y nativos de la zona y para identificar zonas de la amazonía peruana en las que se puedan presentar hechos.* Congreso de la República del Perú. Grupo de Trabajo. https://www4.congreso.gob.pe/congresista/2001/lguerrero/paginas/fiscalizadorao.htm.

Guibernau I Berdún, Maria Montserrat & John Rex (eds) (2010). *The Ethnicity Reader: Nationalism, Multiculturalism and Migration.* Cambridge, MA: Polity Press.

Gustafson, Bret (2009). Manipulating cartographies: Plurinationalism, autonomy, and indigenous resurgence in Bolivia. *Anthropological Quarterly*, 82(4), 985–1016.

(2014). Intercultural bilingual education in the Andes: Political change, new challenges and future directions. In Regina Cortina (ed.), *The Education of Indigenous Citizens in Latin America.* Bristol and Buffalo: Multilingual Matters.

Hale, Charles (2002). Does multiculturalism menace? Governance, cultural rights, and the politics of identity in Guatemala. *Journal of Latin American Studies*, 34(3), 485–535.

(2005). Neoliberal multiculturalism: The remaking of cultural rights and racial dominance in Central America. *Political and Legal Anthropology Review*, 28, 10–28.

Hall, Gillette & Harry A. Patrinos (2005). *Indigenous Peoples, Poverty and Human Development in Latin America: 1994–2004.* Washington, DC: World Bank.

Hall, Stuart (1996). On postmodernism and articulation: An interview with Stuart Hall. In David Morley & Kuan-Hsing Chen (eds.), *Stuart Hall: Critical dialogues in cultural studies.* London: Routledge, 131–50 (reprinted from *Journal of Communication Inquiry*, 1986, 10(2), 45–60).

Handelman, Howard (1975). *Struggle in the Andes: Peasant Political Mobilization in Peru.* Austin: University of Texas Press.

Harvey, David (2007). Neoliberalism as creative destruction. *The Annals of the American Academy of Political and Social Science*, 610, 22–44.

Hasan, Zoya & Martha Craven Nussbaum (2012). *Equalizing Access: Affirmative Action in Higher Education in India, United States, and South Africa.* New Delhi: Oxford University Press.

Haslam, Paul A. & Nasser A. Tanimoune (2016). The determinants of social conflict in the Latin American mining sector: New evidence with quantitative data. *World Development*, 78, 401–19.

Heath, John & Hans Binswanger (1996). Natural resource degradation effects of poverty and population growth are largely policy-induced: The case of Colombia. *Environmental and Development Economics*, 1, 65–84.

Hernandez-Zavala, M., H. Patrinos, C. Sakellariou & J. Shapiro (2006). *Quality of schooling and quality of schools for indigenous students in Guatemala,*

Mexico and Peru. *World Bank Policy Research Paper 3982, Human Development Network, Education Team*. Washington, DC: World Bank.

Hobsbawm, Eric J. (1959). *Primitive rebels: Studies in Archaic Forms of Social Movement in the 19th and 20th Centuries*. Manchester: Manchester University Press.

Hobsbawm, Eric & Terence Ranger (ed.) (1983). *The Invention of Tradition*. Cambridge, MA: Cambridge University Press.

Hobson, Barbara (ed.) (2003). *Recognition Struggles and Social Movements: Contested Identities, Agency and Power*. Cambridge, MA: Cambridge University Press.

Hoffman, Max & Ana I. Grigera (2013). *Climate change, migration, and conflict in the Amazon and the Andes*. Rising tensions and policy options in South America. Report. Center for American Progress. https://www.americanprogress.org/article/climate-change-migration-and-conflict-in-the-amazon-and-the-andes/.

Hoffmann, Odile (2000). Titling collective lands of the Black communities in Colombia, between innovation and tradition. In W. Assies, G. V. D. Haar & A. Hoekema (eds.), *The Challenge of Diversity: Indigenous Peoples and Reform of the State in Latin America*. Amsterdam: Thela Thesis, 123–36.

Honneth, Axel (1995). *The Struggle for Recognition*. Cambridge, MA: Polity Press.

Hooker, Juliet (2005). Indigenous inclusion/black exclusion: Race, ethnicity and multicultural citizenship in Latin America. *Journal of Latin American Studies*, 37(2), 285–310.

Hughes, Neil (2010). Indigenous protest in Peru: The "Orchard Dog" bites back. *Social Movement Studies*, 9(1), 85–90.

Ibarra, Hernán (1999). Intelectuales Indígenas, Neoindigenismo e Indianismo en el Ecuador. *Ecuador Debate*, 48, 71–94

ILO (2013). *Understanding the Indigenous and Tribal People Convention, 1989 (No. 169): Handbook for ILO Tripartite Constituents*. Geneva: ILO. http://www.ilo.org/global/standards/subjects-covered-by-international-labour-standards/indigenous-and-tribal-peoples/WCMS_205225/lang–en/index.htm, accessed 30 July 2015.

INE & UNDP (2006). *Atlas Estadístico de Municipios 2005*. La Paz: INE/UNDP.

Instituto Nacional de Estadistica e Informatica (2014). *Caracteristica Socioeconomicas del productor agropecuario en el Peru*. Lima: INEI. https://www.inei.gob.pe/media/MenuRecursivo/publicaciones_digitales/Est/Lib1177.

Jackson, Jean E. (1995). Culture, genuine and spurious: The politics of Indianness in the Vaupés, Colombia. *American Ethnologist*, 22(1), 3–27.

(2019). *Managing Multiculturalism: Indigeneity and the Struggle for Rights in Colombia*. Stanford: Stanford University Press.

Jackson, Jean E. & Kay B. Warren (2005). Indigenous movements in Latin America, 1992–2004: Controversies, ironies, new directions. *Annual Review of Anthropology*, 34, 549–73.

Jiménez Quispe, Luz (2014). Indigenous leaders and the challenges of decolonization in Bolivia. In Regina Cortina (ed.), *The Education of Indigenous Citizens in Latin America*. Bristol and Buffalo: Multilingual Matters.

Kingsbury, Benedict (1998). "Indigenous peoples" in international law: A constructivist approach to the Asian controversy. *American Journal of International Law*, 92(3), 414–57.

Kohl, Benjamin & Linda C. Farthing (2006). *Impasse in Bolivia: Neoliberal Hegemony and Popular Resistance*. London: Zed Books.

Kohl, James V. (1978) Peasant and revolution in Bolivia, April 9, 1952–August 2, 1953. *The Hispanic American Historical Review*, 58(2), 238–59.

Kuper, Adam (2003). The return of the native. *Current Anthropology*, 44(3), 389–402.

Kymlicka, Will (1995). *Multicultural Citizenship: A Liberal Theory of Minority Rights*. New York: Oxford University Press.

(2001). *Politics in the Vernacular*. Oxford: Oxford University Press.

(2007). *Multicultural Odysseys: Navigating the New International Politics of Diversity*. Oxford: Oxford University Press.

Kymlicka, Will (2013). Neoliberal multiculturalism? In Peter A. Hall & Michèle Lamont (eds.), *Social Resilience in the Neoliberal Era*. Cambridge, MA: Cambridge University Press, 99–125.

Lakhani, Nina (2020). Costa Rica indigenous leader shot amid tensions over land rights. *The Guardian*, 17 February. https://www.theguardian.com/world/2020/feb/17/costa-rica-indigenous-leader-shot-land-rights#:~:text=Mainor%20Ortiz%20Delgado%2C%2029%2C%20a,same%20family%20in%2014%20months.

La Razón (2007). Los indígenas de Apolo amenazan con chaquear en el parque Madidi. *La Razón*. Digital Edition, 18 May.

La República (2002). Un drama de la pobreza. *La República*, 20 January. http://larepublica.pe/politica/351403-editorial-un-drama-de-la-pobreza.

Lacroix, Laurent (2011). La participation de la Confédération Indigène de Bolivie. à la vie politique nationale bolivienne (1982–2010). *Civilisations. Revue internationale d'anthropologie et de sciences humaines*, 60(1), 103–19.

Lama, Abraham (2002). Peru: Indígenas en guerra por sus tierras. Inter Press Service, 25 January. https://ipsnoticias.net/2002/01/peru-indigenas-en-guerra-por-sus-tierras/.

Lamont, Michèle (2018). Addressing recognition gaps: Destigmatization and the reduction of inequality. *American Sociological Review*, 83(3), 419–44.

Lamont, Michèle & Virág Molnár (2002). The study of boundaries in the social sciences. *Annual Review of Sociology*, 28(1), 167–95.

Lapegna, Pablo (2013). Social movements and patronage politics: Processes of demobilization and dual pressure. *Sociological Forum*, 28(4), 842–63.

(2016). Neoliberal politics and moral riots in Bolivia's "Black February". *ISA Symposium for Sociology* e-Forum https://www.isaportal.org/resources/resource/neoliberal-politics-and-moral-riots-in-bolivias-black-february/download/.

Lathrap, Donald W. (1970). *The Upper Amazon. Vol. 70. Ancient Peoples and Places*. New York: Praeger.

Laurie, Nina, Robert Andolina & Sarah Radcliffe (2005). Ethnodevelopment: Social movements, creating experts and professionalising indigenous knowledge in Ecuador. *Antipode*, 37(3), 470–96.

Le Bot, Yvon (2009). *La Grande Révolte Indienne*. Paris: Éditions Robert Laffont.

León, Luis Vázquez (2016). Multiculturalism as a juridical weapon: The use and abuse of the concept of "pueblo originario" in agrarian conflicts in Michoacán, Mexico. In David Lehmann (ed.), *The Crisis of Multiculturalism in Latin America*. New York: Palgrave Macmillan, 35–73.

Levitsky, Steven & Kenneth Roberts (eds.) (2011). *The Resurgence of the Latin American Left*. Baltimore, MD: Johns Hopkins University Press.

Li, Fabiana (2015). *Unearthing Conflict*. Durham, NC: Duke University Press.

Li, Tania M. (2002). Ethnic cleansing, recursive knowledge, and the dilemmas of sedentarism. *International Social Science Journal*, 54(3), 361–71.

Lieberman, Evan S. & Prerna Singh (2012). Conceptualizing and measuring ethnic politics: An institutional complement to demographic, behavioral, and cognitive approaches. *Studies in Comparative International Development*, 47(3), 255–86.

(2017). Census enumeration and group conflict: A global analysis of the consequences of counting. *World Politics*, 69(1), 1–53.

López, Luis Enrique (1998) *Pesquisas en Lingüística Andina*. Puno: Universidad Nacional del Altiplano.

(2005). *De Resquicios a Boquerones. La Educación Inetrcultural Bilingüe in Bolivia*. La Paz: PROEIB Andes and Plural.

(2009). Reaching the unreached: Indigenous intercultural bilingual education in Latin America. Agenda, 1–81.

(2014). Indigenous intercultural bilingual education in Latin America: Widening gaps between policy and practice. In Regina Cortina (ed.), *The Education of Indigenous Citizens in Latin America*. Bristol and Buffalo: Multilingual Matters.

López Pila, Esther (2014). "We don't lie and cheat like the Collas do." Highland–lowland regionalist tensions and indigenous identity politics in Amazonian Bolivia. *Critique of Anthropology*, 34(4), 429–49.

Lucero, José Antonio (2008). *Struggles of Voice: The Politics of Indigenous Representation in the Andes*. Pittsburgh: University of Pittsburgh Press.

(2013). Seeing like an international NGO: Encountering development and indigenous politics in the Andes. In Eduardo Silva (ed.), *Transnational Activism and National Movements in Latin America: Bridging the Divide*. London: Routledge, 96–121.

Lutz, Ellen L. & Kathryn Sikkink (2000). International human rights law and practice in Latin America. *International Organization*, 54(3), 633–59.

Martin, Adrian, Brendan Coolsaet, Esteve Corbera et al. (2016). Justice and conservation: The need to incorporate recognition. *Biological Conservation*, 197, 254–61.

McAdam, Doug, Sidney Tarrow & Charles Tilly (2001). *Dynamics of Contention*. Cambridge, MA: Cambridge University Press.

McCarthy, Cameron (1998). *The Uses of Culture: Education and the Limits of Ethnic Affiliation*. London: Routledge.

McNay, Lois (2008). *Against Recognition*. Cambridge and Malden: Polity.

McNeish, John A. (2002). Globalization and the reinvention of Andean tradition: The politics of community and ethnicity in highland Bolivia. *The Journal of Peasant Studies*, 29(3–4), 228–69.

(2013). Extraction, protest and indigeneity in Bolivia: The TIPNIS effect. *Latin American and Caribbean Ethnic Studies*, 8(2), 221–42.

McSweeney, Kendra & Shahna Arps (2005) A "demographic turnaround": The rapid growth of the indigenous populations in Lowland Latin America. *Latin American Research Review*, 40(1), 3–29.

Merino Acuña, Roger (2015). The politics of extractive governance: Indigenous peoples and socio-environmental conflicts. *The Extractive Industries and Society*, 2(1), 85–92.

(2018). Re-politicizing participation or reframing environmental governance? Beyond indigenous' prior consultation and citizen participation. *World Development*, 111, 75–83.

Middleton, Townsend (2015). *The Demands of Recognition: State Anthropology and Ethnopolitics in Darjeeling*. Stanford: Stanford University Press.

Milano, Flavia & Andrea Sanhueza (2016). Consultas Públicas con Sociedad Civil: Guías para Agencias Ejecutoras Públicas y Privadas. *Interamerican Development Bank*. https://publications.iadb.org/bitstream/handle/11319/ 7499/Consultas-publicas-con-sociedad-civil-Guias-para-agencias-ejecutoras-publicas-y-privadas.pdf?sequence=2.

Miller, David (1999). *Principles of Social Justice*. Cambridge, MA: Harvard University Press.

Mistry, Jayalaxshmi & Andrea Berardi (2016). Bridging indigenous and scientific knowledge: Local ecological knowledge must be placed at the center of environmental governance. *Science*, 352(6291), 1274–75.

Mitchell, William P. (1991). *Peasants on the Edge: Crop, Cult, and Crisis in the Andes*. Austin, TX: University of Texas Press.

Mollett, Sharlene (2011). Racial narratives: Miskito and colono land struggles in the Honduran Mosquitia. *Cultural Geographies*, 18(1), 43–62.

Mougeot, Luc J. A. (1985). Alternative migration targets and Brazilian Amazonia's closing frontier. In John Hemming (ed.), *Change in the Amazon Basin. Volume II: The frontier after a decade of colonization*. Manchester: Manchester University Press, 51–90.

Negrete, Esneyder (2014). El Gobierno no le va a cumplir a nadie. *Confidencial Colombia*, 25 August. http://confidencialcolombia.com/agenda-nacional/el-gobierno-no-le-va-a-cumplir-a-nadie__233406/2014/08/25.

Newing, Helen (2009). Unpicking "community" in community conservation: Implications of changing settlement patterns and individual mobility for the Tamshiyacu Tahuayo Communal Reserve, Peru. In Miguel N. Alexiades (ed.), *Mobility and Migration in Indigenous Amazon: Contemporary Ethnoecological Perspectives*. Oxford: Berghahn Books, pp. 97–114.

Newman, Dwight & Wendy E. Ortega Pineda (2016). Comparing Canadian and Colombian approaches to the duty to consult indigenous communities on international treaties. *Constitutional Forum Constitutionnel*, 25(1), 29–36.

Niezen, Ronald (2003). *The Origins of Indigenism*. Berkeley, CA: University of California Press.

(2010). *Public Justice and the Anthropology of Law*. Cambridge, MA: Cambridge University Press.

Nuitjen, Monique & David Lorenzo (2009). Ritual and rule in the periphery: State violence and local governance in a Peruvian comunidad. In F. Benda-Beckmann, K. Benda-Beckmann & J. Eckert (eds), *Rules of Law and Laws of Ruling: On the Governance of Law*. Farnham and Burlington: Ashgate.

OAS (1987). *Estudio de Casos de Manejo Ambiental: Desarrollo Integrado de un Área en los Trópicos Húmedos – Selva Central del Perú*. Washington DC: OAS. https://www.oas.org/dsd/publications/Unit/oea27s/begin.htm.

Ogburn, Dennis E. (2008). Becoming Saraguro: Ethnogenesis in the context of Inca and Spanish colonialism. *Ethnohistory*, 55(2), 287–319.

Orlove, B. & G. Custred (eds.) (1980). *Land and Power in Latin America: Agrarian Economies and Social Processes in the Andes*. New York: Holmes and Meir.

O'Rourke, Dara & Sarah Connolly (2003). Just oil? The distribution of environmental and social impacts of oil production and consumption. *Annual Review of Environment and Resources*, 28(1), 587–617.

Orta-Martínez, Martí & Matt Finer (2010). Oil frontiers and indigenous resistance in the Peruvian Amazon. *Ecological Economics*, 70, 207–18.

OSAL (2007). *Propuesta de las Organizaciones Indígenas, Originarias, Campesinas y de Colonizadores hacia la Asamblea Constituyente*, CLACSO 22. http://bibliotecavirtual.clacso.org.ar/ar/libros/osal/osal22/AC22Documento.pdf.

Pallares, Amalia (2002). *From Peasant Struggles to Indian Resistance: The Ecuadorian Andes in the Late Twentieth Century*. Norman, OK: University of Oklahoma Press.

Panfichi, A. (2011). Contentious representation and its impact in contemporary Peru. In J. Crabtree (ed.), *Fractured Politics: Peruvian Democracy Past and Present*. London: Institute for Latin American Studies.

Panizza, Francisco (1995). Human rights in the processes of transition and consolidation of democracy. *Political Studies*, 43, 168–88.

Parra, José (2016). The role of domestic courts in international human rights law: The Constitutional Court of Colombia and Free, Prior and Informed Consent. *International Journal on Minority and Group Rights*, 23, 355–81.

Paschel, Tianna S. (2016). *Becoming Black Political Subjects: Movements and Ethno-Racial Rights in Colombia and Brazil*. Princeton, NJ: Princeton University Press.

Paschel, Tianna S. & Mark Q. Sawyer (2008). Contesting politics as usual: Black social movements, globalization, and race policy in Latin America. *Souls*, 10 (3), 197–214.

Paz, Sarela, Rosalva Aída Hernández & Teresa Sierra María (eds.) (2004). *El estado y los indígenas en tiempos del PAN: neoindigenismo, legalidad e identidad*. Tlalpan, México DF: CIESAS-MA Porrúa.

Peeler, John (2003). Social justice and new indigenous politics: An analysis of Guatemala, the Central Andes and Chiapas. In Susan Eckstein & Timothy Wickham Crowley (eds.), *What Justice? Whose Justice? Fighting for Fairness in Latin America*. Berkeley, CA: University of California Press, 257–84.

Pelican, Michaela (2009). Complexities of indigeneity and autochthony: An African example. *American Ethnologist*, 36(1), 52–65.

Pellegrini, Lorenzo & Marco O. Ribera Arismendi (2012). Consultation, compensation and extraction in Bolivia after the "Left Turn": The case of oil exploration in the north of La Paz Department. *Journal of Latin American Geography*, 11(2), 101–18.

Perreault, Tom (2015). Performing participation: Mining, power, and the limits of public consultation in Bolivia. *The Journal of Latin American and Caribbean Anthropology*, 20(3), 433–51.

Perreault, Tom & Barbara Green (2013). Reworking the spaces of indigeneity: The Bolivian ayllu and lowland autonomy movements compared. *Environment and Planning D: Society and Space*, 31(1), 43–60.

Perrier Bruslé, Laetitia (2012). Le conflit du Tipnis et la Bolivie d'Evo Morales face à ses contradictions: analyse d'un conflit socio-environnemental. *EchoGéo*, 26 January. http://echogeo.revues.org/12972, accessed 10 January 2015.

Peters, Pauline (2004). Inequality and social conflict over land in Africa. *Journal of Agrarian Change*, 4(3), 269–314.

Petras, James & Hanry Veltmeyer (2001). Are Latin American peasant movements still a force for change? Some new paradigms revisited. *The Journal of Peasant Studies*, 28(2), 83–118.

Pilapil, Renante D. (2015). *Recognition: Examining Identity Struggles*. Manila: Ateneo de Manila University Press.

Pontificia Universidad Javeriana Cali (PUJC) (2013). *Asesoria y Acompañamiento para el manejo de las relaciones interétnicas e interculturales para el desarrollo rural*. Informe Final, PUJC, May.

Posner, Daniel N. (2005). *Institutions and Ethnic Politics in Africa*. Cambridge, MA: Cambridge University Press.

Postero, Nancy G. (2007). *Now We Are Citizens: Indigenous Politics in Postmulticultural Bolivia*. Palo Alto: Stanford University Press.

Postero, Nancy G. & Leon Zamosc (eds.) (2004). *The Struggle for Indigenous Rights in Latin America*. Portland: Sussex Academic Press.

PRONABEC (2014). Beca 18 Educación Intercultural Bilingue. Expediente técnico 2014, PRONABEC. http://www.pronabec.gob.pe/inicio/publicaciones/documentos/eib_expediente2014.pdf.

  (2015). *Este Año Beca 18 Recibirá a 1223 Jóvenes de Comunidades Nativas Amazónicas*. https://andina.pe/agencia/noticia-este-ano-beca-18-beneficia-a-1223-jovenes-comunidades-nativas-555839.aspx.

Quesada Tovar, Carlos E. (2013). *Derecho a la Consulta Previa para comunidades campesinas*. Master's Dissertation, Universidad Nacional de Colombia.

Rappaport, Joan (2005). *Intercultural Utopias: Public Intellectuals, Cultural Experimentation, and Ethnic Pluralism in Colombia*. Durham, NC: Duke University Press.

Remotti, Francesco (2001). *Contro l'Identità*. Bari: Laterza.

Remy, María Isabel (2010). El asedio desde los márgenes: entre la multiplicidad de conflictos locales y la lenta formación de nuevos movimientos sociales en Perú. In M. Tanaka & F. Jacome (eds.), *Desafíos de la gobernabilidad democrática*. Lima: IDRC/IEP/Canada.

(2013). *Historia de las Comunidades Indígenas y Campesinas del Perú*. Lima: IEP Instituto de Estudios Peruanos.

(2014). *Conflicto y Cambios en la Sociedad Rural*. Lima: Ministerio de Cultura.

Rettberg, A. & Ortiz-Riomalo, J. F. (2016). Golden opportunity, or a new twist on the resource–conflict relationship: Links between the drug trade and illegal gold mining in Colombia. *World Development*, 84, 82–96.

Reyes-García, Victoria, Martí Orta-Martínez & Maximilien Gueze et al. (2012). Does participatory mapping increase conflicts? A randomized evaluation in the Bolivian Amazon. *Applied Geography*, 34, 650–58.

Rice, R. (2012). *The New Politics of Protest: Indigenous Mobilization in Latin America's Neoliberal Era*. Austin, AZ: University of Arizona Press.

Richards, Patricia (2003). Expanding women's citizenship? Mapuche women and Chile's national women's service. *Latin American Perspectives*, 30(2), 249–73.

Richardson, Henry S. (2012). On the sites of remedial justice: Colleges, clinics, and the state. In Zoya Hasan & Martha Craven Nussbaum (eds.), *Equalizing Access: Affirmative Action in Higher Education in India, United States, and South Africa*. New Delhi: Oxford University Press, 22–43.

Ricoeur, Paul (2005). *The Course of Recognition*. Cambridge, MA: Harvard University Press.

Rights and Resources Initiative (2015a). Who owns the land in Latin America? The status of indigenous and community land rights in Latin America. http://www.rightsandresources. org/publication/whoownstheland.

(2015b). Protected areas and the land rights of indigenous peoples and local communities. May. https://rightsandresources.org/wp-content/uploads/RRIReport_Protected-Areas-and-Land-Rights_web.pdf accessed 10 December 2018.

Rivera Cusicanqui, Silvia (1984). *Oprimidos pero no Vencidos: Luchas del Campesinado Aymara y Qhechwa de Bolivia, 1900–1980*. La Paz: HISBOL-CUSTCB.

(1987). Luchas campesinas contemporáneas en Bolivia: El movimiento Katarista: 1970-1980. In René Zavaleta Mercado (ed.), *Bolivia, Hoy*. Méxic D.F.: Siglo XXI.

(1993). La raíz: colonizadores y colonizados. In X. Albó & R. Barrios (eds.), *Violencias Encubiertas en Bolivia*. Vol. 1. La Paz: Cipca/Ayuwiyiri, 27–139.

(2012). *Ch'ixinakax utxiwa*: A reflection on the practices and discourses of decolonization. *South Atlantic Quarterly*, 111(1), 95–109.

(2015). Violencia e interculturalidad: paradojas de la etnicidad en la Bolivia de hoy. Telar: Revista del Instituto Interdisciplinario de *Estudios Latinoamericanos*, 10(15), 49–70.

Roberts, Kenneth (2012). *The Politics of Inequality and Redistribution in Latin America's Post-Adjustment Era*. UNU-Wider Working Paper No. 2012/08. Helsinki: UNU World Institute for Development Economics Research.

Robles, Frances (2016). Una disputa por tierras indígenas provoca una ola de homicidios en Nicaragua. *New York Times ES*, 17 October. https://www.nytimes.com/es/2016/10/17/espanol/una-disputa-por-tierras-indigenas-provoca-una-ola-de-homicidios-en-nicaragua.html/. accessed 10 August 2018.

Rodríguez-Carmona, Antonio (2009). *El Proyectorado: Bolivia tras 20 Años de Ayuda Externa.* La Paz: Plural.

Rodríguez-Garavito, César (2011). Ethnicity.gov: Global governance, indigenous peoples, and the right to prior consultation in social minefields. *Indiana Journal of Global Legal Studies,* 18(1), 263–305.

Rojas, Axel (2011). Gobernar(Se) En Nombre de La Cultura. Interculturalidad y Educación Para Grupos Etnicos En Colombia. *Revista Colombiana de Antropologia,* 47(2), 173–98.

Roldán Ortiga, Roque (2004). *Models for Recognizing Indigenous Land Rights in Latin America.* Washington, DC: World Bank.

Rossi, Federico M. (2017). *The Poor's Struggle for Political Incorporation: The Piquetero Movement in Argentina.* Cambridge, MA: Cambridge University Press.

Rousseau, S. & Dargent, E. (2019). The construction of Indigenous language rights in Peru: A language regime approach. *Journal of Politics in Latin America,* 11(2), 161–80.

Rudel, Thomas K., Ruth Defries, Gregory P. Asner, William F. Laurance (2009). Changing drivers of deforestation and new opportunities for conservation. *Conservation Biology,* 23(6), 1396–405.

Sánchez Aguilar, Aníbal (2015). *Migraciones Internas en el Peru.* Lima: International Migration Organization. https://repository.iom.int/handle/20.500.11788/1490

Sánchez García, Inmaculada (2007). *La educación en la Población Indígena Boliviana. Avances, Deficiencias y Discriminación Sexual.* Fundación CIDEAL http://www.cideal.org.

Sartre, Jean-Paul (1943). *Being and Nothingness: A Phenomenological Essay on Ontology.* New York: Washington Square Press.

Schatz, Edward (ed.) (2009). *Political Ethnography: What Immersion Contributes to the Study of Power.* Chicago & London: University of Chicago Press.

Schilling-Vacaflor, Almut & Riccarda Flemmer (2013). Why is prior consultation not yet an effective tool for conflict resolution? The case of Peru. *GIGA Working Papers* N. 220.

Schmelkes, S., G. Águila & M.A. Núñez (2009). Alfabetización de Jóvenes y Adultos Indígenas En México. In L. E. López & U. Hanemann (eds), *Alfabetización y Multiculturalidad. Miradas Desde América Latina.* Guatemala: UNESCO-UIL, GTZ, 237–90.

Seligmann, Linda J. (1995). *Between Reform & Revolution: Political Struggles in the Peruvian Andes, 1969–1991.* Stanford: Stanford University Press.

Semana (2011). Ataque a Toribío: 460 viviendas afectadas y 480 familias damnificadas, *Semana.* http://www.semana.com/nacion/articulo/ataque-toribio-460-viviendas-afectadas-480-familias-damnificadas/242906-3.

Shah, Alpa (2007). The dark side of indigeneity?: Indigenous people, rights and development in India. *History Compass,* 5(6), 1806–32.

(2010). *In the Shadows of the State: Indigenous Politics, Environmentalism, and Insurgency in Jharkhand, India.* Durham, NC: Duke University Press.

Shneiderman, Sara & Louise Tillin (2015). Restructuring states, restructuring ethnicity: Looking across disciplinary boundaries at federal futures in India and Nepal. *Modern Asian Studies,* 49(1), 1–39.

Sieder, Rachel (ed.) (2002). *Multiculturalism in Latin America: Indigenous Rights, Diversity, and Democracy*. New York: Palgrave Macmillan.

Siegel, Karen M. (2016). Fulfilling promises of more substantive democracy? Post-neoliberalism and natural resource governance in South America. *Development and Change*, 47(3), 495–516.

Sikor, Thomas, Adrian Martin, Janet Fisher & Jun He (2014). Toward an empirical analysis of justice in ecosystem governance. *Conservation Letters*, 7(6), 524–32.

Singh, Prerna & Matthias vom Hau (2016). Ethnicity in time: Politics, history, and the relationship between ethnic diversity and public goods provision. *Comparative Political Studies*, 49(10), 1303–40.

Soria Dall'Orso & Carlos A. M. (2015). Increased relevance and influence of Free Prior and Informed Consent, REDD and green economy principles on sustainable commons management in Peru. *Journal of Sustainable Development Law and Policy*, 5, 4–31.

Sotomayor, Carlos (2009). Apolo, un conflicto entre iguales. In Juan Pablo Chumacero (ed.), *Reconfigurando Territorios: Reforma Agraria, Control Territorial y Gobiernos Indígenas en Bolivia*. La Paz: Fundación Tierra, 121–42.

Spivak, Gayatri C. & Sarah Harasym (eds.) (1990). *The Postcolonial Critic: Interviews, Strategies, Dialogues*. New York: Routledge.

Stavenhagen, Rodolfo (2007). *Los Pueblos Indígenas y sus Derechos*. México: UNESCO.

Stefanoni, Pablo (2006). El nacionalismo indígean en el poder. *Observatorio Social de America Latina*, 7(19), 37–44.

Stein, William W. (1984). Images of the Peruvian Indian peasant in the work of José Carlos Mariátegui. *Historical Reflections*, 11(1), 1–35.

Steinert, Ole Christian (2003). *Ethnic Communities and Ethno-Political Strategies: The Struggle for Ethnic Rights*. PhD thesis, University of Texas Austin. https://repositories.lib.utexas.edu/bitstream/handle/2152/963/steinertpoco36.pdf.

Stephenson, Marcia (2002). Forging an indigenous counterpublic sphere: the Taller de Historia Oral Andina in Bolivia. *Latin American Research Review*, 37(2), 99–118.

Stern, S. (ed.) (1987). *Resistance, Rebellion, and Consciousness in the Andean Peasant World, 18th to 20th Centuries*. Madison, WI: University of Wisconsin Press.

Stock, Anthony (2005). Too much for too few: Problems of indigenous land rights in Latin America. *Annual Review of Anthropology*, 34, 85–104.

Storper, Michael (2005). Society, community, and economic development. *Studies in Comparative International Development*, 39(4), 30–57.

Ströbele-Gregor, Juliana, Olaf Kaltmeier & Cornelia Giebeler (eds) (2010). Fortalecimiento de Organizaciones Indígenas en América Latina: Construyendo Interculturalidad: Pueblos Indígenas, Educación y Políticas de Identidad en América Latina. *GIZ*. https://www.bivica.org/files/ag_interculturalidad.pdf.

Sub-central TIPNIS Comisión de Recorrido (2012). Informe del Recorrido Realizado por Las Cominidades del TIPNIS. https://www.scribd.com/docu ment/133471091/Libro-TIPNIS-Informe-Del-Recorrido.

Sunderlin, William D., Anne M. Larson, Amy E. Duchelle et al. (2014). How are REDD+ proponents addressing tenure problems? Evidence from Brazil, Cameroon, Tanzania, Indonesia, and Vietnam. *World Development*, 55, 37–52.

Sylvain, Renée (2014). Essentialism and the indigenous politics of recognition in Southern Africa. *American Anthropologist*, 116(2), 251–64.

Tanaka, M. (2012). ¿Por qué el Estado no responde adecuadamente a los conflictos sociales? Qué hacer al respecto? *Economia y Sociedad*, 79, 36–43.

Taras, Raymond & Rajat Ganguly (2008). *Understanding Ethnic Conflict: The International Dimension*. New York, San Francisco, Boston, London: Longman.

Tarrow, Sidney (1998). *Power in Movement*. New York: Cambridge University Press.

Tassi, Nico (2010). The "postulate of abundance": Cholo market and religion in La Paz, Bolivia. *Social Anthropology*, 18(2), 191–209.

(2017). *The Native World-system: An Ethnography of Bolivian Aymara Traders in the Global Economy*. Oxford: Oxford University Press.

Taylor, Charles (1992). *Multiculturalism and The Politics of Recognition: An Essay*. Princeton, NJ: Princeton University Press.

Telles, Edward & PERLA (Project on Ethnicity and Race in Latin America) (2014). *Pigmentocracies: Ethnicity, Race and Color in Latin America*. Chapel Hill, NC: University of North Carolina Press.

Thomson, Sinclair (2002). *We Alone Will Rule: Native Andean Politics in the Age of Insurgency*. Madison, WI: University of Wisconsin Press.

Ticona, Esteban (2000). *Organización y Liderazgo Aymara, 1979–1996*. La Paz: Universidad de la Cordillera, AGRUCO.

Tilly, Charles (2005). *Identities, Boundaries, and Social Ties*. Boulder: Paradigm Publishers.

Torrejón, Erika (2002) La República en Flor de la Frontera, escenario de la masacre de 15 personas. *La República*, 1 February. https://larepublica.pe/ politica/348611-la-republica-en-flor-de-la-frontera-escenario-de-la-masacre-de-15-personas-aun-se/

Torres Wong, Marcela (2018). *Natural Resources, Extraction and Indigenous Rights in Latin America: Exploring the Boundaries of Environmental and State-corporate Crime in Bolivia, Peru, and Mexico*. London: Routledge.

Trench, Tim (2005). Representaciones y sus impactos: el caso de los lacandones en la Selva Lacandona. *Liminar*, 3(2), 48–69.

Troyan, Brett (2008). Ethnic citizenship in Colombia: The experience of the Regional Indigenous Council of the Cauca in Southwestern Colombia from 1970 to 1990. *Latin American Research Review*, 43(3), 166–91.

(2015). *Cauca's Indigenous Movement in Southwestern Colombia: Land, Violence, and Ethnic Identity*. Lanham, BO and London: Lexington Books.

UNDP (2013). Pueblos indígenas en América Latina: pese a los avances en la participación política, las mujeres son las más rezagadas. UNDP, 22 May. https://www1.undp.org/content/undp/es/home/news-centre/news/2013/05/22/

pueblos-indigenas-en-america-latina-pese-a-los-avances-en-la-participacion-poli
tica-las-mujeres-son-las-mas-rezagadas-segun-el-pnud/, accessed 10 August 2018.

(2014). *Cauca Análisis de conflictividades y construcción de paz.* UNDP,
December. http://www.co.undp.org/content/dam/colombia/docs/Paz/undp-
co-catatumbo-2014.pdf, accessed 8 December 2018.

UN-REDD (2013). Guidelines on Free Prior and Informed Consent. *FAO/UNDP/
UNEP.* https://www.uncclearn.org/wp-content/uploads/library/un-reddo5.pdf.

Uquillas, Jorge E. & Martien Van Nieuwkoop (2003). Social capital as a factor in
indigenous peoples development in Ecuador. *World Bank Sustainable
Development Working Paper 15.*

Urrutia Valenzuela, Carlos (2017). La regulación del derecho fundamental a la
consulta previa en Colombia. *Ambito Jurídico,* 18 July. https://www
.ambitojuridico.com/bancoconocimiento/constitucional-y-derechos-huma
nos/la-regulacion-del-derecho-fundamental-a-la-consulta-previa-en-
colombia.

Valencia García, Maria del Pilar V. & Zurita, Ivan É. (2010). *Los Pueblos
Indígenas de Tierras Bajas en el Proceso Constituyente Boliviano.* Santa
Cruz: CEJIS.

Van Cott, Donna L. (2000) *The Friendly Liquidation of the Past: The Politics of
Diversity in Latin America.* Pittsburgh: University of Pittsburgh Press.

(2002). Constitutional reform in the Andes: redefining indigenous-state relations. In *Multiculturalism in Latin America* (pp. 45–73). London: Palgrave
Macmillan.

(2005a). *From Movements to Parties in Latin America: The Evolution of Ethnic
Politics.* New York: Cambridge University Press.

(2005b). Building inclusive democracies: Indigenous peoples and ethnic minorities in Latin America. *Democratization,* 12(5), 820–37.

Vargas, María Teresa & Edil Osinaga (2009). ¿En manos de quién están
los bosques en Bolivia? Implicaciones de la tenencia en el manejo
forestal y en los medios de vida rurales. *Estudio de caso.* Roma and Bolivia:
FAO.

Vásquez León, Luis (2016). 'Multiculturalism as a juridical weapon: The use and
abuse of the concept of 'Pueblo Originario' in agrarian conflicts in Michoacán,
Mexico'. In David Lehmann (ed.) *The Crisis of Multiculturalism in Latin
América* (pp. 35–73). New York: Palgrave Macmillan.

Vavrus, Michael J. (2015). *Diversity & Education: A Critical Multicultural
Approach.* New York: Teachers College Press.

Verdad Abierta (2014). La ficha campesina en el rompecabezas territorial de
Cauca. *Verdad Abierta,* 19 May. http://www.verdadabierta.com/lucha-por-
la-tierra/5333-la-ficha-campesina-en-el-rompecabezas-territorial-de-cauca.

Vergara, A., (2011). United by discord, divided by consensus: National and subnational articulation in Bolivia and Peru, 2000–2010. *Journal of Politics in
Latin America,* 3(3), 65–93.

Vergara, Walter, Luciana Gallardo Lomeli, Ana R. Rios et al. (2016). *The
Economic Case for Landscape Restoration in Latin America.* Washington,
DC: World Resources Institute. https://www.wri.org/publication/economic-
case-for-restoration-20x20.

Villanueva, Arturo D. (2004). *Pueblos Indígenas y Conflictos de Tierras*. La Paz: Fundación Tierra.

Viqueira, Juan Pedro (1995). *La Comunidad India en México en los Estudios Antropológicos e Históricos. Anuario 1994*. Tuxtla Gutiérrez, Chiapas: CESMECA-UNICACH.

Wainwright, Joel & Joe Bryan (2009). Cartography, territory, property: Postcolonial reflections on Indigenous counter-mapping in Nicaragua and Belize. *Cultural Geographies*, 16, 153–78.

Ward, Tara (2011). Right to free, prior, and informed consent: Indigenous peoples' participation rights within international law. *Northwestern Journal of Human Rights*, 10, 54–84.

Webber, Jeffrey R. (2011). *From Rebellion to Reform in Bolivia: Class Struggle, Indigenous Liberation and the Politics of Evo Morales*. Chicago, IL: Haymarket Books.

Weitzner, Viviane (2017). "Nosotros Somos Estado": Contested legalities in decision-making about extractives affecting ancestral territories in Colombia. *Third World Quarterly*, 38(5), 1198–214.

Wightman, Ann M. (1990). *Indigenous Migration and Social Change: The Forasteros of Cuzco, 1570–1720*. Durham, NC: Duke University Press.

Williams, Mark & Anthony Bebbington (2008). Water and mining conflicts in Peru. *Mountain Research and Development*, 28(3/4), 190–95. http://snobear .colorado.edu/Markw/Research/08_peru.pdf.

Wimmer, Andreas (2013). *Ethnic Boundary Making, Institutions, Power, Networks*. New York: Oxford University Press.

Wolf, Eric R. (1969). *Peasant Wars of the Twentieth Century*. New York & London: Harper and Row.

World Bank (2010). Indigenous peoples still among poorest in world, but progress reported in some countries. World Bank, 26 April. http://www.worldbank .org/en/news/press-release/2010/04/26/indigenous-peoples-still-among-poorest-in-world-but-progress-reported-in-some-countries.

(2016). A year in the lives of smallholder farmers. *World Bank*, 25 February. http://www.worldbank.org/en/news/feature/2016/02/25/a-year-in-the-lives-of-smallholder-farming-families.

(2018). *Indigenous Latin America in the Twenty-First Century*. Washington, DC: World Bank. http://documents.worldbank.org/curated/en/145891467991974540/pdf/98544-REVISED-WP-P148348-Box394854B-PUBLIC-Indigenous-Latin-America.pdf.

Yashar, Deborah J. (1998). Contesting citizenship: Indigenous movements and democracy in Latin America. *Comparative Politics*, 31(1), 23–42.

(1999). Democracy, indigenous movements, and the postliberal challenge in Latin America. *World Politics*, 52(1), 76–104.

(2005). *Contesting Citizenship in Latin America: The Rise of Indigenous Movements and the Postliberal Challenge*. Cambridge, MA: Cambridge University Press.

Zamosc, León (1986). *The Agrarian Question and the Peasant Movement in Colombia*. Cambridge, MA: Cambridge University Press.

Zaremberg, Gisela & Marcela Torres Wong (2018). Participation on the edge: Prior consultation and extractivism in Latin America. *Journal of Politics in Latin America*, 10(3), 29–58.

Zavala, Virginia (2007). *Avances y Desafíos de La Educación Intercultural Bilingüe En Bolivia, Ecuador y Perú: Estudio de Casos*. Lima: CARE. http://repositorio.minedu.gob.pe/handle/20.500.12799/844.

Index

Note: Page numbers in italic denote figures and page numbers with the suffix n indicate a footnote.

Other Books in the Series (*continued from page ii*)

Cambridge Studies in Comparative Politics

Adam Michael Auerbach, *Demanding Development: The Politics of Public Goods Provision in India's Urban Slums*

David Austen-Smith, Jeffry A. Frieden, Miriam A. Golden, Karl Ove Moene, and Adam Przeworski, eds., *Selected Works of Michael Wallerstein: The Political Economy of Inequality, Unions, and Social Democracy*

S. Erdem Aytaç and Susan C. Stokes, *Why Bother? Rethinking Participation in Elections and Protests*

Andy Baker, *The Market and the Masses in Latin America: Policy Reform and Consumption in Liberalizing Economies*

Laia Balcells, *Rivalry and Revenge: The Politics of Violence during Civil War*

Lisa Baldez, *Why Women Protest: Women's Movements in Chile*

Kate Baldwin, *The Paradox of Traditional Chiefs in Democratic Africa*

Stefano Bartolini, *The Political Mobilization of the European Left, 1860–1980: The Class Cleavage*

Robert H. Bates, *The Political Economy of Development: A Game Theoretic Approach*

Robert H. Bates, *When Things Fell Apart: State Failure in Late-Century Africa*

Mark Beissinger, *Nationalist Mobilization and the Collapse of the Soviet State*

Pablo Beramendi, *The Political Geography of Inequality: Regions and Redistribution*

Nancy Bermeo, ed., *Unemployment in the New Europe*

Carles Boix, *Democracy and Redistribution*

Carles Boix, *Political Order and Inequality: Their Foundations and their Consequences for Human Welfare*

Carles Boix, *Political Parties, Growth, and Equality: Conservative and Social Democratic Economic Strategies in the World Economy*

Catherine Boone, *Merchant Capital and the Roots of State Power in Senegal, 1930–1985*

Catherine Boone, *Political Topographies of the African State: Territorial Authority and Institutional Change*

Catherine Boone, *Property and Political Order in Africa: Land Rights and the Structure of Politics*

Michael Bratton and Nicolas van de Walle, *Democratic Experiments in Africa: Regime Transitions in Comparative Perspective*

Michael Bratton, Robert Mattes, and E. Gyimah-Boadi, *Public Opinion, Democracy, and Market Reform in Africa*

Valerie Bunce, *Leaving Socialism and Leaving the State: The End of Yugoslavia, the Soviet Union, and Czechoslovakia*

Daniele Caramani, *The Nationalization of Politics: The Formation of National Electorates and Party Systems in Europe*

John M. Carey, *Legislative Voting and Accountability*

Kanchan Chandra, *Why Ethnic Parties Succeed: Patronage and Ethnic Headcounts in India*

Eric C. C. Chang, Mark Andreas Kayser, Drew A. Linzer, and Ronald Rogowski, *Electoral Systems and the Balance of Consumer-Producer Power*

José Antonio Cheibub, *Presidentialism, Parliamentarism, and Democracy*

Isabela Mares, *The Politics of Social Risk: Business and Welfare State Development*

Isabela Mares, *Taxation, Wage Bargaining, and Unemployment*

Cathie Jo Martin and Duane Swank, *The Political Construction of Business Interests: Coordination, Growth, and Equality*

Anthony W. Marx, *Making Race, Making Nations: A Comparison of South Africa, the United States, and Brazil*

Daniel C. Mattingly, *The Art of Political Control in China*

Kevin Mazur, *Revolution in Syria: Identity, Networks, and Repression*

Bonnie M. Meguid, *Party Competition between Unequals: Strategies and Electoral Fortunes in Western Europe*

Joel S. Migdal, *State in Society: Studying How States and Societies Constitute One Another*

Joel S. Migdal, Atul Kohli, and Vivienne Shue, eds., *State Power and Social Forces: Domination and Transformation in the Third World*

Eduardo Moncada, *Resisting Extortion: Victims, Criminals and States in Latin America*

Scott Morgenstern and Benito Nacif, eds., *Legislative Politics in Latin America*

Kevin M. Morrison, *Nontaxation and Representation: The Fiscal Foundations of Political Stability*

Layna Mosley, *Global Capital and National Governments*

Layna Mosley, *Labor Rights and Multinational Production*

Wolfgang C. Müller and Kaare Strøm, *Policy, Office, or Votes?*

Maria Victoria Murillo, *Political Competition, Partisanship, and Policy Making in Latin American Public Utilities*

Maria Victoria Murillo, *Labor Unions, Partisan Coalitions, and Market Reforms in Latin America*

Monika Nalepa, *Skeletons in the Closet: Transitional Justice in Post-Communist Europe*

Noah L. Nathan, *Electoral Politics and Africa's Urban Transition: Class and Ethnicity in Ghana*

Simeon Nichter, *Votes for Survival: Relational Clientelism in Latin America*

Richard A. Nielsen, *Deadly Clerics: Blocked Ambition and the Paths to Jihad*

Ton Notermans, *Money, Markets, and the State: Social Democratic Economic Policies since 1918*

Aníbal Pérez-Liñán, *Presidential Impeachment and the New Political Instability in Latin America*

Roger D. Petersen, *Understanding Ethnic Violence: Fear, Hatred, and Resentment in Twentieth-Century Eastern Europe*

Roger D. Petersen, *Western Intervention in the Balkans: The Strategic Use of Emotion in Conflict*

Simona Piattoni, ed., *Clientelism, Interests, and Democratic Representation*

Paul Pierson, *Dismantling the Welfare State? Reagan, Thatcher, and the Politics of Retrenchment*

Marino Regini, *Uncertain Boundaries: The Social and Political Construction of European Economies*

Philipp Rehm, *Risk Inequality and Welfare States: Social Policy Preferences, Development, and Dynamics*

Kenneth M. Roberts, *Changing Course in Latin America: Party Systems in the Neoliberal Era*

For EU product safety concerns, contact us at Calle de José Abascal, 56–1°,
28003 Madrid, Spain or eugpsr@cambridge.org

www.ingramcontent.com/pod-product-compliance
Ingram Content Group UK Ltd.
Pitfield, Milton Keynes, MK11 3LW, UK
UKHW010250140625
459647UK00013BA/1769